Lab Manual for Network+ Guide to Networks, Second Edition

Michael Grice
Tamara Dean

COURSE
TECHNOLOGY

TM

THOMSON LEARNING

Australia • Canada • Mexico • Singapore • Spain • United Kingdom • United States

COURSE TECHNOLOGY

™

THOMSON LEARNING

Lab Manual for Network+ Guide to Networks, Second Edition

is published by Course Technology

Associate Publisher:
Steve Elliot

Senior Editor:
Lisa Egan

Product Manager:
Amy M. Lyon

Developmental Editor:
Jill Batistick

Production Editor:
Melissa Panagos

Technical Editor:
James I. Conrad, Accusource CC, Inc.

Manufacturing Coordinator:
Alexander Schall

Quality Assurance Technical Lead:
Nicole Ashton

Marketing Manager:
Toby Shelton

Associate Product Manager:
Tim Gleeson

Editorial Assistant:
Nick Lombardi

Text Designer:
GEX Publishing Services

Compositor:
GEX Publishing Services

Cover Design:
Julie Malone

Disclaimer
Course Technology reserves the ri
revise this publication and make
changes from time to time in its c
without notice.

ISBN 0-619-12134-3

TABLE OF CONTENTS

INTRODUCTION

Hands-on learning is the best way to master the networking skills necessary for both CompTIA's Network+ exam and a networking career. This book contains dozens of hands-on exercises that apply fundamental networking concepts as they would be applied in the real world. In addition, each chapter offers multiple review questions to reinforce your mastery of networking topics. The organization of this book follows the same organization as Course Technology's *Network+ Guide to Networks, Second Edition*, and using the two together will provide a substantial, effective learning experience. This book is suitable for use in a beginning or intermediate networking course. As a prerequisite, students should have at least six months of computer experience and should be familiar with some basic networking components, such as NICs and patch cables. Passing the A+ certification exam would suffice in lieu of this experience. This book is best used when accompanied by the Course Technology textbook *Network+ Guide to Networks, Second Edition*, or another introduction to networking textbook.

FEATURES

In order to ensure a successful experience for instructors and students alike, this book includes the following features:

- **Network+ Certification Objectives** — Each chapter lists the relevant objectives from the CompTIA Network+ 2001 Exam.
- **Lab Objectives** — Every lab has a brief description and list of learning objectives.
- **Materials Required** — Every lab includes information on network access privileges, hardware, software, and other materials you will need to complete the lab.
- **Completion Times** — Every lab has an estimated completion time, so that you can plan your activities more accurately.
- **Activity Sections** — Labs are presented in manageable sections. Where appropriate, additional Activity Background information is provided to illustrate the importance of a particular project.
- **Step-by-Step Instructions** — Logical and precise step-by-step instructions guide you through the hands-on activities in each lab.
- **Review Questions** — Questions help reinforce concepts presented in the lab.

Note for instructors: Answers to review questions are available on the Course Technology Web site at www.course.com/irc/. Search on this book's ISBN, which is found on the back cover.

Hardware requirements

The following is a list of hardware required to complete all the labs in the book. The hardware requirements for many of the individual labs are less than what is listed.

- Three computers with Pentium 166 MHz CPU or higher processors (400 MHz recommended) with the following features:
  - 128 MB of RAM minimum (256 MB recommended) in each computer
  - A 2-GB hard disk with at least 1 GB of available storage space (4-GB hard disk or larger with at least 2 GB available storage space recommended) in each computer
  - Two additional hard drives
  - A CD-ROM drive
- A telephone line or another type of connection to the Internet (cable, DSL, or faster preferred)
- Two modems
- A dial-up Internet account
- Internet access (this does not need to be through the dial-up account)
- At least four PCI Ethernet network interface cards with the following features:
  - Four with RJ-45 connectors
  - Two with BNC connectors (some network interface cards are available with both RJ-45 and BNC connectors)
  - Two from the following list: 3Com 3C509, 3Com 3C595, 3Com 3C905, Realtek NE2000 compatible, Realtek NE2000 PCI compatible, or ISA/PCI NE2000 compatible
- Category 5 UTP cabling to make cables
- Category 3 UTP cabling to make cables
- At least six Category 5 UTP straight-through patch cables
- At least two Category 5 UTP crossover patch cables
- RJ-45 connectors
- A computer professional's toolkit that includes a Phillips-head screwdriver, a ground strap, and a ground mat
- A networking professional's kit that includes a cable tester, crimper, wire stripper, and a wire cutting tool
- Four 10/100 Ethernet hubs
- Coaxial cable, T-connectors, and terminators
- Two fiber-optic bridges with AUI interfaces
- Two twisted-pair transceivers with an RJ-45 connection on one end and an AUI connection on the other end
- At least six feet of fiber-optic cable
- Access to two analog outside phone lines (or two digital lines and two digital-to-analog converters)

You may choose to install multiple network operating systems on each computer, as this will allow you to boot into a particular operating system when needed for a lab.

SOFTWARE/SETUP REQUIREMENTS

- At least two copies of Windows 2000 Server with Windows 2000 Service Pack 1
- At least one copy of Windows 2000 Professional
- Novell NetWare 5.x network operating system
- Linux Red Hat 7.x
- Microsoft IIS Version 5 installed on Windows 2000 Server
- A web browser such as Internet Explorer (Internet Explorer 5.0 is used in the text)
- Novell Client for Windows NT/2000 4.81
- Anti-virus software such as McAfee's VirusScan
- FREESCO 0.27 downloaded from *www.freesco.org*
- Microsoft Project 2000

ACKNOWLEDGMENTS

Michael Grice: I would like to thank Tamara Dean for her gracious help, and for introducing me to Course Technology. I would also like to thank Lisa Egan for bringing me on this project, Amy Lyon for being so well-organized and enthusiastic, Jill Batistick for making the labs more readable, James Conrad for catching all my mistakes in the first draft, and Nicole Ashton for catching everything that slipped through. Thanks also to all the peer reviewers who worked under very tight deadlines and gave us great feedback: Todd Koonts, Pat Lyon, Brian McCann, Judson Miers, David Pope, Sara Robben, and Chris Ward. Finally, I'd like to thank my lovely wife, Nancy, for her support and patience.

Tamara Dean: A warm thanks to the entire Course Technology team for making this book a reality. In particular, I would like to thank our Product Manager, Amy Lyon, and our Senior Editor, Lisa Egan, for their efficiency, planning, and support. Thanks also to Steve Elliot, Associate Publisher, Melissa Panagos, Production Editor, Nicole Ashton, Quality Assurance Technical Lead, and other editorial, production, and marketing staff who fostered the book from inception to fruition. Kudos to Jill Batistick, our Developmental Editor, for minding the clarity and consistency of our writing through every draft. Thanks also to the Technical Editor, James Conrad, who scrutinized the content and helped to make this lab manual more accurate and complete. Thanks to our dedicated team of peer reviewers: Todd Koonts, Pat Lyon, Brian McCann, Judson Miers, David Pope, Sara Robben, and Chris Ward. Thanks to my coauthor, Michael Grice, for being so diligent, personable, and just plain smart. Finally, thanks to friends and family who've shown enough interest in this series so that they now know the difference between a study guide and a lab manual (or so they say).

CHAPTER ONE

AN INTRODUCTION TO NETWORKING

Labs included in this chapter

➤ Lab 1.1 Understanding Elements of a Network

➤ Lab 1.2 Understanding How Networks Are Used

➤ Lab 1.3 Creating a Free Internet E-mail Account

➤ Lab 1.4 Searching for Networking Jobs

➤ Lab 1.5 Building a Simple Peer-to-Peer Network

Net+ Exam Objectives

Objective	Lab
Identify the purpose, features, and functions of the following network components: hubs, switches, bridges, routers, gateways, CSU/DSU, Network Interface Cards/ISDN adapters/system area network cards, wireless access points, modems	1.1, 1.2,
Recognize the following logical or physical network topologies given a schematic diagram or description: star, bus, mesh, ring, wireless	1.1
Recognize the following media connectors and/or describe their uses: RJ-11, RJ-45, AUI, BNC, ST, SC	1.1, 1.5
Identify the basic capabilities (i.e., client support, interoperability, authentication, file and print services, application support, and security) of the following server operating systems: UNIX/Linux, NetWare, Windows, Macintosh	1.2, 1.5
Define the function of the following remote access protocols and services: RAS, PPP, PPTP, ICA	1.2

LAB 1.1 UNDERSTANDING ELEMENTS OF A NETWORK

Objectives

When first learning about network components, it is often helpful to observe a live network and talk with experienced networking professionals. The concept of segments, connectivity devices, or structured wiring techniques, for example, can be more easily demonstrated on a real network than in a textbook. The goal of this lab is to explore some real-life examples of basic networking concepts. To complete this lab, you will be required to tour your school's computer laboratory or network and identify various networking components at that site. Alternately, your instructor might arrange your class to tour a business's network with a willing network professional.

After completing this lab, you will be able to:

➤ Identify and sketch the organization's network topology

➤ Identify the nodes on a real-life network

➤ Identify a network's network operating system and client software

➤ Identify protocols used by the network

Materials Required

This lab will require the following:

➤ A network professional or instructor willing to give you a tour of your school's computer laboratory or data center or a network professional willing to give you a tour of a network at a business, school, or other site

➤ Pencil and paper

Estimated completion time: **3 hours**

ACTIVITY

1. If you cannot tour your school's computer laboratory or data center, contact a business, school, or other organization and ask to interview the person in charge of their network. Explain that your purpose is purely educational and that you desire to learn more about networking. Also, explain that you will need to take notes.

2. Make the visit and with the guidance of the network administrator, observe the organization's network. Remember to ask for details about the network's topology, hardware, operating system, and protocols.

3. On a separate piece of paper, draw the site's network topology, using boxes to represent the components such as computers and printers. Draw lines to

connect the components. You might also use network-diagramming software such as Microsoft Visio in order to diagram the network.

4. On your diagram, label servers with the letter "S," workstations with the letter "W," and printer with the letter "P." Label devices used to connect other devices together (such as a hub) with a "C." If you are unsure about a network component, label the box with the letter "O" for "other."

5. Ask the networking professional or instructor for specifics about the network operating system (NOS) types and versions and the client types and versions used within this network. Record this information.

6. Record the make and model of any network interface cards (NICs). Note how many different types of NICs this network uses. If the number of different types is high (for example, over six), ask the network administrator how this variability affects network maintenance and troubleshooting.

7. Record the protocols used in the network.

8. If you toured an outside organization's network, thank the person you interviewed. Follow up later with a letter of thanks.

Certification Objectives

Objectives for the Network+ Exam:

➤ Identify the purpose, features, and functions of the following network components: hubs, switches, bridges, routers, gateways, CSU/DSU, Network Interface Cards/ISDN adapters/system area network cards, wireless access points, modems

➤ Recognize the following logical or physical network topologies given a schematic diagram or description: star, bus, mesh, ring, wireless

➤ Recognize the following media connectors and/or describe their uses: RJ-11, RJ-45, AUI, BNC, ST, SC

Review Questions

1. Which of the following best describes a network's physical topology?
   a. the method by which multiple nodes transmit signals over a shared communications channel
   b. the physical layout of a network
   c. the organization of a network's cable and wireless infrastructure
   d. the software used to ensure reliable connections between nodes on a network

2. Which of the following is the most popular type of modern network architecture?
   a. client/server
   b. terminal/mainframe
   c. peer-to-peer
   d. mainframe/dial-up

3. Which of the following elements is not required for a client to connect to a server on a client/server LAN?

   a. protocols

   b. media

   c. e-mail account

   d. client software

4. Which of the following are examples of client/server network operating systems? (Choose all that apply.)

   a. Windows 98

   b. Windows 2000 Server

   c. UNIX

   d. NetWare

5. Network protocols are used to do which of the following? (Choose all that apply.)

   a. to ensure reliable delivery of data

   b. to determine the nearest printer for a print job

   c. to interpret keyboard commands

   d. to indicate the source and destination addresses for data packets

6. On a client/server network, clients may have only one protocol installed at any time. True or False?

7. A significant difference between the peer-to-peer and client/server network types is that a peer-to-peer network _____.

   a. is more difficult to set up

   b. does not allow for resource sharing between workstations

   c. does not usually provide centralized management for shared resources

   d. is more secure

8. Why is it necessary for each client on a client/server network to have a unique address?

LAB 1.2 UNDERSTANDING HOW NETWORKS ARE USED

Objectives

As with network components, network services can be better understood through observing a live network than through simply reading a textbook. The goal of this lab is to help you learn more about how network services, such as remote access services and Internet services, are used in the real world. In addition, this lab will help you understand the importance of these services to an organization.

Server hardware includes the IBM xSeries 370, the Sun Enterprise 420R, and the Dell PowerEdge 7150 servers. Typical examples of software used for File and Print Services include the Windows 2000, Netware 5.x, and Linux/Unix network operating systems. Typical examples of software used in communication services include Routing and Remote Access Services in Windows 2000 and NetWare Connect in Netware 5.0.

Typical examples of software used for communication services include Microsoft Exchange Server, Novell's GroupWise, and Sendmail on UNIX and Linux. Many different software products may be used for Internet services. Examples include Microsoft's Internet Information Services (IIS) on Windows Servers and the Apache HTTP Server on UNIX or Linux servers, both of which are World Wide Web (WWW) servers. Examples of software used for management services include Novell's ManageWise, Microsoft Systems Management Server, and Hewlett-Packard OpenView Network Node Manager.

To do this lab, your instructor may arrange for you to tour your school's computer laboratory or network, or another organization's network. If you do not have access to a school's network, you may arrange your own tour with a willing network professional.

After completing this lab, you will be able to:

> ➤ Identify the types of network services used by an organization

> ➤ Describe the software and hardware used to supply these network services

> ➤ Identify the consequences for the organization if any of these services were to fail

Materials Required

This lab will require the following:

> ➤ A network professional or instructor willing to give you a tour of your school's computer laboratory or data center or a network professional willing to give you a tour of a network at a business, school, or other site. The network should include at least one server.

> ➤ Pencil and paper

Estimated completion time: **2 hours**

ACTIVITY

1. If you cannot tour your school's computer laboratory or data center, contact the network professional at the site. As in Lab 1.1, explain that your purpose is educational and that you will be taking notes about the network.

2. Make the visit and observe the network. Ask for descriptions of the network's File and Print Services, communications services, Internet services, and management services.

3. Record the software and hardware of the servers using File and Print Services. Ask your instructor or the person giving the tour for the business purpose or purposes fulfilled by these services for this organization.

4. Record the software and the hardware of the servers using communication services. What business purpose or purposes do these services fulfill for this organization?

5. Record the software and the hardware of the servers using e-mail services. What business purpose or purposes do these services fulfill for this organization?

6. Record the software and hardware of the servers using Internet services. What business purpose or purposes do these services fulfill for this organization?

7. Record the software and hardware of the servers using management services. What business purpose or purposes do these services fulfill for this organization?

8. Ask the network administrator to explain how the failure of the services described in Steps 3 through 7 would affect that organization. What steps have they taken to minimize the consequences of these failures?

Certification Objectives

Objectives for the Network+ Exam:

➤ Identify the purpose, features, and functions of the following network components: hubs, switches, bridges, routers, gateways, CSU/DSU, Network Interface Cards/ISDN adapters/system area network cards, wireless access points, modems

➤ Identify the basic capabilities (i.e., client support, interoperability, authentication, file and print services, application support, and security) of the following server operating systems: UNIX/Linux, NetWare, Windows, Macintosh

➤ Define the function of the following remote access protocols and services: RAS, PPP, PPTP, ICA

Review Questions

1. Which of the following network connectivity issues could be solved through the use of a communications server?
   a. A temporary employee does not have privileges to modify the files he needs to edit.
   b. A professor cannot connect to the Internet from his workstation on a university's LAN.
   c. An inventory control person in a warehouse needs to scan the bar codes of hundreds of auto parts into a networked database.
   d. A traveling salesperson needs to upload her sales figures to a database on the company's home network from her hotel room.

2. Which of the following is an example of a LAN's Internet service?
   a. Web site hosting
   b. translating data between two disparate e-mail systems
   c. saving a week's worth of data from a database to a backup tape
   d. issuing valid Internet IP addresses on a dynamic basis to multiple clients

3. Which of the following are advantages to using print services on a large LAN? (Choose all that apply.)

   a. Sharing printers between multiple clients can make printing faster for each client.

   b. Sharing printers between multiple clients reduces purchasing costs.

   c. Sharing printers between multiple clients saves maintenance efforts for printers.

   d. Sharing printers between multiple clients reduces per page printing costs.

4. Which two of the following network services together allow only appropriate personnel within an organization to access confidential files across a LAN?

   a. communications services

   b. Internet services

   c. management services

   d. file services

   e. print services

5. What would happen to the performance of a single server if it suddenly began to run all of the services mentioned in this lab?

6. Which of the following services would be considered management services? (Choose all that apply.)

   a. load balancing between servers

   b. granting access rights to files

   c. maintaining records of each client's network address

   d. enabling multiple users to share the same printer

7. As a network administrator, what concern might you have about establishing a remote access (or communications) server for your network?

   a. the availability of phone lines for remote users

   b. the modification of file access rights for users when they are mobile

   c. the assignment of printer device drivers to remote users

   d. the potential security risk of allowing users to remotely log on to your network

8. When used in the context of e-mail services, a gateway performs which of the following functions?

   a. routes e-mail messages from one LAN client to another client on the same LAN

   b. encrypts e-mail messages before they are transmitted from a LAN to the Internet

   c. allows two dissimilar e-mail programs to accept and interpret each others' messages

   d. manages the Inboxes and Outboxes for multiple users on a LAN

5. Based on what you learned during this lab or personal experience, identify two potential disadvantages to using a free e-mail account as opposed to one that you registered with an Internet Service Provider (ISP)?

6. Which of the following is mail-server software (and not mail-client software)?
   a. Netscape Communicator
   b. Microsoft Outlook
   c. Eudora
   d. Microsoft Exchange

LAB 1.4 SEARCHING FOR NETWORKING JOBS

Objectives

During this lab, you will search for jobs online. Many companies are now advertising their jobs nationally online. Additionally, many local papers now place their classified advertisements online so that they reach a larger audience. This means that you can search for jobs both nationally and regionally online. If you don't know the address of your local newspaper's Web site, your local reference librarian will know. This lab uses the Chicago Tribune's Web site as an example.

After completing this lab, you will be able to:

➤ Use the Internet to search for a job

➤ Identify the types of networking skills that are in demand, both nationally and regionally

Materials Required

This lab will require the following:

➤ A computer with access to the Internet

➤ A Web browser

Estimated completion time: **30 minutes**

ACTIVITY

1. Start your Internet browser.

2. Go to **www.hotjobs.com**.

3. Type **Network** in the Quick Job Search/Enter Keyword(s): text box, and then click the **Search** button.

4. Record the number of jobs that were returned. _____

5. Click the first job title in the list.

6. Record the job title. _____

7. Scroll down and notice that you can click the Apply to Job link at the bottom in order to apply for the job online. Do not apply for the job.

8. Type **www.chicagotribune.com** in the Address bar of your browser.

9. Click the **Classified** link.

10. Click the **Jobs** link.

11. Select **No Location Specified** from the Where do you want to work? drop-down list.

12. Select **IT/MIS** (an abbreviation for Information Technology/Management Information Services) from the Select a Job Category drop-down list. Type **networking** in the blank below it.

13. Click the **Go!** button.

14. Click the link to the first job listed. Record the title. _____

15. Exit the Web browser.

Certification Objectives

Objectives for the Network+ Exam:

This lab does not directly map to an objective on the exam. However, it does teach a skill that is valuable to networking professionals.

Review Questions

1. Based on your search of networking jobs, arrange the following skills in the order in which you think they would be most marketable:
   - Fiber-optic cable installation expertise
   - 10Base5 networking expertise
   - Knowledge of Windows 2000 Server
   - Network+ certification
   - Knowledge of NetWare 5.x
   - Project management experience
   - Cisco router configuration expertise

2. List at least three benefits of obtaining a networking certification, such as CompTIA's Network+. _____

3. Order the following organizations according to the number and sophistication of networking professionals they are most likely to hire.
   - A chain of three taverns located within one medium-sized city
   - A state university with 20,000 students
   - An insurance company with field offices in 20 cities across the state
   - The federal government's social security agency and its offices across the country
   - A regional hospital with five area clinics
   - A local flooring store

4. Order the organizations listed in Review Question 3 according to their need for network security specialists. _____

LAB 1.5 BUILDING A SIMPLE PEER-TO-PEER NETWORK

Objectives

Peer-to-peer networks are commonly found in offices where only a handful of users have access to networked computers, as they do not scale well and do not provide good security. However, peer-to-peer networks are an excellent choice in a few situations because they are simple and inexpensive to configure. A home office with three to five computers and only a couple of users, for example, would make a good candidate for peer-to-peer networking.

The goal of this lab is to become familiar with the methods for establishing a simple peer-to-peer network. During this lab you will be introduced to the hardware and software required to connect two workstations so that they can share each other's resources, such as files and CD-ROM drives.

Materials Required

This lab will require the following:

➤ Two computers running Windows 2000 Professional, with Ethernet NICs with RJ-45 connectors, powered on for five minutes prior to the beginning of the lab

➤ A CD-ROM drive for one of the computers

➤ Access to both computers as an administrator (with different administrator passwords)

➤ Client for Microsoft Networks and File and Printer Sharing for Microsoft Networks installed on both computers

➤ Crossover cable with RJ-45 connectors at either end

➤ A CD with data files on it

Estimated completion time: **30 minutes**

ACTIVITY

1. Plug one end of the crossover cable into the NIC in one machine and the other end into the NIC in the other machine. A link light on both NICs illuminates, indicating that each NIC has successfully connected.

2. On each machine, press **Ctrl + Alt + Del**. The Windows 2000 login dialog box appears.

3. Log into both machines as an administrator or as a user with equivalent rights.

4. Insert the CD-ROM in the CD-ROM drive. If both machines have a CD-ROM drive, select one at random.

5. Right-click the **My Network Places** icon on the desktop, and then click **Properties**.

6. Click the **Advanced** menu at the top of the window, and then click **Network Identification**. The System Properties dialog box appears.

7. Click the **Network Identification** tab, if necessary, and then click **Properties**. Change the name of the computer to **CDROM**.

8. At the bottom of the dialog box, click **Workgroup**. Type **NetPlus** for the name of the workgroup, and then click **OK**. A message box appears, welcoming you to the NetPlus workgroup. Click **OK**. A dialog box appears, indicating that you must reboot the computer for the changes to take effect.

9. Click **OK** to close the dialog box, and then click **OK** again to close the System Properties dialog box.

10. The Systems Settings Change dialog box appears. Cick **Yes** to reboot the computer.

11. After logging back into the computer, click **Start**, point to **Programs**, click **Accessories**, and then click **Windows Explorer**. Find the icon for the CD-ROM drive in the left pane of Windows Explorer. Right-click the **CD-ROM** icon and then click **Properties**.

12. Click the **Sharing** tab.

13. Click **Share this folder**, then type a share name of **SHAREDFILES**.

14. Click **OK** to exit. You have now shared the CD-ROM drive on this computer so that the other can access it.

15. On the computer without the CD-ROM disk inserted, right-click **My Network Places**, and then click **Properties**.

CHAPTER TWO

NETWORKING STANDARDS AND THE OSI MODEL

Labs included in this chapter

➤ Lab 2.1 Networking Standards Organization
➤ Lab 2.2 The OSI Model
➤ Lab 2.3 Investigating IEEE 802.11 Standards
➤ Lab 2.4 Determining the MAC Address of a Windows 2000 Computer
➤ Lab 2.5 Understanding Frame Types

Net+ Exam Objectives

Objective	Lab
Specify the main features of 802.2 (LLC), 802.3 (Ethernet), 802.5 (token ring), 802.11b (wireless), and FDDI networking technologies, including: speed, access, method, topology, media	2.1, 2.3, 2.5
Identify the seven layers of the OSI model and their functions	2.2
Identify the OSI layers at which the following network components operate: hubs, switches, bridges, routers, network interface cards	2.2
Recognize the following logical or physical network topologies given a schematic diagram or description: star, bus, mesh, ring, wireless	2.3
Given an example, identify a MAC address	2.4
Given a troubleshooting scenario, select the appropriate TCP/IP utility from among the following: tracert, ping, netstat, nbtstat, arp, ipconfig, ifconfig winipcfg, nslookup	2.4
Given output from a diagnostic utility (e.g., tracert, ping, ipconfig, etc.), identify the utility and interpret the output	2.4
Identify the basic capabilities (i.e., client support, interoperability, authentication, file and print services, application support, and security) of the following server operating systems: UNIX/Linux, NetWare, Windows, Macintosh	2.5
Given a network configuration, select the appropriate NIC and network configuration settings (DHCP, DNS, WINS, protocols, NetBIOS/host name, etc.)	2.5

Lab 2.1 Networking Standards Organization

Objectives

Networking standards play an important role in the technologies you will use during your networking career. Most importantly, a networking standard allows vendors of many different manufacturers to produce products that work together. The extent to which a standard is approved and accepted by the industry also helps determine how widely it is used.

In this lab you will explore the standards set by two organizations. The first is ANSI (American National Standards Institute), which is an organization composed of more than 1000 representatives from industry and government who together determine standards for the electronics industry in addition to other fields, such as chemical and nuclear engineering, health and safety, and construction. The second is ISO (International Organization for Standardization), which is a collection of standards organizations representing 130 countries whose headquarters is located in Geneva, Switzerland. The ISO's goal is to establish international technological standards to facilitate global exchange of information and barrier-free trade.

After completing this lab, you will be able to:

> ➤ Understand the purpose of networking standards organizations

Materials Required

This lab will require the following:

> ➤ A computer with an Internet connection and a Web browser
> ➤ Pencil and paper

Estimated completion time: **20–25 minutes**

Activity

1. Open your Internet browser.

2. Go to **www.ansi.org**. The ANSI home page appears.

3. Click the **ABOUT ANSI** link. The About ANSI page appears.

4. Read the information about this organization, and click the **NEXT** link at the bottom of the page to proceed to the next page.

5. Review the complete explanation of the purpose of ANSI. There are several pages, which you can navigate between using the arrow buttons at the bottom of the page.

6. Write a summary of the purpose of ANSI.

   _____

   _____

   _____

   _____

   _____

7. Go to **www.iso.ch**. The ISO home page appears on your screen. Click the **enter** link at the bottom of the page.

8. Click the **About ISO** link. The What are standards? page appears with several hyperlinks on the left side of the screen. Scroll down to see the information that is referenced in the hyperlinks on the What are standards? page.

9. Read the information about this organization and write a summary of its purpose.

   _____

   _____

   _____

   _____

   _____

10. Exit the Web site and the Web browser.

Certification Objectives

Objectives for the Network+ Exam:

➤ Specify the main features of 802.2 (LLC), 802.3 (Ethernet), 802.5 (token ring), 802.11b (wireless), and FDDI networking technologies, including: speed, access, method, topology, media

Review Questions

1. What standards organization represents the United States in setting international standards?

   a. ANSI

   b. ISO

   c. ITU

   d. CCITT

2. What standards organization promotes development and education in the electrical engineering and computer science fields?

   a. ISO

   b. ANSI

   c. IEEE

   d. ITU

3. What is the geographical area to which ISO's standards apply?
   a. the world
   b. the United States
   c. North America
   d. the northern hemisphere

4. What standards organization is part of the United Nations?
   a. EIA
   b. ANSI
   c. IEEE
   d. ITU

5. Which standards organization specifies methods for installing network cabling in a building?
   a. ANSI
   b. ITU
   c. EIA
   d. IEEE

6. Which of the following is addressed by an IEEE standard?
   a. the type of media used by Ethernet networks
   b. the size of an RJ-45 plug
   c. the API used for network telephony
   d. the optimal environmental conditions for a telecommunications closet

LAB 2.2 THE OSI MODEL

Objectives

Because you can't see the communication that occurs between two nodes on a network, it may help to rely on a model that depicts how the communication takes place. The model commonly used to describe network communications is called the Open Systems Interconnection (OSI) Model. It's important to note that the OSI Model describes only what transpires when two computer systems communicate. It does not describe how an application launches on a single computer, for example, or how network cabling should be installed. In this lab, you will learn more about the OSI Model by drawing a representation of a data packet as it moves between a source and destination on the network.

After completing this lab, you will be able to:

➤ Identify the functions of the layers of the OSI Model

➤ Identify the networking devices that transform data at each layer of the OSI Model

Materials Required

This lab will require the following:

➤ Pencil and paper

Estimated completion time: **15 minutes**

 ## ACTIVITY

1. Draw a small rectangle that represents the payload data to be sent between two computers on a network. For example, you may simply want to write "text" in the rectangle.

2. Directly above the rectangle, draw another identical rectangle. Now append a small box to the left of the rectangle that represents the information added to the data as the data traverses the Physical layer of the OSI Model. To the right of the new, elongated rectangle write "Physical layer."

3. Repeat Step 2 for the Data Link layer, drawing a rectangle identical to the one now pictured for the Physical layer above the Physical layer and appending boxes that represent the fields added to the data as it traverses the Data Link layer of the OSI Model. If you do not know the proper abbreviations for every added field, simply make a notation that indicates what type of information would be added at each layer.

4. Repeat the same process for the Network, Transport, Session, Presentation, and Application layers of the OSI Model. Notice how the data field's size increases as it moves up the layers.

5. Once you have diagrammed the data from the Physical to the Application layer and for the Network, Data Link, and Physical layers, indicate one type of device that could modify the data at each layer.

Certification Objectives

Objectives for the Network+ Exam:

➤ Identify the seven layers of the OSI Model and their functions

➤ Identify the OSI layers at which the following network components operate: hubs, switches, bridges, routers, network interface cards

Review Questions

1. Which layer of the OSI Model is responsible for encrypting data before it is transmitted?
   a. Physical
   b. Session
   c. Presentation
   d. Application

2. At which layer of the OSI Model is a logical address appended to a data frame?
   a. Physical
   b. Data Link
   c. Transport
   d. Network

3. Which of the following is a function of the Transport layer?
   a. assigning a physical address
   b. determining the best path for data between two nodes
   c. issuing electrical signals onto a wire
   d. arranging data in proper sequence at their destination

4. Which layer of the OSI Model deals with cable specifications?
   a. Physical
   b. Data Link
   c. Network
   d. Transport

5. Which layer of the OSI Model can be called "the traffic cop" because it manages communication?
   a. Data Link
   b. Network
   c. Presentation
   d. Session

6. To what layer of the OSI Model do routers belong?
   a. Transport
   b. Network
   c. Session
   d. Application

7. Which of the following is a function of the Data Link layer?
   a. arranging data in proper sequence at their destination
   b. encrypting data prior to transmission
   c. dividing data into distinct frames
   d. issuing electrical signals onto a wire

8. What part of a data frame checks to make sure that the data arrived exactly as it was sent?

   a. CRC

   b. start delimiter

   c. payload

   d. padding

LAB 2.3 INVESTIGATING IEEE 802.11 STANDARDS

Objectives

Now that you have discovered more about the standards organizations that establish conventions for networking hardware and software, you can explore a specific networking standard in more detail. Although some standards, such as IEEE's 802.3 Ethernet standard, are well-established and widely accepted in the industry, other newer standards are not as universally understood. One example of a newer standard is the IEEE 802.11b standard that describes a method of connecting LAN nodes through wireless communication. The goal of this lab is to introduce you to the emerging standards for wireless networking that fall under the auspices of the IEEE 802.11 Committee.

After completing this lab, you will be able to:

➤ Identify the purpose of the IEEE Standards Committees

➤ Identify standards for wireless networking

➤ Describe the difficulties involved in developing wireless networking standards

Materials Required

This lab will require the following:

➤ A computer with access to the Internet and a Web browser

Estimated completion time: **15 minutes**

ACTIVITY

1. Open your Web browser.

2. Go to **www.webopedia.com**.

3. Type **802.11** in the Search box, and then click the **Go!** button.

4. The definition of the 802.11 specifications appears, along with a series of links to further information at the bottom. In your own words, write the definition of the 802.11 standard.

4. Type **ipconfig /all**, and look for the MAC address in the output. The MAC address is called the Physical Address in the output of the ipconfig command. Record the MAC address of this computer.

_____

5. Type **exit**. The command prompt window closes.

Certification Objectives

Objectives for the Network+ Exam:

➤ Given an example, identify a MAC address

➤ Given a troubleshooting scenario, select the appropriate TCP/IP utility from among the following: tracert, ping, netstat, nbtstat, arp, ipconfig, ifconfig winipcfg, nslookup

➤ Given output from a diagnostic utility (e.g., tracert, ping, ipconfig, etc.), identify the utility and interpret the output

Review Questions

1. What is the purpose of the MAC address?
   a. to indicate the type of protocol a workstation or server uses
   b. to uniquely identify a node's network interface
   c. to signify the type of encryption scheme an application requires
   d. to indicate the maximum time to live for a data packet

2. MAC addresses are initially assigned by the _____.
   a. NIC manufacturer
   b. network administrator
   c. workstation user
   d. central numbering authority on the Internet

3. The MAC address of two computers can be the same. True or False?

4. Which of the following is a valid MAC address?
   a. AD005G211L9
   b. 188.23.65.88
   c. 238800ACD403
   d. 100.100.100.1

5. What is the purpose of the Block ID?
   a. to represent the NIC manufacturer
   b. to represent the server's NOS version
   c. to represent the maximum throughput a network interface can handle
   d. to represent the type of plug a NIC requires

6. Where in a MAC address does the Device ID appear?
  a. in the first six digits
  b. in the second six digits
  c. in the first twelve digits
  d. in the second twelve digits

7. Which of the following is synonymous with "MAC address"?
  a. physical address
  b. network address
  c. logical address
  d. host address

LAB 2.5 UNDERSTANDING FRAME TYPES

Objectives

The purpose of this lab is to help you understand the importance of choosing the correct frame type when communicating with Novell NetWare servers. Each frame type follows a different networking standard. A Novell 4.x and higher server, running IPX, will use the 802.2 frame type by default. A Novell server running a version of the NOS lower than 4.x along with IPX will use 802.3 frame types by default. A Novell server running TCP/IP will use Ethernet_II as the frame type.

After completing this lab you will be able to:

➤ Configure frame types on a Windows 2000 server

➤ Identify incompatible frame types

Materials Required

This lab will require the following:

➤ One computer running Novell NetWare 5.x Server with an internal network number of 13 and a network number of A

➤ One computer running Microsoft Windows 2000 Server with the NWLink IPX/SPX/NetBIOS Compatible Transport protocol installed

➤ Microsoft GSNW (Gateway Services for NetWare) loaded on the Windows 2000 server

➤ Access as an administrator to the Windows 2000 server

Estimated completion time: **20–25 minutes**

ACTIVITY

1. On the Windows 2000 computer, press **Control + Alt + Delete**. The Log On to Windows screen appears.

2. Log on as an administrator or a user with equivalent privileges. The Windows 2000 desktop appears.

3. On the Windows 2000 computer, right-click **My Network Places**, and then click **Properties**. The Network and Dial-up Connections window appears.

4. Right-click **Local Area Connection**, and then click **Properties**. The Local Area Connection Properties dialog box opens.

5. Click **NWLink IPX/SPX/NetBIOS Compatible Transport Protocol** in the list of components used by this connection. The entry is highlighted.

6. Click **Properties**. The NWLink IPX/SPX/NetBIOS Compatible Transport Protocol Properties dialog box opens.

7. In the General tab, change the Internal network number to **13**.

8. Click **Manual frame type detection**. In the next step, you will manually select the frame type.

9. Click **Add**. The Manual Frame Detection dialog box opens. In this dialog box, you can select a frame type and a network number.

10. Click **Ethernet 802.3** in the Frame type list box. Selecting this frame type will prevent the Windows 2000 server from communicating with the Novell 5.x server, because the Novell server defaults to 802.2 frame types.

11. In the Network number text box, type **A**. This is the same network number as the Novell 5.0 server. Click **OK** to create the frame type and network number and to close the Manual Frame Detection dialog box. Click **OK** to close the dialog box.

12. Close the Local Area Connection Properties box.

13. Double-click the **My Network Places** icon, and then double-click **Entire Network**. If you do not see the Netware or Compatible Network icon, click the **hyperlink** in the left pane of the window for the entire contents of the network. The Netware or Compatible Network icon appears. Double-click the **Netware or Compatible Network** icon.

14. Look for the Novell server in My Network Places.

Certification Objectives

Objectives for the Network+ Exam:

➤ Specify the main features of 802.2 (LLC), 802.3 (Ethernet), 802.5 (token ring), 802.11b (wireless), and FDDI networking technologies, including: speed, access, method, topology, media

➤ Identify the basic capabilities (i.e., client support, interoperability, authentication, file and print services, application support, and security) of the following server operating systems: UNIX/Linux, NetWare, Windows, Macintosh

➤ Given a network configuration, select the appropriate NIC and network configuration settings (DHCP, DNS, WINS, protocols, NetBIOS/host name, etc.)

Review Questions

1. If you modify the frame type used by a server, you must modify the frame type used by its clients to be the same in order for those clients to communicate with the server. True or False?

2. Which of the following networks use 802.3 frames? (Choose all that apply.)
   a. 10BaseT
   b. 10Base5
   c. ATM
   d. Token Ring

3. Which of the following networks uses 802.5 frames?
   a. 10BaseT
   b. 10Base5
   c. ATM
   d. Token Ring

4. Which protocol is the most likely to be used on modern networks?
   a. IPX/SPX
   b. TCP/IP
   c. AppleTalk
   d. NetBEUI

5. What is the default frame type for a server running Novell 5.x?
   a. 802.2
   b. 802.3
   c. Ethernet_II
   d. 802.12

LAB 3.1 USING ADDRESS RESOLUTION PROTOCOL (ARP)

Objectives

The goal of this lab is to help you learn about the Address Resolution Protocol, or ARP. ARP is critical to the function of TCP/IP because it associates physical address information from the second layer of the OSI Model (a MAC address) to the third layer (an IP address).

The ARP cache is a database that maps Layer 3 IP addresses (logical addresses) to Layer 2 MAC addresses (physical addresses). In Windows 2000, if an ARP cache entry is not used within two minutes, it is deleted. If it is reused, it will remain in the cache for another two minutes (up to a maximum of 10 minutes). ARP can be a valuable troubleshooting tool for discovering the identity of a machine whose IP address you know, or for solving the problem of two machines trying to use the same IP address.

After completing this lab, you will be able to:

➤ View the ARP cache

➤ Place an IP address to MAC address mapping in the ARP cache

➤ Understand the purpose of ARP

Materials Required

This lab will require the following:

➤ Two networked computers running Microsoft Windows 2000 Server or Windows 2000 Professional with TCP/IP installed and running on each computer

---

Estimated completion time: **10 minutes**

ACTIVITY

1. Log on to both computers.

2. On each computer, click **Start**, point to **Programs**, point to **Accessories**, and then click **Command Prompt**. The Command Prompt screen appears, displaying the D:\> prompt (your command prompt may be another letter, such as C:).

3. On each computer, type **ipconfig /all**. The TCP/IP settings for this computer display.

4. Record the IP address of each computer:
   Computer one

   _____

   Computer two

   _____

5. Record the physical address of each computer:
   Computer one

   _____

   Computer two

   _____

6. At computer one, type **arp /?**. This will show you a list of all the options you can use with the arp command, and a brief description of how to use them. You can find information about almost any command by typing /? after it in a command prompt.

7. Type **arp –a** at the command prompt. You may see a mapping of IP addresses to MAC (physical) addresses, as shown in Figure 3-1. This mapping is stored in the ARP cache. More likely, however, you will see a message indicating that no entries are found in the ARP cache.

```
D:\>arp -a

Interface: 160.100.100.112 on Interface 3
  Internet Address        Physical Address        Type
  160.100.100.22          00-e0-29-22-eb-b6       dynamic

D:\>
```

Figure 3-1   Results of the arp command

6. At computer one, type **ping** followed by the IP address of computer two. For example, if the IP address of computer two is 160.100.100.200, you would type ping 160.100.100.200. This command sends an Internet Control Message Protocol (ICMP) message to the second computer requesting a response. Note, however, that the computer must first make an ARP request to find the other computer's MAC address.

7. At the command prompt on computer one, type **arp –a** again. Record the result.

   _____

8. At the command prompt on computer two, type **arp –a** again. Record the result.

   _____

9. Compare the physical address of computer one to the physical address(es) found with the arp command on computer two. Additionally, compare the physical address of computer two to the physical address(es) found with the arp command on computer one. What do you notice about the two MAC addresses?

   _____

10. Close the Command Prompt window on both computers.

Certification Objectives

Objectives for the Network+ Exam:

➤ Give an example, identify a MAC address

➤ Define the purpose, function and/or use of the following protocols within TCP/IP: IP, TCP, UDP, FTP, TFTP, SMTP, HTTP, HTTPS, POP3/IMAP4, TELNET, ICMP, ARP, NTP

Review Questions

1. What does the "R" in ARP stand for?
   a. registration
   b. resolution
   c. resource
   d. remote

2. What is the purpose of the ARP cache?
   a. to retain a table of IP addresses and their associated host names
   b. to dynamically supply IP addresses to hosts logging on to a network
   c. to retain a table of IP addresses and their associated MAC addresses
   d. to retain recently accessed files from the Internet

3. Which of the following network components is responsible for generating ARP requests?
   a. NIC
   b. connector
   c. cable
   d. modem

4. What is the maximum amount of time an entry will remain in an ARP cache?
   a. one minute
   b. 10 minutes
   c. 60 minutes
   d. indefinitely, until the cache is manually cleared

5. Which of the following network nodes would not maintain an ARP cache?
   a. workstation
   b. server
   c. bridge
   d. repeater

6. ARP operates at the Application layer of the OSI Model. True or False?

LAB 3.2 REMOVING AND REINSTALLING THE TCP/IP PROTOCOL ON A WINDOWS 2000 SERVER

3

Objectives

The goal of this lab is to help you learn about removing and installing the TCP/IP protocol. Without a Network layer protocol, a networked node cannot interconnect with dissimilar networks, which limits the network's size and capabilities. Without a network protocol like TCP/IP, the Internet would not be possible. Because you have to configure Network layer addresses, however, network protocols are more complex to configure than Physical layer addresses, which typically require no configuration. In this lab, you will also configure IP address information.

After completing this lab, you will be able to:

➤ Remove the TCP/IP protocol from a computer

➤ Set IP address and subnet mask properties for a Windows 2000 Server computer

Materials Required

This lab will require the following:

➤ One computer with Microsoft Windows 2000 Server or Professional installed on it

Estimated completion time: **15–20 minutes**

ACTIVITY

1. Press **Ctrl + Alt + Del**. The Log On Windows screen appears.

2. Log on to the Microsoft Windows 2000 Server computer as an administrator.

3. Right-click the **My Network Places** icon, and then click **Properties**. The Network and Dial-up Connections window appears.

4. Right-click the **Local Area Connection** icon, and then click **Properties**. The Local Area Connection dialog box opens.

5. Click **Internet Protocol (TCP/IP)**. Internet Protocol (TCP/IP) is highlighted.

6. Click **Uninstall**. A warning message appears, indicating that removing this protocol will remove it from all connections.

7. Click **Yes**. The TCP/IP protocol is removed and the Local Network dialog box opens, indicating that you must shut down and restart the computer before the new settings will take effect.

8. Click **Yes** to restart the computer.

9. Once the computer has restarted, log on as an administrator.

10. Right-click the **My Network Places** icon, and then click **Properties**. The Network and Dial-up Connections window appears.

11. Right-click the **Local Area Connection** icon, and then click **Properties**. The Local Area Connection dialog box opens.

12. Click the **Install** button. The Select Network Component Type dialog box opens. Click **Protocol** and then click **Add**. The Select Network Protocol dialog box opens.

13. Click **Internet Protocol (TCP/IP)**, and then click **OK**. The TCP/IP protocol is added and the Local Area Connection Properties dialog box opens.

14. Select **Internet Protocol (TCP/IP)**, and then click **Properties**. The Internet Protocol (TCP/IP) Properties dialog box opens, as shown in Figure 3-2. Here you can enter the computer's IP address and subnet mask properties.

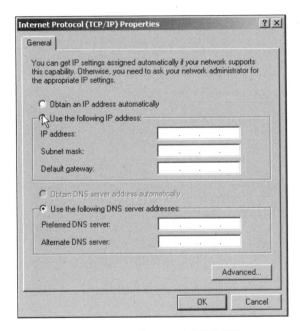

Figure 3-2   Internet Protocol (TCP/IP)

15. Click the **Use the following IP address:** option button, as shown in Figure 3-2. The IP address:, Subnet mask:, and Default gateway: text boxes become enabled.

16. Type **172.25.100.105** as the IP address for your computer in the IP address: text box.

17. Click the **Subnet mask:** text box. A default subnet mask appears. Record the default subnet mask.

3

18. Type **172.25.100.1** in the Default gateway: text box.

19. Click **OK**. The Local Area Connection Properties box appears again.

20. Click **OK** to exit the box.

21. Click **Start**, point to **Programs**, click **Accessories**, and then click **Command Prompt**.

22. At the command prompt, type **ipconfig**. The IP address and subnet mask that you noted in Steps 17 through 19 should appear.

23. Close the Command Prompt window and any other application windows that are still open.

Certification Objectives

Objectives for the Network+ Exam:

➤ Identify IP addresses (IPv4, IPv6) and their default subnet masks

➤ Define the purpose, function and/or use of the following protocols within TCP/IP: IP, TCP, UDP, FTP, TFTP, SMTP, HTTP, HTTPS, POP3/IMAP4, TELNET, ICMP, ARP, NTP

Review Questions

1. Which of the following protocols forms the basis of all Internet traffic?
   a. NetBIOS
   b. IPX/SPX
   c. TCP/IP
   d. AppleTalk

2. At which layer of the OSI Model does IP operate?
   a. Physical
   b. Data Link
   c. Transport
   d. Network

3. Which of the following is a valid TCP/IP address?
   a. 1.1.1.1
   b. EF-34-AA-0B-2A-C6
   c. 543.78.100.92
   d. FF-FF-FF-FF-FF-FF

4. What does the "T" in TCP/IP stand for?
   a. Transmission
   b. Transport
   c. Telecommunications
   d. Terminal

5. List the steps required to add another protocol, such as IPX/SPX, to a Windows 2000 computer.

6. Which of the following protocols is not routable?
   a. NetBEUI
   b. IPX/SPX
   c. TCP/IP
   d. AppleTalk

7. What type of TCP/IP network uses a default subnet mask of 255.255.0.0?
   a. Class A
   b. Class B
   c. Class C
   d. Class D

8. Which of the following subprotocols within the TCP/IP suite is connectionless?
   a. TCP
   b. IP
   c. Telnet
   d. FTP

LAB 3.3 UNBINDING THE TCP/IP PROTOCOL ON A NOVELL NETWARE 5.x SERVER

Objectives

The goal of this lab is to help you learn how to unbind the TCP/IP protocol on a Novell NetWare 5.x server. Additionally, you will learn how to configure a NetWare 5.x server with an IP address and a subnet mask. Binding is the process of associating a protocol to a NIC. A protocol must be bound to a computer's NIC before the computer can communicate with other computers on a network. Because running several different protocols in a network can add unnecessary complexity and overhead, you will want to reduce the number of protocols when possible by unbinding them from servers and clients.

After completing this lab, you will be able to:

➤ Explain the necessity of binding protocols

➤ Bind and unbind the TCP/IP protocol on a Novell NetWare 5.x server

Materials Required

This lab will require the following:

➤ A computer running Novell NetWare 5.x Server and running the TCP/IP protocol with an IP address of 165.100.100.100

> ➤ A NIC driver on the NetWare 5.x server with a known name, such as the SMCPWRII driver

> ➤ A Windows 2000 Professional computer running the TCP/IP protocol, with Client Services for NetWare installed

> ➤ Administrator access to both computers

> ➤ All networking equipment necessary to allow the computers to communicate on a network

Estimated completion time: **15 minutes**

ACTIVITY

1. Log on to the Windows 2000 computer as an administrator.

2. Click **Start**, point to **Programs**, point to **Accessories**, and then click **Command Prompt**.

3. Type **ping 165.100.100.100**. You should see four reply statements listing the IP address of the computer you are pinging, the number of bytes sent, the time in milliseconds, and the Time To Live, or TTL, value. (TTL indicates how long a data packet may circulate on the network before being discarded.)

4. Go to the Novell server computer and type **unbind ip from smcpwrii** at the prompt. If the NIC driver has a different name, substitute its name for smcpwrii. A screen similar to Figure 3–3 appears.

Figure 3-3   Unbinding the IP protocol from the NIC

5. At the Windows 2000 Professional computer, attempt to ping the Novell NetWare 5.i server again, as in Step 3. Record the result.

_____

6. At the Novell server, bind the IP protocol to the NIC again by typing **bind ip to smcpwrii addr=165.100.100.100 mask=255.255.0.0**.

7. Attempt to ping the server from the client computer. Record the result.

_____

8. Close the Command Prompt window.

Certification Objectives

Objectives for the Network+ Exam:

➤ Identify IP addresses (IPv4, IPv6) and their default subnet masks

➤ Define the purpose, function and/or use of the following protocols within TCP/IP: IP, TCP, UDP, FTP, TFTP, SMTP, HTTP, HTTPS, POP3/IMAP4, TELNET, ICMP, ARP, NTP

Review Questions

1. Which of the following best describes the concept of binding?
   a. installing a NIC on a computer's system board
   b. attaching a computer's NIC to a cable
   c. assigning a logical address to a computer's client software
   d. associating a protocol with a computer's network interface

2. What protocol used to be required for NetWare servers using version 3.11?
   a. NetBEUI
   b. IPX/SPX
   c. TCP/IP
   d. AppleTalk

3. If a protocol is not bound to a NIC, the computer cannot be accessed over the network. True or False?

4. What protocol would you need to install on a Windows 2000 computer if you want to access a Novell server that uses only the IPX/SPX protocol?
   a. NetBEUI
   b. IPX/SPX
   c. TCP/IP
   d. AppleTalk

5. What is the default protocol used on both Windows 2000 Server and NetWare 5.x?
   a. NetBEUI
   b. IPX/SPX
   c. TCP/IP
   d. AppleTalk

6. How many protocols can be bound on one server?
   a. only one
   b. no more than two
   c. no more than three
   d. as many as are necessary

LAB 3.4 CHANGING THE BINDING ORDER ON A MULTIPROTOCOL NETWORK

Objectives

The goal of this lab is to help you understand how the binding order affects network performance. On many networks, multiple protocols are necessary in order to meet the requirements of multiple clients and servers. Clients in your network might use TCP/IP to communicate with UNIX and Linux servers, IPX to communicate with NetWare servers, and NetBEUI to communicate with Windows 2000 servers.

Multiple protocols may be bound and running on a computer. However, this adds complexity and overhead to your network. Windows computers will also attempt to use protocols in the order specified by the binding order. If it can't use the first protocol to use a network resource, it will go on to the next, and so on. To conserve network resources and improve performance, you should place the most frequently used protocols at the top of the binding list.

After completing this lab, you will be able to:

➤ Change the protocol binding order on Microsoft Windows 2000 computers

➤ Discuss how the binding order affects network performance

Materials Required

This lab will require the following:

➤ One computer with Microsoft Windows 2000 Server or Microsoft Windows 2000 Professional running TCP/IP, NWLink, and NetBEUI

➤ All networking equipment necessary to allow the computers to communicate on a network

Estimated completion time: **10–15 minutes**

ACTIVITY

1. Log on to the Windows 2000 computer as an administrator.

2. Right-click the **My Network Places** icon, and then click **Properties**. The Network and Dial-up Connections window appears.

3. Click the **Advanced** menu at the top of the window, and select **Advanced Settings**. The Advanced Settings dialog box opens, as shown in Figure 3-4.

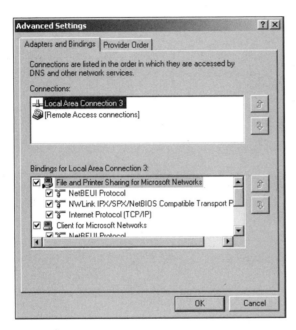

Figure 3-4   Advanced Settings dialog box

4. Observe the list of services that are running on your computer. In Windows 2000, a service is bound to a protocol, and then the protocol is bound to a NIC.

5. Record the binding order for the Client for Microsoft Networks.

_____

6. Click the **protocol** on the bottom of the list, and then click the **up arrow** to the right of the bindings box until the protocol is at the top of the list.

7. Click the **Provider Order** tab, if necessary. A list of network providers appears, as shown in Figure 3-5. Record the order of network providers.

_____

3

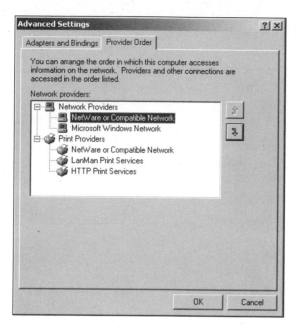

Figure 3-5   Provider Order tab

8. Click **Microsoft Windows Network** to select it. If it is at the top of the list, move it to the bottom with the down arrow key. If it is at the bottom of the list, move it to the top.

9. Click **OK**. The changes are written to the Registry.

10. Click the **Advanced** menu at the top of the window, and select **Advanced Settings** to open the Advanced Settings dialog box again. Record the new binding order.

_____

11. Set your binding order for the Client for Microsoft Networks to reflect the original settings you recorded in Step 5.

12. Click the **Provider Order** tab. Set the provider order to reflect the original settings recorded in Step 7.

13. Close the Advanced Settings dialog box and any open windows.

Certification Objectives

Objectives for the Network+ Exam:

➤ Differentiate between the following network protocols in terms of routing, addressing schemes, interoperability and naming conventions: TCP/IP, IPX/SPX, NetBEUI and AppleTalk

➤ Identify the basic capabilities (i.e., client connectivity, local security and authentication) of network clients

Review Questions

1. On a Windows 2000-based network, services are bound to protocols and protocols are bound to NICs. True or False?

2. If you are using both IPX/SPX and TCP/IP on a network that uses a Windows 2000 server to supply users with applications and data sharing space and a NetWare 4.11 server to manage a tape backup device, what binding order should you use on the Windows 2000 server?

3. For which of the following network components is binding order a factor in performance? (Choose all that apply.)
   a. workstation
   b. server
   c. hub
   d. switch

4. If you install the Windows 2000 Server operating system and choose to install NetBEUI as well as TCP/IP, what will the default binding order be?
   a. TCP/IP, NetBEUI
   b. NetBEUI, TCP/IP
   c. The binding order cannot be predicted.
   d. The binding order will vary depending on the selections made during installation.

5. What is the best binding policy in order to optimize performance on a Windows-based network?
   a. The most frequently used interfaces should be at the top of the order.
   b. The most infrequently used interfaces should be at the top of the order.
   c. The most frequently used protocols should be at the top of the order.
   d. Binding order does not affect performance on a Windows-based network.

LAB 3.5 DISABLING UNNECESSARY PROTOCOLS

Objectives

The goal of this lab is to help you learn how to disable protocols that are not being used. You will often be able to configure multiple network clients to use only one or two network protocols. Disabling or removing a protocol will reduce network traffic and the load on your servers. On a computer with multiple NICs, you may find it useful to disable a protocol on one interface and leave it enabled on another. The clients on the network attached to one NIC might need that protocol, while the clients on the network attached to the other NIC do not.

3

After completing this lab, you will be able to:

➤ Disable unnecessary protocols

➤ Enable necessary protocols

Materials Required

This lab will require the following:

➤ One Microsoft Windows 2000 Server computer running the TCP/IP, NWLink, and NetBEUI protocols

➤ One Microsoft Windows Professional workstation computer running the TCP/IP, NWLink, and NetBEUI protocols

➤ All networking equipment necessary to allow the computers to communicate on a network

Estimated completion time: **20–25 minutes**

ACTIVITY

1. Log on to the Windows 2000 Professional computer as an administrator.

2. Double-click the **My Network Places** icon. The My Network Places window appears.

3. Double-click the **Entire Network** icon. The Entire Network window appears.

4. In the left portion of the window, click the link to view the entire contents of the network. The Microsoft Windows Network and NetWare or Compatible Network icons appear.

5. Double-click the **Microsoft Windows Network** icon. A list of workgroups or domains appears. Verify that the Windows 2000 Server computer is here.

6. Log on to the Windows 2000 Server computer as an administrator.

7. Right-click the **My Network Places** icon, and click **Properties**. The Network and Dial-up Connections window appears.

8. Right-click the **Local Area Connection** icon, and then click **Properties**. The Local Area Connection Properties dialog box opens, with a check box to the left of each protocol, client, and service listed. Record the protocols running on this computer.

9. Uncheck the **NetBEUI Protocol, Internet Protocol (TCP/IP), NWLink NetBIOS,** and **NWLink IPX/SPX/NetBIOS Compatible Transport Protocol** check boxes.

10. Click **OK.** The Network Connections dialog box opens, warning you that several services and clients will not function properly without the protocols you are disabling. Click **Yes** to continue. The changes are written to the Registry. The Local Area Connection Properties dialog box appears again.

11. Click **OK.** Repeat Steps 1 through 5 to attempt to connect to the Windows 2000 Server computer. Record your observations.

_____

12. Log on to the Windows 2000 Server computer. If you see a dialog box indicating that one or more services have failed on startup, click **OK.**

13. Repeat Steps 7 and 8. Check the **NetBEUI Protocol, Internet Protocol (TCP/IP), NWLink NetBIOS, NWLink IPX/SPX/NetBIOS Compatible Transport Protocol** check boxes. Additionally, the check boxes for any clients or services, including the Client for Microsoft Networks and File and Printer Sharing for Microsoft Networks, will be empty. In order to reactivate the disabled clients and services, click all the check boxes in the list so that they all contain a check mark.

14. Click **OK.**

15. Click **Yes** when prompted to restart your computer.

16. Repeat Steps 1 through 5 from the Windows 2000 Professional computer to attempt to connect to the Windows 2000 Server computer. Record your observations.

_____

_____

Certification Objectives

Objectives for the Network+ Exam:

➤ Differentiate between the following network protocols in terms of routing, addressing schemes, interoperability and naming conventions: TCP/IP, IPX/SPX, NetBEUI and AppleTalk

➤ Identify the basic capabilities (i.e., client connectivity, local security and authentication) of network clients

Review Questions

1. It is prudent to install and bind all four major protocol suites on your server, regardless of whether they are going to be used. True or False?

2. Why would a network administrator choose to disable one of two network interfaces on a server?
   a. because it is infrequently used
   b. because it is faulty
   c. because it is not as fast as the other
   d. because it is incapable of handling certain protocols

3. What would happen if the TCP/IP binding on a Windows 2000 server's only interface, which had previously been bound to both TCP/IP and IPX/SPX, was disabled?
   a. Clients would not be able to access the server's resources via TCP/IP.
   b. Clients would not be able to access the server at all.
   c. Only those clients running TCP/IP would be able to access the server's resources.
   d. Clients would be able to access the server's resources via both TCP/IP and IPX/SPX, but TCP/IP-based services would be slower.

4. Why would a network administrator choose to unbind a protocol on a server?
   a. because it is only occasionally used, and as long as it remains bound it is using server resources
   b. because it is no longer used, and as long as it remains bound it is using server resources
   c. because it is interfering with traffic using other protocols
   d. because it has proven to be unstable with certain applications

5. Besides TCP/IP, what needs to be bound to a client's NIC in order for it to log on to a Windows 2000 server?
   a. Client for Microsoft Networks
   b. Gateway Services for NetWare
   c. IPX/SPX
   d. NWLink

6. Why is NetBEUI not routable?
   a. because it does not contain a subprotocol at the Application layer of the OSI Model
   b. because it does not contain Network layer addressing information
   c. because it is incompatible with modern routing techniques
   d. because its data frames are too large and slow to be practically routed

CHAPTER FOUR

TRANSMISSION BASICS AND NETWORKING MEDIA

Labs included in this chapter

➤ Lab 4.1 Learning Media Characteristics

➤ Lab 4.2 Creating a 10BaseT Crossover Cable to Connect Two Computers

➤ Lab 4.3 Comparing 10BaseT and 100BaseT Transmission

➤ Lab 4.4 Understanding How a 10BaseT Cable Fails

➤ Lab 4.5 Understanding Cable Types

Net+ Exam Objectives

Objective	Lab
Recognize the following media connectors and/or describe their uses: RJ-11, RJ-45, AUI, BNC, ST, SC	4.1, 4.2
Choose the appropriate media type and connectors to add a client to an existing network	4.1, 4.3
Given a wiring task, select the appropriate tool (e.g., wire crimper, media tester/certifier, punch down tool, tone generator, optical tester, etc.)	4.2, 4.4
Given a network scenario, interpret visual indicators (i.e., link lights, collision lights, etc.) to determine the nature of the problem	4.2, 4.4, 4.5
Specify the characteristics (e.g., speed, length, topology, cable type, etc.) of the following: 802.3 Ethernet standards, 10BaseT, 10BaseTX, 10Base2, 10Base5, 10BaseFX, Gigabit Ethernet	4.3, 4.5
Specify the main features of 802.2 (LLC), 802.3 (Ethernet), 802.5 (Token Ring), 802.11b (wireless), and FDDI networking technologies, including speed, access, method, topology and media	4.3
Given a network troubleshooting scenario involving a wiring/infrastructure problem, identify the cause of the problem (i.e., bad media, interference, network hardware)	4.4, 4.5

4. What is the purpose of using terminators on a 10Base2 network?
   a. to eliminate noise
   b. to eliminate signal bounce
   c. to eliminate EMI
   d. to eliminate crosstalk

5. What is the maximum throughput of a 10Base5 network?
   a. 5 Mbps
   b. 10 Mbps
   c. 50 Mbps
   d. 100 Mbps

6. On a 10BaseT network, attenuation is addressed through the use of which of the following?
   a. amplifiers
   b. multiplexers
   c. repeaters
   d. RF generators

7. What is the maximum allowable segment length on a 10BaseT network?
   a. 85 feet
   b. 85 meters
   c. 185 feet
   d. 100 meters

8. Why is the maximum segment length on a 10Base2 network longer than that of a 10BaseT network?
   a. because 10Base2 allows fewer nodes to connect to a shared channel, thus reducing attenuation
   b. because 10Base2 uses a bus topology, which is less susceptible to attenuation
   c. because 10Base2 uses terminators, which eliminate attenuation
   d. because 10Base2 uses coaxial cable, which is better shielded from noise than UTP

LAB 4.2 CREATING A 10BASET CROSSOVER CABLE TO CONNECT TWO COMPUTERS

Objectives

The goal of this lab is to teach you how to make your own cable in order create a simple peer-to-peer network. Proper cabling is critical to the functioning of any wire-bound network. You may find it necessary to make cables from time to time. Many companies do make their own cables to save money. Additionally, knowing how to make cables makes it easier to troubleshoot cabling problems.

Normal patch cables, those whose wire terminations are identical in both of the two plugs, are known as straight-through cables. Networking professionals may also call them patch cables. Another kind of cable is a crossover cable. In this type of cable, the transmit and receive pins in one of the cable's plugs must be reversed. A crossover cable allows two workstations to connect directly to each other (without using a connectivity device in between).

After completing this lab, you will be able to:

> ➤ Directly connect two computers with an RJ-45 crossover cable by plugging one end of the cable into the NIC of one computer and the other end of the cable into the NIC of the second computer

> ➤ Use a cable tester to ensure cable integrity

Materials Required

This lab will require the following:

> ➤ At least 10 feet of Category 5 cable

> ➤ Two RJ-45 connectors

> ➤ Two computers running Windows 2000 Professional with an Ethernet NIC with an RJ-45 connector

> ➤ Access as an administrator to both computers

> ➤ A network crimper

> ➤ A wire stripper

> ➤ A cable tester

> ➤ A wire cutting tool

Estimated completion time: **25–30 minutes**

ACTIVITY

1. Use the wire cutter to make a clean cut at both ends of the UTP cable.

2. Use the wire stripper to remove one inch (or less) of the sheath from one end of the UTP cable. Take care not to damage the insulation on the twisted pairs inside.

3. Slightly separate the four wire pairs, but keep the pairs twisted around each other.

4. Hold the RJ-45 connector so that the opening faces you and the plastic flap is on the bottom. Use a crimping tool to connect the wires in the RJ-45 connector, matching their color to their correct pin number, as described in Table 4-1. You have now completed one end of the cable.

Table 4-1   Pin numbers and color codes for creating a straight-through cable end

Pin number	Pair number	Use	Color
1	2	Transmit	White with green stripe
2	2	Receive	Green
3	3	Transmit	White with orange stripe
4	1	Receive	Blue
5	1	Transmit	White with blue stripe
6	3	Receive	Orange
7	4	Transmit	White with brown stripe
8	4	Receive	Brown

5. Repeat Steps 1 through 3 for the other end of the twisted-pair cable.

6. Hold the RJ-45 connector so that the opening faces you and the plastic flap is on the bottom, just as you did in Step 4. If you flip the RJ-45 connector over, the cable will not work. Use a crimping tool to connect the wires in the RJ-45 connector, matching their color to their correct pin number, as described in Table 4-2. This crosses the transmit and receive wires (both positive and negative), which allows the computers to communicate when connected. After completing this step, your crossover cable will be ready to use.

Table 4-2   Pin numbers and color codes for creating a crossover cable end

Pin number	Pair number	Use	Color
1	3	Transmit	White with orange stripe
2	3	Receive	Orange
3	2	Transmit	White with green stripe
4	1	Receive	Blue
5	1	Transmit	White with blue stripe
6	2	Receive	Green
7	4	Transmit	White with brown stripe
8	4	Receive	Brown

7. Plug each end of the cable into the cable tester, as shown in Figure 4-1. If the lights on the tester turn on, proceed to the next step. If not, recrimp the ends of the cable and repeat Step 1.

8. Remove the cable ends from the cable tester.

9. Connect one end of the cable to the NIC of one computer.

10. Connect the other end of the same cable to the NIC of the second computer. The lights on each NIC turn on.

Figure 4-1   Cable tester used to ensure that the cable was created correctly

11. On one computer, press **Ctrl + Alt + Del**. The Log On to Windows screen appears.

12. Enter an administrator user name and password, and then click **OK**. The Windows 2000 desktop appears.

13. Double-click the **My Network Places** icon. The My Network Places window appears.

14. Double-click the **Entire Network** icon. The Entire Network window appears.

15. If the Entire Network window does not contain any icons, click the link on the left that says you may also view the entire contents of the network. Icons for various network types appear. Double-click the **Microsoft Windows Network** icon. A list of workgroups displays.

16. Double-click the workgroup for the other computer. A list of folders on the other computer displays.

17. Close all open windows, and log off the computer.

Certification Objectives

Objectives for the Network+ Exam:

➤ Given a wiring task, select the appropriate tool (e.g., wire crimper, media tester/certifier, punch down tool, tone generator, optical tester, etc.)

➤ Recognize the following media connectors and/or describe their uses: RJ-11, RJ-45, AUI, BNC, ST, SC

➤ Given a network scenario, interpret visual indicators (i.e., link lights, collision lights, etc.) to determine the nature of the problem

Review Questions

1. What is one use for a crossover cable?
   a. to connect a hub and a workstation
   b. to connect a workstation to a wall jack
   c. to directly connect two workstations
   d. to connect a workstation to a modem

2. Which of the following tools would be useful in creating a patch cable for a 100BaseT network?

   a. screwdriver

   b. crimper

   c. soldering iron

   d. pliers

3. In twisted-pair wire, how does the twist ratio affect transmission? (Choose all that apply.)

   a. The more twists per inch, the less crosstalk transmission will suffer.

   b. The more twists per inch, the slower transmission will go.

   c. The more twists per inch, the more attenuation transmission will suffer.

   d. The more twists per inch, the faster transmission will go.

4. What is the maximum speed at which Category 3 UTP can transmit data?

   a. 1 Mbps

   b. 10 Mbps

   c. 100 Mbps

   d. 1 Gbps

5. What type of cable would connect a workstation to the wall jack in the work area of a 10BaseT network?

   a. straight-through cable

   b. crossover cable

   c. coaxial cable

   d. punch-down cable

6. What type of cable is required for 100BaseFX?

   a. coaxial cable

   b. UTP

   c. STP

   d. fiber-optic cable

7. Which of the following are characteristics of a Thicknet network? (Choose all that apply.)

   a. vampire taps

   b. transceiver cable

   c. BNC connectors

   d. RJ-45 connectors

8. Which of the following would be the best medium for an environment that is subject to heavy EMI?

   a. fiber-optic cable

   b. RF

   c. infrared

   d. UTP

LAB 4.3 COMPARING 10BaseT AND 100BaseT TRANSMISSION

Objectives

The goal of this lab is to help you understand the differences between the two most popular forms of Ethernet transmission, 10BaseT and 100BaseT. You will often have to choose between different types of media, even within the same network. For instance, servers typically require faster media than most workstations, and some workstations will require faster media than others.

After completing this lab, you will be able to:

➤ Configure a NIC to use either the 10BaseT or 100BaseT standard

➤ Measure the throughput on an Ethernet network

➤ Compare throughput on 10BaseT and 100BaseT networks

➤ Recognize that actual throughput may not reach the maximum throughput specified for a network

Materials Required

This lab will require the following:

➤ A Windows 2000 Server computer that contains a 10/100 Ethernet NIC and that has File and Printer Sharing for Microsoft Networks installed

➤ A workgroup named Laboratory on the Windows 2000 server

➤ A shared folder named "NetPlus" on the Windows 2000 server that contains the file driver.cab copied from C:\WINNT\Driver Cache\i386

➤ A Windows 2000 Professional computer that contains a 10/100 Ethernet NIC, that has File and Printer Sharing for Microsoft Networks installed, and that has a workgroup name of Laboratory

➤ Administrator access to both computers

➤ A 10–Mbps hub

➤ A 100–Mbps hub

➤ Two straight-through Category 5 (or higher) UTP cables to connect the computers to a hub

Estimated completion time: **25–30 minutes**

ACTIVITY

1. Plug both computers into the 10-Mbps hub. Lights appear on both NICs.

2. Log on to the Windows 2000 Professional computer as an administrator.

3. Double-click the **My Network Places** icon.

4. Double-click **Entire Network**.

5. If the Microsoft Windows Network icon does not appear in the Entire Network window, click the link in the left part of the window that says you may also view the entire contents of the network.

6. Double-click **Microsoft Windows Network**.

7. Double-click the **Laboratory** workgroup.

8. Double-click the icon for the Windows 2000 Server computer. A dialog box asking you to log on opens.

9. Log on to the Windows 2000 Server computer as an administrator. You might not need to log in if the administrator account has the same name and password on both machines.

10. Right-click the **NetPlus** shared folder, and then click **Map Network Drive**.

11. Choose driver letter Z: from the drop-down menu as the drive letter for the network drive, then click **Finish**.

12. Click **Start**, point to **Settings**, then click **Control Panel**. The Control Panel appears.

13. Double-click the **Administrative Tools** icon. The Administrative Tools window appears.

14. Double-click the **Performance** icon. The Performance window appears.

15. Right-click the graph in the right pane of the window, and then click **Add Counters**.

16. Click **Network Interface** from the drop-down menu underneath Performance object.

17. Click **Bytes Received/sec** to highlight it in the list underneath the Select counters from list option.

18. Click your network card from the list of network cards found underneath the Select instances from list option.

19. Click the **Add** button. Bytes received per second is graphed. Click the **Close** button.

20. Click **Start**, point to **Programs**, point to **Accessories**, and then click **Command Prompt**.

21. At the command prompt, type **mkdir C:\temp**.

22. At the command prompt, type **notepad throughput.bat**. A dialog box asking if you would like to create the file opens.

23. Click **Yes**. The Notepad window appears.

4

24. In Notepad, type the following three lines:
    :COPY
    copy Z:\driver.cab C:\temp
    goto COPY

25. Close Notepad. A dialog box opens, asking if you want to save the changes. Click **Yes**.

26. At the command prompt, type **throughput**. The batch file now continuously copies the file onto this computer from the shared folder on the Windows 2000 Server computer.

27. After a minute, record the number of bytes received per second. Multiply this number by 8 to find the number of bits received per second. Record the number of bits received per second and compare it to the bandwidth of the hub.

_____

28. At the command prompt, press **Ctrl + C** to stop the batch file. Type **Y** and press **Enter** when asked to terminate the batch job.

29. Plug the cables from both computers into the 100-Mbps hub. The lights on each NIC turn on.

30. At the command prompt on the Windows 2000 Professional computer, type **throughput**.

31. After a minute, record the number of bytes received per second. Multiply this number by 8 to find the number of bits received per second and compare it to the bandwidth of the hub.

_____

32. At the command prompt, press **Ctrl + C** to stop the batch file. Type **Y** and press **Enter** when asked to terminate the batch job. Close the Performance window and any other open windows, and log off the computer.

33. Compare the number of bits received per second with the 10-Mbps hub and the 100-Mbps hub.

Certification Objectives

Objectives for the Network+ Exam:

➤ Specify the characteristics (e.g., speed, length, topology, cable type, etc.) of the following: 802.3 Ethernet standards, 10BaseT, 10BaseTX, 10Base2, 10Base5, 10BaseFX, Gigabit Ethernet

➤ Choose the appropriate media type and connectors to add a client to an existing network

➤ Specify the main features of 802.2 (LLC), 802.3 (Ethernet), 802.5 (Token Ring), 802.11b (wireless), and FDDI networking technologies, including speed, access, method, topology and media

Review Questions

1. What might cause a 10BaseT network to experience an average throughput of less than 10 Mbps? (Choose all that apply.)
   a. heavy traffic on the network
   b. excessive noise
   c. too many protocols bound on the server
   d. a mix of different network operating systems on the servers

2. What is the maximum number of routers a data packet may traverse on a 100BaseT network?
   a. 2
   b. 3
   c. 4
   d. 5

3. Which of the following networks would be the most scalable?
   a. 10Base2
   b. 10Base5
   c. 10BaseT
   d. Token Ring

4. What does the "T" in 10BaseT and 100BaseT stand for?
   a. transmission
   b. transport layer
   c. twisted pair
   d. transparent

5. Which of the following is not capable of full duplexing?
   a. 10BaseT
   b. 100BaseTX
   c. 100BaseT4
   d. 100BaseFX

6. What type of media do wireless networks use? (Choose all that apply.)
   a. UTP
   b. alpha wave
   c. infrared
   d. radio frequency

7. What type of cable is required for a 100BaseT network?
   a. CAT3 or higher
   b. CAT5 or higher
   c. CAT6 or higher
   d. CAT7 or higher

8. Where would you find a plenum cable?
    a. above the ceiling tiles in an office
    b. in an outdoor cable trench that leads to a building
    c. between a hub and a punch-down panel
    d. between a workstation and a wall jack

4

LAB 4.4 UNDERSTANDING HOW A 10BASET CABLE FAILS

Objectives

The goal of this lab is to help you understand why the placement of the wires in a 10BaseT cable is so important. Seemingly complex network problems can often be a result of a faulty cable. Verifying the integrity of network cabling is often an important first step in solving network problems.

After completing this lab, you will be able to:

➤ Identify the problem associated with an incorrectly wired 10BaseT cable

Materials Required

This lab requires the following:

➤ At least 10 feet of Category 5 (or higher) unshielded twisted-pair cable

➤ Four RJ-45 connectors

➤ Two computers running Windows 2000, using Ethernet NICs with RJ-45 connectors, with File and Printer Sharing for Microsoft Networks installed, and with a workgroup named Laboratory

➤ Administrator access to both computers

➤ A network crimper

➤ A wire stripper

➤ A wire cutting tool

➤ Completion of Lab 4.2

Estimated completion time: **35 minutes**

ACTIVITY

1. Repeat Steps 1–3 of Lab 4.2 for the other end of the twisted-pair cable.

2. Using a crimping tool, connect the wires in the RJ-45 connector, matching their colors to the pin number listed in Table 4–3. This results in an incorrectly made cable.

3. Connect the ends of the cable to each computer. If the network adapter lights on each computer will not turn on, proceed with the next step. If they do, you accidentally made a correctly wired cable, and you need to begin this lab again.

4. On one computer, press **Ctrl+Alt+Del**. The Log On to Windows screen appears.

5. Enter an administrator user name and password, and click **OK**. The Windows 2000 desktop appears.

Table 4-3   Pin numbers and color codes for creating an incorrect cable end

Pin number	Pair number	Color
1	4	Brown
2	4	White with brown stripes
3	1	White with blue stripes
4	3	White with orange stripes
5	3	Orange
6	1	Blue
7	2	White with green stripes
8	2	Green

6. Double-click **My Network Places**. Double-click **Entire Network**. If the Microsoft Windows Network icon does not appear, click the link at the left that indicates that you may also view the entire contents of the network. Double-click **Microsoft Windows Network**. Double-click the **Laboratory workgroup**.

7. Notice that you cannot see the other computer in the list.

8. Log off the computer.

9. Using the wire cutting tool, cut the end of the cable about one inch from the RJ-45 connector. The RJ-45 connector should drop off.

10. Rewire and recrimp the cable. Connect one end of the cable to the NIC in each of the computers.

11. Repeat Step 7 again. You should now see the second computer appear in the list.

Certification Objectives

Objectives for the Network+ Exam:

➤ Given a wiring task, click the appropriate tool (e.g., wire crimper, media tester/certifier, punch down tool, tone generator, optical tester, etc.)

➤ Given a network scenario, interpret visual indicators (i.e., link lights, collision lights, etc.) to determine the nature of the problem

➤ Given a network troubleshooting scenario involving a wiring/infrastructure problem, identify the cause of the problem (i.e., bad media, interference, network hardware)

Review Questions

1. What pin number is used for transmitting a positive signal on an RJ-45 straight-through patch cable?
   a. 1
   b. 2
   c. 5
   d. 6

2. Which of the following could be a symptom of a damaged patch cable between a workstation and the wall jack on a 10BaseT network? (Choose all that apply.)
   a. The workstation cannot send or receive data to or from the network.
   b. The workstation and other workstations in the same office cannot send or receive data to or from the network.
   c. The workstation can send data to the network, but cannot receive data from the network.
   d. All workstations on the same segment can send data to the network, but cannot receive data from the network.

3. How does bend radius affect transmission?
   a. Transmission will not be successful until the bend radius has been reached.
   b. Transmission cannot occur at the bend radius.
   c. Transmission will be unreliable after the bend radius is exceeded.
   d. Transmission will be less secure after the bend radius is exceeded.

4. How many wire pairs are in a typical Category 3 cable?
   a. 2
   b. 3
   c. 4
   d. 6

5. Which of the following types of cable is most likely to be used on a Token Ring network?
   a. CAT1
   b. CAT3
   c. CAT4
   d. CAT7

6. What organization is responsible for establishing structured wiring standards?
   a. TIA/EIA
   b. ANSI
   c. ITU
   d. FCC

LAB 4.5 UNDERSTANDING CABLE TYPES

Objectives

The goal of this lab is to help you understand the necessity of using the correct cable type for a given hub. Use of the proper media is essential to the proper function of a network, regardless of whether you are building a new network or upgrading an existing one.

After completing this lab, you will be able to:

➤ Identify the proper cable type for a particular hub

Materials Required

This lab will require the following:

➤ An Ethernet 100-Mbps hub

➤ At least 10 feet of Category 3 cable with RJ-45 connectors

➤ At least 10 feet of Category 5 (or higher) cable with RJ-45 connectors

➤ A computer running Windows 2000 Professional that is not attached to a network

➤ An Ethernet 100-Mbps NIC inside the computer

Estimated completion time: **15 minutes**

ACTIVITY

1. Plug the RJ-45 connector on one end of the cable into the NIC of the Windows 2000 computer and plug the RJ-45 connector on the other end into the hub. The lights should not turn on.

2. Replace the Category 3 cable with the completed Category 5 cable. The light should now turn on.

3. Explain why the link light turned on with the Category 5 cable but not with the Category 3 cable.

Certification Objectives

Objectives for the Network+ Exam:

➤ Given a network scenario, interpret visual indicators (i.e., link lights, collision lights, etc.) to determine the nature of the problem

➤ Specify the characteristics (e.g., speed, length, topology, cable type, etc.) of the following: 802.3 Ethernet standards, 10BaseT, 10BaseTX, 10Base2, 10Base5, 10BaseFX, Gigabit Ethernet

➤ Given a network troubleshooting scenario involving a wiring/infrastructure problem, identify the cause of the problem (e.g.., bad media, interference, network hardware)

4

Review Questions

1. Which of the following differentiates Category 5 from Category 3 UTP? (Choose all that apply.)
   a. Category 5 has a higher twist ratio.
   b. Category 5 has a thicker sheath.
   c. Category 5 is more flexible.
   d. Category 5 is more expensive.

2. What type of cable contains two wire pairs and is suited for voice communications?
   a. Category 1
   b. Category 4
   c. Category 5
   d. Category 7

3. How many wire pairs in a cable are used for communicating over a 100BaseTX network?
   a. 1
   b. 2
   c. 3
   d. 4

4. Which of the following has the highest twist ratio?
   a. Category 1
   b. Category 3
   c. Category 4
   d. Enhanced Category 5

LAB 5.1 THE BUS TOPOLOGY

Objectives

The goal of this lab is to teach you about the importance of terminators in a bus topology. A bus topology is one in which a single channel is shared by all networks attached to a network or network segment. On a bus network, a node issues data to the channel, and the destination node picks it up. Terminators are required to stop signals after they have reached the end of the wire. Without these devices, signals on a bus network would travel endlessly between the two ends of the network—a phenomenon known as signal bounce—and new signals could not get through, resulting in a range of problems from degraded performance to outright failure.

After completing this lab, you will be able to:

➤ Network computers together in a bus network topology

➤ Explain what happens when a bus network is not terminated

Materials Required

This lab will require the following:

➤ Two computers running Microsoft Windows 2000 Server or Windows 2000 Professional with NICs with BNC connectors, arranged in a bus topology

➤ Microsoft Client for Windows and File and Printer Sharing for Microsoft Networks enabled on both computers, and a workgroup named NetPlus configured for each computer

➤ The necessary coaxial cable and T-connectors to connect the two computers

➤ Two terminators inserted at the two ends of the coaxial cable

➤ Access as an administrator to both computers

Estimated completion time: 20 minutes

ACTIVITY

1. Log on to one computer as an administrator. The Windows 2000 desktop appears.

2. Double-click the **My Network Places** icon. The My Network Places screen appears with the name of the other computer.

3. Double-click the **Entire Network** icon. The Entire Network screen appears.

4. If the Microsoft Windows Network icon does not appear in the right pane of the window, click the link in the left pane that says you may also view the entire contents of the network.

5. Double-click the **Microsoft Windows Network** icon. A list of workgroups displays, including the icon for the NetPlus workgroup

6. Double-click the icon for the NetPlus workgroup. A list of computers in that workgroup displays, including the name of the other computer.

7. Click **File** on the menu bar, and then click **Close**. The window closes.

8. Unscrew the terminator on one end of the network.

9. Repeat Steps 1 through 4 on the same computer again.

10. Double-click the **Microsoft Windows Network** icon. A dialog box with an error message opens, indicating that the list of servers for this workgroup is not available.

11. Click **OK** to exit the dialog box.

12. Reinsert the terminator and repeat Steps 1 through 5.

13. Log off the computer.

Certification Objectives

Objectives for the Network+ Exam:

➤ Recognize the following logical or physical network topologies given a schematic diagram or description: star, bus, mesh, ring, wireless

➤ Specify the characteristics (e.g., speed, length, topology, cable type, etc.) of the following technologies: 802.3 (Ethernet) standards, 10BaseT, 100BaseT, 100BaseTX, 10Base2, 10Base5, 100BaseFX, Gigabit Ethernet

➤ Recognize the following media connectors and/or describe their uses: RJ-11, RJ-45, AUI, BNC, ST, SC

➤ Choose the appropriate media type and connectors to add a client to an existing network

Review Questions

1. How many terminators would be required on a bus network that contains 20 workstations, one server, and three printers?
   a. 1
   b. 2
   c. 5
   d. 20

2. Which of the following topologies requires a terminator? (Choose all that apply.)
   a. star
   b. bus
   c. ring
   d. mesh

3. Which of the following types of Ethernet networks requires terminators? (Choose all that apply.)
   a. 10Base2
   b. 10Base5
   c. 10BaseT
   d. 100BaseTX

4. What type of device is used as a terminator on a Thinnet network?
   a. 5-MHz generator
   b. 5-Mbps multiplexer
   c. 50-MHz transmitter
   d. 50-ohm resistor

5. Signal bounce is a phenomenon that affects a network at which layer of the OSI Model?
   a. Physical
   b. Data Link
   c. Network
   d. Transport

LAB 5.2 THE STAR TOPOLOGY

Objectives

The goal of this lab is to understand how to create a star topology. In a star topology, every node on the network is connected through a central device, such as a hub. Star topologies are usually built with twisted-pair or fiber cabling. Any single cable on a star network connects only two devices (for example, a workstation and a hub), so a cabling problem will affect two nodes at most. This makes star topologies very flexible and fault-tolerant.

Star topologies form the basis of most modern LANs. You can scale a network in a star topology easily by connecting the central device in the star to other networks. In this lab, you will connect two computers to separate hubs and then connect the hubs.

After completing this lab, you will be able to:

➤ Create a star topology network

➤ Combine two star topology networks

Materials Required

This lab will require the following:

➤ Two computers running Microsoft Windows 2000 Server or Professional with the TCP/IP and NetBEUI protocols loaded and bound to the NICs of both computers

> ➤ Administrator access to both computers

> ➤ Both computers residing in a workgroup named NetPlus

> ➤ Two Ethernet eight-port hubs with a crossover or uplink port, or a Category 5 cable if it is necessary to connect the hubs

> ➤ Three Category 5 twisted-pair cables

Estimated completion time: **20 minutes**

5

ACTIVITY

1. Power on the two computers and the two hubs.

2. Connect one end of one cable to port 5 of one of the hubs, and connect the other end of the same cable to the Windows 2000 Server computer's NIC. The lights on port 5 of the hub and on the Windows 2000 Server computer's NIC should turn on. (On some devices, the lights will flicker on and off; this is normal activity.)

3. Repeat Step 2 for the Windows 2000 Professional computer.

4. Connect the third cable to the uplink port of one hub and to port 1 of the second hub. After you connect the two hubs, you should see lights on the uplink port of the first hub and on port 1 of the second hub. The uplink port is designed to allow you to connect two hubs together with a straight-through cable. However, some hubs still require a crossover cable in order to make a successful connection.

5. On the Windows 2000 Server computer, log on as an administrator.

6. Double-click the **My Network Places** icon. Double-click the **Entire Network** icon. If the icon for Microsoft Windows Network does not appear in the right pane of the window, click the link in the left pane that says you may also view the entire contents of the network.

7. Double-click the **Microsoft Windows Network**. The icon for the NetPlus workgroup appears. Double-click the **NetPlus** icon. The Windows 2000 Professional computer appears.

8. Exit My Network Places.

9. Unplug one of the RJ-45 connectors from one of the ports. The light on that port and the light on the corresponding NIC should turn off.

10. Attempt to connect to the Windows 2000 Professional computer by repeating Steps 6 and 7. A dialog box opens indicating that the workgroup is not accessible and that the list of servers for this workgroup is not currently available.

11. Plug the connector back into the port, and exit My Network Places.

Certification Objectives

Objectives for the Network+ Exam:

➤ Recognize the following logical or physical network topologies given a schematic diagram or description: star, bus, mesh, ring, wireless

➤ Specify the characteristics (e.g., speed, length, topology, cable type, etc.) of the following technologies: 802.3 (Ethernet) standards, 10BaseT, 100BaseT, 100BaseTX, 10Base2, 10Base5, 100BaseFX, Gigabit Ethernet

➤ Recognize the following media connectors and/or describe their uses: RJ-11, RJ-45, AUI, BNC, ST, SC

➤ Choose the appropriate media type and connectors to add a client to an existing network

Review Questions

1. Which of the following is most likely to be at the center of a workgroup connected in the star topology?
   a. bus
   b. tone generator
   c. modem
   d. hub

2. How many cables are necessary to connect four workstations and one server in a star topology?
   a. at least four
   b. at least five
   c. at least eight
   d. at least ten

3. Which of the following LEDs can indicate whether a workstation connected to a hub is actually sending and receiving data to and from the network?
   a. link
   b. power
   c. uplink
   d. bus

4. In a star topology, the failure of one node will not necessarily bring down the entire network. True or False?

5. Which of the following is an advantage of using a star network over using a bus network?
   a. It is more scalable.
   b. It is less expensive to create.
   c. It is easier to install.
   d. It requires less connectivity hardware.

6. Which of the following types of networks use some form of star topology? (Choose all that apply.)
   a. 10Base2
   b. 10Base5
   c. 10BaseT
   d. 100BaseTX

Lab 5.3 Building a Daisy Chain

5

Objectives

The goal of this lab is learn about the types of topologies you might realistically find in an enterprise LAN. A daisy chain is a linked series of devices. It is inexpensive to set up because the hubs are modular. In an enterprise network, this type of topology is often called a serial backbone. Although this lab will use hubs and Category 5 cabling, enterprise backbones often use switches instead of hubs. In addition, the backbones will use fiber-optic cable instead of Category 5 cable between the switches.

After completing this lab, you will be able to:

➤ Identify common enterprise backbone topologies

➤ Build a simple version of a common enterprise backbone

Materials Required

This lab will require the following:

➤ Four 10-Mbps Ethernet hubs, or four 10/100-Mbps Ethernet hubs set to connect at 10 Mbps

➤ Five Category 5 cables

➤ Three Category 5 crossover cables, if required, to connect the hubs

➤ Two computers running Microsoft Windows 2000 Server or Windows 2000 Professional, with RJ-45 NICs and the TCP/IP protocol bound, with Client for Microsoft Networks and File and Printer Sharing for Microsoft Networks installed and enabled, and with some drivers or folders shared on both PCs

➤ Access as an administrator to both computers

➤ Both computers residing in a workgroup named NetPlus

Estimated completion time: **20 minutes**

ACTIVITY

1. Power on each hub and each computer.

2. Plug the end of one of the Category 5 cables into a port in one of the hubs. Plug the other end of this cable into the uplink port of one of the other hubs. On both hubs a link light turns on. If not, use a crossover cable to connect the two hubs. The uplink port is designed to allow two hubs to be connected with a straight-through cable, but for some hubs, a crossover cable may still be necessary.

3. Connect one of the remaining two hubs to one of the two hubs you connected in Step 2. Connect the remaining hub to the hub you just connected. Now you have a chain of four hubs connected to each other. Each connection on each hub should now have a link light turned on.

4. Plug the RJ-45 connector from one of the Category 5 cables into a data port on one of the hubs on the end. Plug the other end into the NIC in the back of one of the computers. A link light appears on both the hub and the NIC.

5. Repeat Step 4 by connecting the other computer into the hub at the other end of the chain.

6. On one of the computers, log on as an administrator.

7. Double-click the **My Network Places** icon. The My Network Places window appears.

8. Double-click the **Entire Network** icon. The Entire Network window appears. If no icons appear in the right pane of the Entire Network window, click the link in the left pane that says you may view the entire contents of the network.

9. Double-click the **Microsoft Windows Network** icon. The icon for the NetPlus workgroup appears.

10. Double-click the icon for the **NetPlus** workgroup. An icon for the other computer appears. Browse through directories and files on the other computer.

11. Record how many hubs a packet sent from one computer must travel through to reach the other computer. How does this compare to the maximum allowed for 10BaseT Ethernet?

Certification Objectives

Objectives for the Network+ Exam:

➤ Recognize the following media connectors and/or describe their uses: RJ-11, RJ-45, AUI, BNC, ST, SC

➤ Recognize the following logical or physical network topologies given a schematic diagram or description: star, bus, mesh, ring, wireless

➤ Identify the purpose, features and functions of the following network components: hubs, switches, bridges, routers, NICs

Review Questions

1. What type of port connects one hub to another in a daisy-chain fashion?
   a. output port
   b. patch panel port
   c. uplink port
   d. external port

2. When connecting hubs in a daisy-chain fashion on a 10BaseT network, what is the maximum number of hubs you may connect?
   a. 2
   b. 3
   c. 4
   d. 5

3. When connectivity devices are connected in a daisy-chain fashion, what type of backbone do they create?
   a. parallel
   b. serial
   c. collapsed
   d. distributed

4. What type of network access method is used on a ring network?
   a. CSMA/CA
   b. CSMA/CD
   c. demand priority
   d. token passing

5. Which of the following is the most popular hybrid topology used on modern Ethernet networks?
   a. star-wired bus
   b. star-wired ring
   c. ring-wired star
   d. bus-wired star

6. What is risky about daisy-chaining hubs on a 100BaseT network?
   a. Too many hubs may cause errors in addressing data for their proper destination.
   b. Too many hubs may cause the network to exceed its maximum length.
   c. Too many hubs will increase the attenuation of a data signal.
   d. Too many hubs will increase the possibility for errors in data encryption and decryption.

5

LAB 5.4 USING NETWORK MONITOR TO VIEW DATA PACKETS

Objectives

The goal of this lab is to show you how to look at data on a network on a packet-by-packet basis. In viewing packets through network monitoring software, you can learn about the data's network access method, Network and Transport layer protocols, packet size, and error-checking routines, among other attributes. When troubleshooting network problems, you will often find it useful to look at the packets themselves. You can use your knowledge of how the packets should look to identify what the problem might be.

After completing this lab, you will be able to:

➤ Identify the portions of a data packet

➤ Use Microsoft's Network Monitor utility

Materials Required

This lab will require the following:

➤ Two computers (one running Microsoft Windows 2000 Server and the other Microsoft Windows 2000 Professional) with the following protocols loaded and bound to the NICs of both computers: TCP/IP, NW Link IPX/SPX Compatible Transport, and NetBEUI

➤ Microsoft Network Monitor installed on the Windows 2000 Server computer

➤ The networking equipment and cables necessary to connect both computers together

Estimated completion time: **25 minutes**

ACTIVITY

1. Log on to the Windows 2000 Server computer as an administrator. The Windows 2000 desktop appears.

2. Click **Start**, point to **Programs**, point to **Administrative Tools**, and then click **Network Monitor**. The Network Monitor window appears. If the Select Default Network dialog box opens, click **OK** twice to select the default network. This dialog box will appear only if you have not run Network Monitor on this computer before.

3. Click **Capture**, and then click **Start**. Network Monitor begins capturing data packets.

4. On the Windows 2000 Professional computer, log on as Administrator and double-click the **My Network Places** icon.

5. Double-click the **Entire Network** icon. If you do not see the Microsoft Windows Network icon, click the link in the left pane to view the entire network.

6. Double-click the **Microsoft Windows Network** icon. Double-click the **workgroup** for the Windows 2000 Server computer. Attempt to browse files on this computer. The point of this step is to generate enough activity to produce a good sample representation of captured data in Network Monitor. Continue browsing for at least one minute.

7. On the Windows 2000 Server computer, go back to Network Monitor, click **Capture**, and then click **Stop**.

8. Click **Capture**, and then click **Display Captured Data**. The Network Monitor Capture Summary window appears, showing information on captured packets arranged in rows and columns.

9. Locate and double-click an **SMB** or **SAP** entry in the Protocol column. Three panes appear, as shown in Figure 5-1. The top pane contains a list of captured packets, the middle pane highlights the parts of the captured packets, and the bottom pane shows the whole packet in hexadecimal.

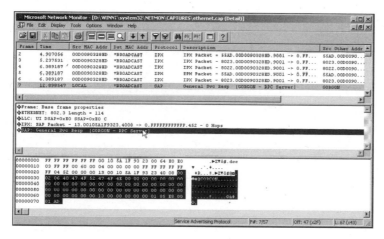

Figure 5-1   Data captured in Network Monitor

10. In the middle pane, a series of plus signs displays. Double-click the **+** next to the word ETHERNET. Information about the Ethernet portion of the packet displays.

11. Identify the MAC address of the destination computer in this packet. Record the result.

12. Locate the MAC address of the source computer for this captured packet. Record the result.

_____

13. Exit Network Monitor without saving the captured data.

14. Log off both computers.

Certification Objectives

Objectives for the Network+ Exam:

➤ Identify the seven layers of the OSI model and their functions

➤ Differentiate between the following network protocols in terms of routing, addressing schemes, interoperability, and naming conventions: TCP/IP, IPX/SPX, NetBEUI, AppleTalk

➤ Identify the basic capabilities (i.e., client support, interoperability, authentication, file and print services, application support, and security) of the following server operating systems: UNIX/Linux, NetWare, Windows, Macintosh

Review Questions

1. What is the purpose of the checksum?
   a. to ensure that data arrive in the proper sequence
   b. to ensure that data are properly encrypted and decrypted
   c. to ensure that data arrive at their intended destination
   d. to ensure that data arrive whole and intact

2. How many times is a checksum calculated when a packet of data is sent from a source computer to a destination computer that resides on the same segment?
   a. 1
   b. 2
   c. 3
   d. 4

3. What type of address identifies the source of data in a frame?
   a. MAC
   b. logical
   c. network
   d. host

4. What part of a data frame is responsible for making sure that packets are reassembled in their original order after they arrive at their destination?
   a. CRC
   b. sequence number
   c. source address
   d. padding

5. What is the minimum size of an Ethernet packet?
   a. 56 bytes
   b. 64 bytes
   c. 128 bytes
   d. 256 bytes

6. If an Ethernet packet doesn't meet the minimum size, what field is used to address this problem?
   a. checksum
   b. payload
   c. padding
   d. sequence number

LAB 5.5 EXAMINING DIFFERENT TYPES OF ETHERNET FRAMES

Objectives

Vendors have used several different types of Ethernet frames over the years. As a network administrator, you will probably encounter more than one type, particularly if you support more than one version of the NetWare operating system. The goal of this lab is to help you distinguish between Ethernet frame types on a packet-by-packet basis. Scrutinizing packets can sometimes help you resolve difficult troubleshooting issues, such as when equipment from two different vendors using different types of Ethernet packets will not communicate with each other.

After completing this lab, you will be able to:

➤ Distinguish between different types of Ethernet packets

➤ Resolve problems due to the use of incompatible frame types

Materials Required

This lab will require the following:

➤ Administrator access to a computer running Windows 2000 Server with Gateway (and Client) Services for NetWare installed

➤ A computer running Netware 5.x

➤ The following IPX networks bound to the NetWare computer's NIC: network number 8022 with frame type Ethernet_802.2, network number 8023 with frame type Ethernet_802.3 frame, and network number 55AD with frame type Ethernet_SNAP

➤ The networking equipment and cabling installed to network the two computers together so that the NetWare server is visible in My Network Places

Estimated completion time: **30 minutes**

ACTIVITY

1. On the Windows 2000 server, click **Start**, point to **Programs**, point to **Administrative Tools**, and click **Network Monitor**.

2. Click **Capture**, and then click **Start**. Network Monitor begins capturing packets.

3. Let Network Monitor capture packets for two minutes. During this time, the NetWare server will broadcast Ethernet packets of all three frame types.

4. Click **Capture**, and then click **Stop and View**. A list of packets captured displays.

5. In the Src Other Addr column, IPX packets have an address consisting of the network number followed by the MAC address (such as 8022.00D0090328ED).

6. In the Src Other Addr column, a packet with an address beginning with the network number 8022 indicates a packet with a frame type of IEEE 802.3 or Novell Ethernet 802.2. Double-click this **packet**. Detailed information about the packet appears, as shown in Figure 5-2.

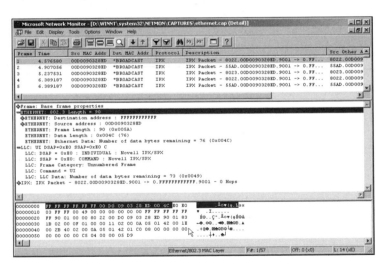

Figure 5-2   IEEE 802.3 or Novell Ethernet 802.2 frame

7. In the middle pane of the Network Monitor window, double-click the **line** containing a plus symbol next to the word ETHERNET:. Detailed information about the Ethernet portion of the frame appears. Identify the parts of the Ethernet portion of the frame.

8. Double-click the **line** containing a plus symbol next to the word LLC:. Identify the parts of the LLC portion of the frame.

9. In the top pane, in the Src Other Addr column, click the **packet** with an address beginning with 8023. Detailed information about a frame of the Novell proprietary 802.3 type appears, as shown in Figure 5-3.

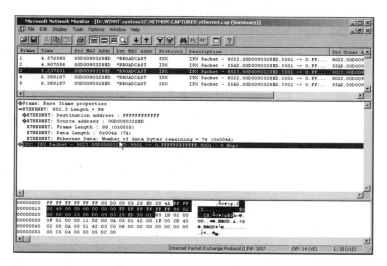

Figure 5-3   Novell proprietary 802.3 frame

10. In the middle pane of the Network Monitor window, double-click the **line** containing a plus symbol next to the word ETHERNET:. Detailed information about the Ethernet portion of the frame appears. Identify the parts of the Ethernet portion of the frame.

11. In the top pane, in the Src Other Addr column, click the **packet** with an address beginning with 55AD. Detailed information about a frame of the IEEE 802.3 SNAP type appears, as shown in Figure 5-4.

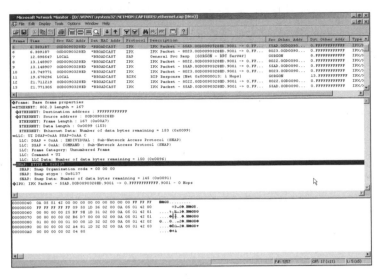

Figure 5-4   IEEE 802.3 SNAP frame

12. In the middle pane of the Network Monitor window, double-click the **line** containing a plus symbol next to the word ETHERNET:. Detailed information about the Ethernet portion of the frame appears. Identify the parts of the Ethernet portion of the frame.

13. Double-click the **line** containing a plus symbol next to the word LLC:. Identify the parts of the LLC portion of the frame.

14. Double-click the **line** containing a plus symbol next to the word SNAP:. Identify the parts of the SNAP portion of the frame.

15. Close Network Monitor without saving any changes.

Certification Objectives

Objectives for the Network+ Exam:

➤ Specify the main features of 802.2 (LLC), 802.3 (Ethernet), 802.5 (Token Ring), 802.11b (wireless), and FDDI networking technologies, including: speed, access, method, topology, media

➤ Identify the basic capabilities (i.e., client support, interoperability, authentication, file and print services, application support, and security) of the following server operating systems: UNIX/Linux, NetWare, Windows, Macintosh

➤ Given a network configuration, select the appropriate NIC and network configuration settings (DHCP, DNS, WINS, protocols, NetBIOS/host name, etc.)

Review Questions

1. What type of Ethernet frame can be used with NetWare 5.x? (Choose all that apply.)
   a. 802.2
   b. 802.3 SNAP
   c. 802.5
   d. Ethernet_II

2. Under what menu would you find the Network Monitor utility on a Windows 2000 server?
   a. Accessories
   b. Administrative Tools
   c. Control Panel
   d. Monitor Tools

3. What switching technique do Ethernet networks use?
   a. circuit
   b. packet
   c. message
   d. cell

4. In message switching, data is on a dedicated channel for the duration of the transmission. True or False?

5. What type of switching does a telephone call over the PSTN use?
   a. circuit
   b. packet
   c. message
   d. cell

6. What does "LLC" stand for?
   a. last logical communication
   b. lower–link control
   c. low–level command
   d. logical–link control

5

LAB 6.1 CREATING A MULTI-HOMED COMPUTER BY INSTALLING TWO NICS

Objectives

Network adapters (also called network interface cards, or NICs) are connectivity devices that enable a workstation, server, printer or other node to receive and transmit data over the network media. In most modern network devices, NICs contain the data transceiver, which is the device that transmits and receives data signals.

NICs belong to both the Physical layer and Data Link layers of the OSI Model because they apply data signals to the wire and assemble or disassemble data frames. They do not, however, analyze the data from higher layers. A router, on the other hand, operates at the Network layer of the OSI Model and can interpret higher-layer logical addressing information.

In this lab, you will take the first step to creating a simple router consisting of two NICs, two hubs and a single computer. Routers are used to interconnect dissimilar networks, and the presence of two NICs in a computer allows that computer to connect to two different networks. In the process, you will also gain experience in how to physically install and properly configure the TCP/IP properties for NICs.

After completing this lab, you will be able to:

> ➤ Physically install NICs

> ➤ Make a multi-homed computer using two NICs

> ➤ Configure TCP/IP properties on NICs

Materials Required

This lab will require the following:

> ➤ A PC running Windows 2000 Server named SERVER01 with at least two PCI bus slots available and no NICs currently installed

> ➤ Administrator access to the Windows 2000 Server computer

> ➤ Two Ethernet 10/100 PCI NICs with RJ-45 connectors that can be found on the Windows 2000 hardware compatibility list (HCL). The HCL shows all the hardware that has been shown to be compatible with Windows 2000. You can find the HCL by connecting to the Internet and pointing your browser to the following URL: *www.microsoft.com/hcl/default.asp.*

> ➤ Two Ethernet hubs

> ➤ Two Category 5 or higher straight-through (not crossover) patch cables

> ➤ A toolkit with a Phillips-head screwdriver, a ground mat, and a ground strap

Estimated completion time: **45 minutes**

ACTIVITY

1. Power off the computer.

2. Unplug the power cord from the computer.

3. Place the ground strap on your wrist and attach it to the ground strap underneath the computer.

4. Remove any screws from the computer's case.

5. Remove the computer case.

6. Choose a vacant PCI slot on the system board where you will insert the NIC. Remove the metal slot cover from the slot you will use.

7. Place the NIC in the slot.

8. Attach the NIC to the system unit with the Phillips-head screwdriver. This will secure the NIC in place.

9. Replace the cover.

10. Reinsert the screws on the cover.

11. Connect one end of one cable to one NIC. Connect the other end of the same cable to one of the hubs.

12. Plug in the computer and turn it on. Plug in the hub.

13. Log on as an administrator. The Windows 2000 desktop appears, and a dialog box indicating that Windows 2000 has discovered new hardware opens briefly.

14. Right-click **My Network Places**, and then click **Properties**. The Network and Dial-up Connections window appears, with an icon for Local Area Connection.

15. Right-click the **Local Area Connection** icon, and then click **Properties**.

16. Click **Internet Protocol (TCP/IP)** to highlight it, and then click **Properties**.

17. Click **Use the following IP address**. The IP Address, Subnet mask, and Default gateway text boxes are highlighted.

18. In the IP Address: text box, type **192.168.100.100**.

19. In the Subnet mask: text box, type **255.255.255.0**.

20. Leave the Default gateway: text box blank.

21. Click **OK**. You return to the Local Area Connection Properties window.

22. Click **OK** again.

23. Repeat Steps 1 through 22 for the second NIC. In Step 14, you will see icons for both Local Area Connection and Local Area Connection 2. For Local Area Connection 2, make the IP address **172.16.100.100**, the subnet mask **255.255.0.0**, and the default gateway blank.

24. After the Windows 2000 Server is running, look at the lights on each NIC and at the port lights on the hub. They should be on. If they are not on, check the cabling. You may also need to turn off the computer, unplug it and verify that each NIC is firmly seated inside the computer.

Certification Objectives

Objectives for the Network+ Exam:

➤ Identify the purpose, features and functions of the following network components: hubs, switches, bridges, routers, gateways, CSU/DSU, network interface cards, wireless access points, modems

➤ Identify the OSI layers at which the following network components operate: hubs, switches, bridges, routers, network interface cards

➤ Given a network configuration, select the appropriate NIC and network configuration settings (DHCP, DNS, WINS, protocols, NetBIOS/host name, etc.)

Review Questions

1. Which of the following devices operates at the Physical layer of the OSI Model? (Choose all that apply.)
   a. NIC
   b. hub
   c. bridge
   d. router

2. What type of address does a router interpret?
   a. physical address
   b. MAC address
   c. Block ID
   d. network address

3. Which of the following connectivity devices takes the most time to interpret the data frames it receives?
   a. hub
   b. bridge
   c. MAU
   d. router

4. On a typical 100BaseT network, where would you find transceivers?
   a. in the NICs
   b. in the operating systems

c. in the UPSs

d. in cabling

5. Which of the following is a difference between a router and a hub?

a. A router is less sophisticated than a hub.

b. A router operates at the Transport layer of the OSI Model, while a hub operates at the Data Link layer of the OSI Model.

c. A router operates at the Network layer of the OSI Model, while a hub operates at the Physical layer of the OSI Model.

d. A router regenerates signals, while a hub interprets addressing information to ensure that data are directed to their proper destination.

6. In which of the following networking scenarios would a router be the optimal connectivity device?

a. a home network with five users who want to share documents that are stored on one of the five workstations

b. a WAN that connects a college physics department with a classroom in a high school on the other side of town

c. a LAN that connects 10 users, a server, and a printer at a small business

d. a peer-to-peer LAN that connects eight users to provide a shared database

7. What is one function of a NIC's device driver?

a. to interpret IP addressing information

b. to interpret commands from the operating system

c. to interpret electrical signals from the wire

d. to interpret encrypted data

LAB 6.2 ACTIVATING ROUTING AND REMOTE ACCESS IN WINDOWS 2000

Objectives

In Lab 6.1, you created a router by adding two NICs to a computer running Windows 2000 Server. In this lab, you will activate Routing and Remote Access (RRAS) so that the Microsoft Windows 2000 Server software will pass packets between different networks. You will also look at the routing table of the new router, and you will add a static route to it. A routing table is a means of associating node addresses with their location on the network. All network computers have routing tables. However, computers that do not route between different networks have very small routing tables.

After completing this lab, you will be able to:

➤ Activate and configure RRAS on a Windows 2000 server

➤ Show the routing table of a Windows 2000 server configured as a network router

➤ Add a static route to a Windows 2000 server configured as a network router

Materials Required

This lab will require the following:

➤ Completion of Lab 6.1

➤ Administrator access to two additional computers running Windows 2000 Professional

➤ Ethernet 10/100 NICs that have RJ-45 jacks and that are found on the Windows 2000 HCL for each of the Windows 2000 Professional computers

➤ TCP/IP installed on each Windows 2000 Professional computer

➤ Two Ethernet hubs

➤ One Windows 2000 Professional computer assigned an IP address of 172.16.100.200, a netmask of 255.255.0.0, and a default gateway of 172.16.100.100, and the other Windows 2000 Professional computer assigned an IP address of 192.168.100.200 and a netmask of 255.255.255.0

➤ Two Category 5 or higher straight-through (not crossover) patch cables

Estimated completion time: **45 minutes**

ACTIVITY

1. On the Windows 2000 server, click **Start**, point to **Programs**, point to **Administrative Tools**, and then click **Routing and Remote Access**.

2. In the left pane of the window, click the name of the server to select it. Click **Action**, and then click **Configure and Enable Routing and Remote Access**. The Routing and Remote Access Server Setup Wizard appears.

3. Click **Next**. The Common Configurations screen appears.

4. Click **Network router**, and then click **Next**. The Routed Protocols screen appears.

5. Click **Next**. The Demand-Dial Connections screen appears.

6. Click the **No** option, and then click **Next**.

7. Click **Finish**. The Routing and Remote Access Server Setup Wizard saves your settings and starts the Routing and Remote Access Service. Close the Routing and Remote Access window.

8. Plug the RJ-45 connector of one of the Category 5 cables into one of the hubs. Plug the other end of the cable into the NIC in the back of one of the Windows 2000 Professional computers.

9. Repeat the previous step, connecting the other computer into the other hub.

10. Log on to the Windows 2000 Professional computer configured with the IP address of 192.168.100.200 as an administrator. Click **Start**, point to **Programs**, point to **Accessories**, and then click **Command Prompt**. The Command Prompt window appears.

11. Type **ping 172.16.100.200**. If the output does not indicate that the computer has received four replies from 172.16.100.200, repeat Step 8 and Step 9 before continuing, switching the hubs to which each computer is attached.

12. Repeat Step 11 with the Windows 2000 Professional computer configured with the IP address of **172.16.100.200**.

13. At the command prompt, type **ping 192.168.100.200**. The output indicates that this computer has received four replies from the other computer. You have now successfully used the Windows 2000 Server computer as a router.

14. Right-click the **My Network Places** icon, and then click **Properties**.

15. Right-click the **Local Area Connection** icon, and then click **Properties**.

16. Click **Internet Protocol (TCP/IP)**, and then click **Properties**. The Internet Protocol (TCP/IP) Properties window appears. Click **Advanced**. The Advanced TCP/IP Settings window appears.

17. Click the **Add** button beneath the IP addresses window at the top of the screen. The TCP/IP Address dialog box opens.

18. Type **10.1.1.1** in the IP address: text box. Type **255.0.0.0** in the Subnet mask: text box.

19. Click **Add**. You have just configured this computer with a second IP address, which it can also use to communicate with other computers. You are returned to the Advanced TCP/IP Settings window.

20. Click **OK** to close this window, click **OK** to close the Internet Protocol TCP/IP Settings window, and then click **OK** to close the Local Area Connection Properties window.

21. On the Windows 2000 Server computer, click **Start**, point to **Programs**, point to **Accessories**, and then click **Command Prompt**.

22. Type **route print**. The computer prints a list of its interfaces and its routing table. Notice that there is no route to any IP address or network beginning with 10. See Figure 6-1 for an example of a routing table on a Windows 2000 Server computer configured as a router.

6

Figure 6-1   Routing table of a Windows 2000 Server computer configured as a router

23. Type **ping 10.1.1.1**. The computer responds with "Request timed out" four times.

24. Type **route add 10.0.0.0 mask 255.0.0.0 172.16.100.200**. This tells the router to add a route to any machine with a network number of 10.0.0.0 and a netmask of 255.0.0.0 through the computer with the IP address of 172.16.100.200. Because the IP address 10.1.1.1 is a secondary IP address, we can only access it through the computer with the IP address of 172.16.100.200.

25. Type **ping 10.1.1.1**. The computer responds with "Reply from 10.1.1.1" four times.

26. Type **route print**. The computer prints its routing table. In the Network Destination column, the route you added in Step 24, 10.0.0.0, displays.

27. Return to the Command Prompt window you opened earlier on the computer configured with the IP address of 192.168.100.200. Type **ping 10.1.1.1**. The computer responds with "Reply from 10.1.1.1" four times. You have now successfully used the static route you configured on the Windows 2000 Server computer.

28. Close the Command Prompt windows on the computers.

Certification Objectives

Objectives for the Network+ Exam:

➤ Identify the purpose, features and functions of the following network components: hubs, switches, bridges, routers, gateways, CSU/DSU, network interface cards, wireless access points, modems

➤ Given output from a diagnostic utility (e.g,, tracert, ping, ipconfig, etc.), identify the utility and interpret the output

➤ Given a remote connectivity scenario (e.g., IP, IPX, dial-up, PPPoE, authentication, physical connectivity, etc.), configure the connection

➤ Identify the basic capabilities (i.e., client support, interoperability, authentication, file and print services, application support, and security) of the following server operating systems: UNIX/Linux, NetWare, Windows, Macintosh

➤ Given a network configuration, select the appropriate NIC and network configuration settings (DHCP, DNS, WINS, protocols, NetBIOS/host name, etc.)

Review Questions

1. To what network class does the following IP address belong: 10.0.0.0?
   a. Class A
   b. Class B
   c. Class C
   d. Class D

2. What is the default subnet mask for a Class B network?
   a. 255.0.0.0
   b. 255.255.0.0
   c. 255.255.255.0
   d. 255.255.255.255

3. What is the purpose of a routing table on a TCP/IP-based network?
   a. to associate the NetBIOS names of nodes with their IP addresses
   b. to associate the IP addresses of nodes with their host names
   c. to associate the IP addresses of nodes with their locations on the network
   d. to associate the host names of nodes with their MAC addresses

4. What does a successful response from the ping command indicate?
   a. that a node is powered on
   b. that a node is physically connected to the network
   c. that a node is running the Windows 2000 operating system
   d. that a node is connected to the network and is running TCP/IP successfully

5. What command would you use to add a node's IP address, netmask, and network location interface to a routing table?
   a. route add
   b. add host
   c. add node
   d. route open

6. In the default ping command on a Windows 2000 Professional workstation, how many replies will you receive if the test is successful?
   a. 1
   b. 2
   c. 3
   d. 4

7. What menu option sequence would you choose to set up Routing and Remote Access service on a Windows 2000 server?
   a. Start, Settings, Network and Dial-up Connections, Connection Properties, Network, Routing and Remote Access
   b. Start, Programs, Administrative Tools, Routing and Remote Access
   c. Start, Programs, Accessories, Routing and Remote Access
   d. Start, Network and Dial-up Connections, Programs, Routing and Remote Access

LAB 6.3 ACTIVATING A ROUTING PROTOCOL ON WINDOWS 2000 SERVER

Objectives

Finding the best route for data to take across the network is one of the most valued and sophisticated functions performed by a router. The term "best path" refers to the most efficient route from one node on a network to another. The best path in a particular situation depends on the number of hops between nodes, the current network activity, the unavailable links, the network transmission speed, and the topology. To determine the best path, routers communicate with each other through routing protocols. The goal of this lab is to increase your knowledge of routing protocols.

After completing this lab, you will be able to:

➤ Explain the function of various routing protocols

➤ Install Routing Information Protocol (RIP)

Materials Required

This lab will require the following:

➤ Two computers running Microsoft Windows 2000 Server with the TCP/IP protocol installed

➤ One Windows 2000 server that has a name of SERVER01, an IP address of 192.168.100.100, a subnet mask of 255.255.255.0, and a blank default gateway entry

➤ A second Windows 2000 server with a name of SERVER02, an IP address of 172.16.100.100, a subnet mask of 255.255.0.0, and a blank default gateway

➤ Routing and Remote Access disabled on both computers

➤ One Ethernet 10- or 100-Mbps hub

➤ An Ethernet 10/100 NIC installed in each Windows 2000 server

➤ Two Category 5 or higher straight-through cables, one to connect each computer to the hub

➤ Access as administrator to both computers

Estimated completion time: **45 minutes**

Activity

1. Log on to the Windows 2000 Server computer named SERVER01 as an administrator. The Windows 2000 desktop appears.

2. Click **Start**, point to **Programs**, point to **Accessories**, and click **Command Prompt**. Type **route print** to show the computer's routing table. Record the networks listed in the Network Destination column. _____
_____   _____

3. Configure Routing and Remote Access on this computer as you did in Steps 1 through 7 of Lab 6.2. Do not close the Routing and Remote Access window when you are done.

4. In the left pane of the Routing and Remote Access window, click the **+** next to the SERVER01 icon. A tree of options appears below the SERVER01 icon.

5. Click the **+** next to the IP Routing icon. More options appear underneath the IP Routing icon.

6. Right-click the **General** icon, and then click **New Routing Protocol**.

7. Click **RIP Version 2 for Internet Protocol**, and then click **OK**. A RIP icon appears in the left pane on the same tree as the General icon while the Windows 2000 Server computer installs the Routing Information Protocol.

8. Right-click the new **RIP** icon, and then click **New Interface**. The New Interface for RIP Version 2 for Internet Protocol window appears.

9. Click **Local Area Connection**, and then click **OK** to add the interface. The RIP Properties – Local Area Connection Properties window appears.

10. Click **OK** to close the window and finish adding the interface. An icon for local area connection appears in the right pane of the Routing and Remote Access window.

11. Enable Routing and Remote Access on the other computer, SERVER02, by repeating Steps 3 through 10. Instead of clicking the SERVER01 icon, click the SERVER02 icon. After RIP for IP is installed on both computers, they will dynamically share their routing tables within a minute.

12. In the left pane of the Routing and Remote Access window, right-click the **RIP** icon, and then click **Show Neighbors**. The other computer appears in the SERVER01 – RIP Neighbors window.

13. Repeat Step 2 on the computer named SERVER02. Record the additional routes you find in the routing table. _____   _____
_____

6

Certification Objectives

Objectives for the Network+ Exam:

➤ Identify the purpose, features and functions of the following network components: hubs, switches, bridges, routers, gateways, CSU/DSU, network interface cards, wireless access points, modems

➤ Identify the basic capabilities (i.e., client support, interoperability, authentication, file and print services, application support, and security) of the following server operating systems: UNIX/Linux, NetWare, Windows, Macintosh

➤ Given a network configuration, select the appropriate NIC and network configuration settings (DHCP, DNS, WINS, protocols, NetBIOS/host name, etc.

Review Questions

1. What does RIP stand for?
   a. Regulated Interaction Protocol
   b. Routing Information Protocol
   c. Response Interpretation Protocol
   d. Registered Installation Protocol

2. In order to determine the best path to transfer data, routers communicate using routing protocols such as TCP/IP. True or False?

3. What is the term for the period of time it takes for routers on a network to recognize a new best path for data if the previous best path is down?
   a. decision time
   b. convergence time
   c. routing time
   d. determination time

4. Which routing protocol is commonly used for Internet backbones?
   a. OSPF
   b. RIP for IP
   c. EIGRP
   d. BGP

5. Under what circumstances might the best path not equal the shortest distance between two nodes?
   a. when a communications link has been recently added to the network
   b. when a communications link is suffering congestion
   c. when a router experiences routing protocol errors
   d. when the media on the shortest path is different from the media on the best path

6. Which protocol was developed by Cisco Systems and has a fast convergence time but is supported only on Cisco routers?

   a. OSPF

   b. RIP for IP

   c. EIGRP

   d. BGP

7. What does "OSPF" stand for?

   a. open shortest path first

   b. overhead system path forwarding

   c. overlook system packet forwarding

   d. open session peer first

6

LAB 6.4 SETTING UP A FLOPPY DISK LINUX ROUTER

Objectives

Routers may run many different types of software and hardware, including Windows-based servers. Most organizations do not use servers as routers, however. Instead, they purchase dedicated hardware that runs an operating system optimized for routing. This operating system software is simpler than a network operating system and does not always have a graphical user interface, as does Microsoft Windows. In this lab, you will build a router on a floppy disk. You will install a version of Linux on the floppy disk, and you can run the software by booting up a computer with the floppy disk.

After completing this lab, you will be able to:

➤ Compare and contrast different types of router software

➤ Configure a router

Materials Required

In this lab, you will need the following:

➤ A computer running Microsoft Windows 2000 Server or Windows 2000 Professional with a floppy drive and two NICs from the following list: 3Com 3C509, 3Com 3C595, 3Com 3C905, Realtek NE2000 compatible, Realtek NE2000 PCI compatible, or ISA/PCI NE2000 compatible

➤ The computer configured to boot from a floppy disk

➤ IRQ and I/O port address information if ISA NICs are used

➤ The FREESCO 0.27 software downloaded from *www.freesco.org* and unzipped into a folder named C:\freesco

➤ A formatted floppy disk

➤ A second computer running Windows 2000 Professional with a NIC, configured with an IP address of 192.168.100.200, a netmask of 255.255.255.0, and a default gateway of 192.168.100.100

➤ A third computer running Windows 2000 Professional with a NIC, configured with an IP address of 172.16.100.200, a netmask of 255.255.0.0, and a default gateway of 172.16.100.100

➤ Two Category 5 (or higher) crossover cables

Estimated completion time: **45 minutes**

ACTIVITY

1. Log on as an administrator to the Windows 2000 computer that contains the FREESCO software in this location: C:\freesco.

2. Click **Start**, point to **Programs**, point to **Accessories**, and then click **Command Prompt**.

3. Type **cd C:\freesco**.

4. Put the floppy disk into the floppy drive. At the command prompt, type **make_fd**. Press **Enter** when prompted to do so. The computer copies the FREESCO files onto the floppy disk.

5. After the copy is completed, click **Start**, click **Shut Down**, and select **Restart** from the What do you want the computer to do? drop-down list in the Shut Down Windows dialog box. Click **OK**. The computer reboots from the floppy disk.

6. Press **Enter** at the boot: prompt, or wait five seconds for the router to begin booting automatically.

7. At the router.inet login: prompt, type **root** to log on.

8. At the Password: prompt, type **root** again. The [Linux] prompt appears.

9. Type **setup**, and then press **Enter**. A screen giving an overview of the setup process appears, indicating that you need to press the Enter key to continue.

10. Press **Enter**. A list of options displays, with the Choice prompt at the bottom of the screen.

11. Type **e** for Ethernet router, and then press **Enter**. A screen prompting you for the hostname of this computer appears. At each step, the program displays additional information about the options you might enter.

12. At the prompt, type **NetPlus**, and then press **Enter**. The Domain name prompt appears.

13. Press **Enter** to accept the default setting. The Autodetect modems now? y/n prompt appears.

14. Type **n** at the prompt, and then press **Enter**. The How many network interface cards do you have [1–3] prompt appears.

15. Type **2**, and then press **Enter**. The I/O Port address of first Ethernet card prompt appears, with the default setting in brackets.

16. Now you will enter the settings for each NIC. A PCI NIC will automatically configure itself. If you use an ISA NIC, you will need to manually enter the I/O port address and the IRQ number. If the NIC is a PCI NIC, type **0** (the default entry). If the NIC is an ISA NIC, type the I/O port address. Press **Enter**. The IRQ line of first Ethernet card prompt appears.

17. If the NIC is a PCI NIC, type **0**. If the NIC is an ISA NIC, type the IRQ number. Press **Enter**. The I/O port address of second Ethernet card prompt appears.

18. If the NIC is a PCI NIC, type **0**. If the NIC is an ISA NIC, enter the I/O port address. The IRQ line of second Ethernet card prompt appears.

19. If the NIC is a PCI NIC, type **0**. If the NIC is an ISA NIC, enter the IRQ number. Press **Enter**. The Use DHCP client to configure first network interface prompt appears.

20. Press **Enter**. The Interface name of the first network, eth0/eth1/eth2 etc prompt, appears.

21. Press **Enter**. The IP address of first network interface prompt appears.

22. Type **192.168.100.100**, and then press **Enter**. The Network mask prompt appears.

23. Type **255.255.0.0**, and then press **Enter**. The IP range prompt appears.

24. Type **–** , and then press **Enter**. The Interface name of second network eth1/eth0:1/eth2 etc prompt appears.

25. Press **Enter**. The IP address of second network interface prompt appears.

26. Type **172.16.100.100**, and the press **Enter**. The Network mask prompt appears.

27. Type **255.255.0.0**, and then press **Enter**. The IP Range prompt appears.

28. Type **–** , and then press **Enter**. The Enable caching DNS server y/s/n prompt appears.

29. Type **n**, and then press **Enter**. The Enable DHCP server y/s/n prompt appears.

30. Type **n**, and then press **Enter**. The Enable public HTTP server y/s/n prompt appears.

6

31. Type **n**, and then press **Enter**. The Enable time server and router control via HTTP y/s/n prompt appears.

32. Type **n**, and then press **Enter**. The Enable Print Server(s) y/s/n prompt appears.

33. Type **n**, and then press **Enter**. The Enable telnet server y/s/n prompt appears.

34. Type **n**, and then press **Enter**. The Savers – screen(min),hdd(x5 sec) 0 –off prompt appears.

35. Press **Enter**. The Swap file size in Megabytes (on boot device). 0 – disable prompt appears.

36. Type **0**, and then press **Enter**. The Do you want to enable extra modules/programs y/n prompt appears.

37. Press **Enter**. The Log size in bytes. syslog,logins_log prompt appears.

38. Press **Enter**. The Host gateway (if exists, otherwise – '-') prompt appears.

39. Type **–**, and then press **Enter**. The Primary DNS address (usually your provider's DNS) prompt appears.

40. Press **Enter**. The Secondary DNS address (otherwise – '-') prompt appears.

41. Type **–**, and then press **Enter**. The ISP http proxy address, (otherwise '-') prompt appears.

42. Type **–**, and then press **Enter**. The Do you want to export services y/n prompt appears.

43. Type **n**, and then press **Enter**. The computer requests a new root password.

44. Type **netplus**, and then press **Enter**.

45. To verify the password, type **netplus** again, and then press **Enter**. The computer will now prompt you for a Web Admin password. Type **network**. Type it again when prompted to do so.

46. Press **Enter**. A list of options and a Choice prompt display.

47. Type **s**, and then press **Enter**. The computer saves your setting and asks you to reboot for the new settings to take effect.

48. At the [Linux] prompt, type **reboot**. The computer reboots. Press **Enter** at the boot: prompt, or wait for the router to boot automatically.

49. Power on the other two computers.

50. Plug in the end of one of the crossover cables into the NIC in the back of the first PC, and plug the other end into the NIC in the back of the router. The link lights on both NICs turn on.

51. Repeat the previous step with the other computer.

52. Log on to the computer configured with the IP address of 192.168.100.200. Click **Start**, point to **Programs**, point to **Accessories**, and then click **Command Prompt**.

53. Type **ping 172.16.100.200**. If the response does not indicate that it received four replies from 172.16.100.200, you may have to reverse the order in which the crossover cables are plugged into the back of the router.

54. Repeat Steps 49 and 50, typing **ping 192.168.100.200** instead. Four replies received from the other computer display.

55. On the router, type the user name **root** at the NetPlus.inet login: prompt, and then press **Enter**. Type **netplus** at the Password: prompt.

56. At the [Linux] prompt, type **netstat –rn**. The router displays its routing table.

57. Remove the floppy disk and reboot the computer back into Windows

Certification Objectives

Objectives for the Network+ Exam:

➤ Identify the purpose, features and functions of the following network components: hubs, switches, bridges, routers, gateways, CSU/DSU, network interface cards, wireless access points, modems

➤ Given output from a diagnostic utility (e.g., tracert, ping, ipconfig, etc.), identify the utility and interpret the output

➤ Identify the basic capabilities (i.e., client support, interoperability, authentication, file and print services, application support, and security) of the following server operating systems: UNIX/Linux, NetWare, Windows, Macintosh

➤ Given a network configuration, select the appropriate NIC and network configuration settings (DHCP, DNS, WINS, protocols, NetBIOS/host name, etc.)

Review Questions

1. Which of the following could serve as routers? (Choose all that apply.)
   a. a modem
   b. a Windows 2000 Professional workstation
   c. a hub
   d. a Linux server

2. A modular router is one that can hold interfaces for different kinds of networks. True or False?

3. In which Layer of the OSI Model does a router operate?
   a. Physical
   b. Data Link
   c. Network
   d. Transport

4. What is an advantage of using Linux over Windows 2000 as a router operating system?

   a. Linux requires less overhead, and can therefore route faster.

   b. Linux can handle multiple different types of protocols, thus connecting dissimilar networks.

   c. Linux can use more different types of routing protocols, thus making it more flexible.

   d. Linux provides more router commands, thus making it more customizable.

5. What type of routing requires the network administrator to manually edit a routing table?

   a. dynamic

   b. manual

   c. static

   d. forced

LAB 6.5 SETTING UP A LINUX FLOPPY DISK BRIDGE

Objectives

In this lab, you will build a Linux bridge on a floppy disk, much like you built a router on a floppy disk in Lab 6.4. A bridge works at Layer 2 of the OSI Model and is a more sophisticated device than a hub. A bridge learns the MAC addresses of machines that send it packets, and it associates each MAC address it learns with one of its ports. However, little or no configuration is usually required for a bridge. Many switches are little more than faster bridges with more ports.

After completing this lab, you will be able to:

➤ Build and configure a bridge on a floppy disk

➤ Network two computers together with a bridge

Materials Required

This lab will require the following:

➤ A computer running Microsoft Windows 2000 Server or Windows 2000 Professional with a floppy drive and two NICs from the following list: 3Com 3C509, 3Com 3C595, 3Com 3C905, Realtek NE2000 compatible, Realtek NE2000 PCI compatible, or ISA/PCI NE2000 compatible

➤ The computer configured to boot from a floppy disk

➤ IRQ and I/O port address information if ISA NICs are used

➤ The FREESCO 0.27 distribution downloaded from *www.freesco.org* and unzipped into a folder named C:\freesco

➤ A formatted floppy disk

➤ Two computers running Microsoft Windows 2000 Server or Windows 2000 Professional, each with a NIC and with the NetBEUI protocol, Client for Microsoft Networks, File and Printer Sharing for Microsoft Networks installed with a workgroup name of NetPlus

➤ Two Category 5 or higher crossover cables

Estimated completion time: **45 minutes**

ACTIVITY

1. Log on as an administrator to the Windows 2000 computer.

2. Click **Start**, point to **Programs**, point to **Accessories**, and then click **Command Prompt**. The Command Prompt window appears.

3. Type **cd C:\freesco**.

4. Put the floppy disk into the floppy drive. At the command prompt, type **make_fd**. The computer copies the FREESCO files onto the floppy disk.

5. After the copy is completed, click **Start**, click **Shut Down**, and select **Restart** from the What do you want the computer to do? drop-down list in the Shut Down Windows dialog box. Click **OK**. The computer reboots from the floppy disk.

6. Press the **Enter** key at the boot: prompt, or wait five seconds for the router to begin booting automatically.

7. At the router.inet login: prompt, type **root** to log on.

8. At the Password: prompt, type **root**. The [Linux] prompt appears.

9. Type **setup**, and then press **Enter**. A screen giving an overview of the setup process appears, indicating that you need to press the Enter key to continue.

10. Press **Enter**. A list of options displays, with the Choice prompt at the bottom of the screen.

11. Type **b** to select an Ethernet Bridge, and then press **Enter**. The computer asks how many network interface cards you have.

12. Type **2**, and then press **Enter**. The computer asks for the I/O port address of the first Ethernet card.

13. Now you will enter information about the NIC. A PCI NIC will configure itself, but you will need to add additional information for an ISA NIC. If the NIC is a PCI NIC, type **0** (the default entry). If the NIC is an ISA NIC, enter

WANS AND REMOTE CONNECTIVITY

Labs included in this chapter

➤ Lab 7.1 Establishing Remote Connectivity Using Fiber-Optic Bridges

➤ Lab 7.2 Pricing WAN Services

➤ Lab 7.3 Connecting to an Internet Service Provider in Windows 2000

➤ Lab 7.4 Configuring a Remote Access Server

➤ Lab 7.5 Creating a VPN with the Point-to-Point Tunneling Protocol

---

Net+ Exam Objectives	
Objective	**Lab**
Identify the purpose, features and functions of the following network components: hubs, switches, bridges, routers, gateways, CSU/DSU, network interface cards/ISDN adapters/system area network cards, wireless access points, modems	7.1, 7.3
Recognize the following media connectors and/or describe their uses: RJ-11, RJ-45, AUI, BNC, ST, SC	7.1
Choose the appropriate media type and connectors to add a client to an existing network	7.1
Identify the basic characteristics (e.g., speed, capacity, media) of the following WAN technologies: Packet switching vs. circuit switching, ISDN, FDDI, ATM, Frame Relay, SONET/SDH , T1/E1, T1/T3, OCx	7.2
Identify the purpose and characteristics of fault tolerance	7.2
Define the function of the following remote access protocols and services: RAS, PPP, PPTP, ICA	7.3, 7.4, 7.5
Given a remote connectivity scenario (e.g., IP, IPX, dial-up, PPPoE, authentication, physical connectivity, etc.), configure the connection	7.3, 7.4, 7.5
Given a troubleshooting scenario involving a remote connectivity problem (e.g., authentication failure, protocol configuration, physical connectivity), identify the cause of the problem	7.3, 7.4, 7.5
Given a troubleshooting scenario involving a small office/home office network failure (e.g., xDSL, cable, home satellite, wireless, POTS), identify the cause of the failure	7.3
Identify the basic capabilities (i.e., client support, interoperability, authentication, file and print services, application support, and security) of the following server operating systems: UNIX/Linux, NetWare, Windows, Macintosh	7.4, 7.5

LAB 7.1 ESTABLISHING REMOTE CONNECTIVITY USING FIBER-OPTIC BRIDGES

Objectives

In this lab, you will simulate a WAN connection with two fiber-optic bridges, which can be connected with fiber-optic cable. With the exception of a wireless WAN such as a satellite link, many of the WAN links you might encounter today travel over fiber-optic cable. Sometimes businesses located in closely grouped buildings will share an expensive WAN connection to the Internet, using fiber-optic cable to connect their buildings. The fiber-optic cable is made with a transmit and receive connection on each end.

After completing this lab, you will be able to:

➤ Simulate a WAN by installing a fiber-optic bridge that connects two separate LANs

➤ Understand WAN connectivity

Materials Required

This lab will require the following:

➤ Two computers running Windows 2000 Server or Windows 2000 Professional, with TCP/IP, Client for Microsoft Networks, and File and Printer Sharing for Microsoft Networks installed and a workgroup named NetPlus

➤ An IP address of 192.168.1.1 configured on one computer and an IP address of 192.168.1.2 configured on the other computer

➤ Administrator access to both computers

➤ Shared directories on each computer

➤ Two Ethernet hubs

➤ A NIC for each computer

➤ Two fiber-optic bridges with AUI interfaces

➤ Two twisted-pair transceivers with an RJ-45 connector on one end and an AUI connector on the other end

➤ At least six feet of fiber-optic cable ready to connect to the bridges

➤ Four Category 5 (or higher) UTP cables

Estimated completion time: **15 minutes**

ACTIVITY

1. Power on both computers.

2. Plug the RJ-45 connector on one end of a UTP cable into one of the ports on one hub. Plug the RJ-45 connector on the other end of the cable into the NIC in the back of one of the computers.

3. Repeat Step 2 with the other computer and the other hub. Each computer is now connected to one of the hubs.

4. Plug the RJ-45 connector on one end of a UTP cable into the uplink port on one hub.

5. Plug the RJ-45 connector on the other end of the same UTP cable into the RJ-45 end of one of the transceivers.

6. Connect the AUI end of the transceiver used in the previous step to one of the fiber-optic bridges.

7. Plug the RJ-45 connector on one end of another UTP cable into the uplink port on the second hub.

8. Connect the RJ-45 connector on the other end of the UTP cable used in the previous step into the RJ-45 end of the second transceiver.

9. Connect the AUI end of the second transceiver to the second fiber-optic bridge.

10. Connect one of the transmit and receive ends of the fiber-optic cable to one bridge.

11. Connect the other transmit and receive end of the same fiber-optic cable to the second bridge. Now the two hubs are connected by fiber, simulating a WAN connection between them, as shown in Figure 7-1.

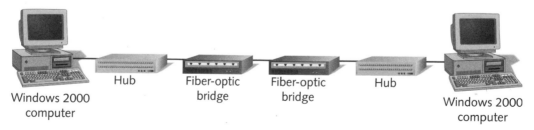

Windows 2000 computer   Hub   Fiber-optic bridge   Fiber-optic bridge   Hub   Windows 2000 computer

Figure 7-1   Diagram of completed network

12. Log on to a Windows 2000 computer that is connected to one of the LANs.

Estimated completion time: **30 minutes**

ACTIVITY

1. Call a local Internet service provider or telephone company and ask to speak with someone about the cost and availability of high-speed Internet links for businesses. Identify the name of the organization you called.

   _____

2. Explain to the person you are connected with that you are doing research for a school project on the pricing of Internet links. Give your name, the name of the networking class you are taking, and the name of your school.

3. For T-1 service, ask if the service is available in your area. If the service is available, ask if there are any geographic restrictions on the service. For instance, some services may not be available in all areas because the necessary infrastructure has not yet been built. Record the geographic availability of the service.

   _____

4. If the service is available, ask for the bandwidth of the service. T-1 service should be available in most areas. If not, go to Step 8. Record the bandwidth.

   _____

5. Ask for the monthly cost of the service. Make sure to ask if you would be billed a flat fee, or whether your bill would change depending on how much you used the service. Record the monthly costs.

   _____

6. Ask if any additional equipment is required for the service and if the company provides it. Additionally, ask if the hardware charge is a flat fee or a monthly charge. If so, ask for the typical price of the additional equipment. Record the cost of additional equipment expected.

   _____

7. Ask about any initial setup fees that you might be charged. Typical setup fees include the installation of the T-1 line itself. Record the cost of the setup fees.

   _____

8. Repeat Step 3 through Step 7, this time referencing DSL.

9. Repeat Step 3 through Step 7, this time referencing ISDN.

10. Repeat Step 3 through Step 7, this time referencing POTS connection with a modem.

11. For each service, calculate the cost of any setup and installation fees and the cost of equipment required (excluding monthly charges for hardware). Record the setup, installation and equipment costs.

   _____

12. For each service, calculate the cost of two years of monthly service, including any monthly charges for hardware. If the service is billed based on usage, estimate the cost based on medium usage. Record the cost of two years of service.

_____

13. For each service, compare the costs calculated in Step 11 and Step 12.

Certification Objectives

Objectives for the Network+ Exam:

➤ Identify the basic characteristics (e.g., speed, capacity, media) of the following WAN technologies: Packet switching vs. circuit switching, ISDN, FDDI, ATM, Frame Relay, SONET/SDH , T1/E1, T1/T3, OCx

➤ Identify the purpose and characteristics of fault tolerance

7

Review Questions

1. Which of the following best describes the function of a CSU?
   a. It transmits several signals over a single channel.
   b. It separates a single channel into multiple channels.
   c. It terminates a digital signal and ensures connection integrity.
   d. It converts the digital signal used by connectivity devices into the digital signal sent through the cabling.

2. What is the purpose of a mutliplexer?
   a. to transmit several signals over a single channel
   b. to separate a single channel into multiple channels
   c. to terminate a digital signal and ensure connection integrity
   d. to convert the digital signal used by connectivity devices into the digital signal sent via the cabling

3. What is the maximum segment length for a T1 line using STP?
   a. 600 meters
   b. 6000 meters
   c. 6000 feet
   d. 6 kilometers

4. A fractional T1 can be leased in multiples of _____ Kbps.
   a. 24
   b. 48
   c. 64
   d. 72

10. Click the **I connect through a phone line and a modem** option button, and then click **Next**.

11. If the Choose Modem window appears, select your modem from the drop-down list. Otherwise, go to Step 12.

12. Enter the area code and telephone number of the ISPs dial-up modem pool, and then click **Next**.

13. Enter the user name and password for the account, and then click **Next**.

14. Type **NetPlus Internet** in the Connection name: text box, and then click **Next**.

15. Click the **No** option button, and then click **Next**.

16. Click **Finish**. Internet Explorer and the Dial-up Connection dialog box open. The Dial-up Connection dialog box contains the connection name, user name, and password you configured earlier.

17. Click **Connect**. The modem dials and the computer connects to the Internet. A dialog box opens indicating that you have connected to the Internet.

18. Click **OK** to close the dialog box.

Certification Objectives

Objectives for the Network+ Exam:

➤ Identify the purpose, features and functions of the following network components: hubs, switches, bridges, routers, gateways, CSU/DSU, network interface cards/ISDN adapters/system area network cards, wireless access points, modems

➤ Define the function of the following remote access protocols and services: RAS, PPP, PPTP, ICA

➤ Given a remote connectivity scenario (e.g., IP, IPX, dial-up, PPPoE, authentication, physical connectivity, etc.), configure the connection

➤ Given a troubleshooting scenario involving a remote connectivity problem (e.g., authentication failure, protocol configuration, physical connectivity) identify the cause of the problem

➤ Given a troubleshooting scenario involving a small office/home office network failure (e.g., xDSL, cable, home satellite, wireless, POTS), identify the cause of the failure

Review Questions

1. What are two differences between PPP and SLIP?
   a. SLIP can handle only asynchronous transmission, while PPP can handle both asynchronous and synchronous transmission.
   b. SLIP encapsulates traffic according to its original Network layer protocol, while PPP masks SLIP traffic as IP-based data.

    c. SLIP cannot carry Network layer protocols other than TCP/IP, while PPP can carry any Network layer protocol.

    d. SLIP is compatible with only NetWare servers, while PPP is compatible with both NetWare and Windows NT/2000 servers.

2. Which of the following is one primary difference between PPP and PPTP?

    a. PPP can handle only asynchronous transmission, while PPTP can handle both asynchronous and synchronous transmission.

    b. PPP encapsulates traffic according to its original Network layer protocol, while PPTP masks PPP traffic as IP-based data.

    c. PPP cannot carry Network layer protocols other than TCP/IP, while PPTP can carry any Network layer protocol.

    d. PPP is compatible with only NetWare servers, while PPTP is compatible with both NetWare and Windows NT/2000 servers.

3. Which of the following is the most secure remote access protocol?

    a. SLIP

    b. PPP

    c. RAS

    d. PPTP

4. Which of the following best describes the asynchronous communications method?

    a. Data that is transmitted and received by nodes must conform to a timing scheme.

    b. Data that is transmitted and received by nodes do not have to conform to any timing scheme.

    c. Data that is transmitted and received by nodes are subject to resequencing by each connectivity device through which they pass.

    d. Data that is transmitted and received by nodes require an additional sequencing bit to ensure they are reassembled in the proper order.

5. If your ISP uses DHCP to assign TCP/IP information to a dial-up connection, which of the following must you still specify in your connection parameters?

    a. the type of server into which you are dialing

    b. your workstation's IP address

    c. the network's DHCP server address

    d. the network's subnet mask

6. Which of the following clients is most likely to use dial-up networking on a daily basis?

    a. an executive at a corporate headquarters who participates in regular video conferences over the Web

    b. a home health care nurse who visits patients in their homes and must transmit data to her clinic office after each visit

     c. a geneticist who works in a lab of 25 scientists and who must upload molecular modeling information to the company's server at the headquarters a few miles away from the lab

     d. a government agent who enters census data in a database at a federal office building

---

LAB 7.4 CONFIGURING A REMOTE ACCESS SERVER

Objectives

In this lab, you will create a dial-up server and connect to it from a client. Although modem connections over the PSTN are slower than other types of WAN connections, the public telephone network is almost universally available. Even when faster types of connections are available, you can use a dial-up connection as a backup. Additionally, you or the users in your network may use a dial-up connection to connect to the office network or check e-mail when traveling. A salesperson, for example, might be on the road a large percentage of the time and have no network access besides her dial-up connection. By dialing into a dial-up server with Routing and Remote Access Server (RRAS), a remote user can check e-mail, share files, and use the network just as if she were locally connected to the network.

In Windows 2000, keep in mind that you need to specifically enable a user to dial in remotely to a Windows 2000 server. Even if the server has a modem and is configured to accept incoming calls, it may reject a call if a user does not have dial-in permission.

After completing this lab, you will be able to:

➤ Configure RRAS to allow a Windows 2000 server to accept dial-up connections

Materials Required

This lab will require the following:

➤ A computer running Windows 2000 Server with a NIC and with TCP/IP configured as the only network protocol, an IP address of 192.168.72.1, a subnet mask of 255.255.255.0, a workgroup of NetPlus, and Routing and Remote Access installed but not activated

➤ A client computer running Windows 2000 Server or Windows 2000 Professional configured with TCP/IP as the only network protocol

➤ Administrator access to both computers

➤ A user account named netplus on the Windows 2000 Server with a known password, configured with sufficient rights to dial into the Windows 2000 server

➤ Modems installed and configured on both machines

➤ Two phone lines; or you may also work with a partner or in teams and have each computer in two different locations, each with its own phone line

➤ Knowledge of the telephone number of the phone line to which the Windows 2000 server is attached

➤ Two phone cords with RJ-11 connectors on both ends that are long enough to reach the wall outlet

Estimated completion time: **25 minutes**

ACTIVITY

1. Power on both computers.

2. Connect one end of a phone cord into the back of the modem installed on the Windows 2000 server, and connect the other end into the wall outlet.

3. Log on to the Windows 2000 server as an administrator.

4. Click **Start**, point to **Programs**, point to **Administrative Tools**, and then click **Routing and Remote Access**. The Routing and Remote Access window appears.

5. Click **Action**, and then click **Configure and Enable Routing and Remote Access**. The Routing and Remote Access Server Setup Wizard appears.

6. Click **Next**. The Common Configurations window appears.

7. Click the **Remote access server** option button. Click **Next**. The Remote Client Protocols window appears.

8. Click **Next**. The Network Selection window appears.

9. Click the **Local Area Connection** option button. This assigns remote clients to that network for addressing and dial-up access. Click **Next**. The IP Address Assignment window appears.

10. Click the **From a specified range of addresses** option button. The Address Range Assignment window appears. Click **Next**.

11. Click **New**. The New Address Range dialog box opens. In the Start IP address: text box, type **192.168.72.5**. In the Number of addresses: text box, type **10**. This assigns 10 IP addresses to incoming dial-up clients, beginning with 192.168.72.5. The dialog box completes the End IP address: text box. Click **OK**.

12. Click **Next**. The Managing Multiple Remote Access Servers window appears.

13. Click the **No, I don't want to set up this server to use RADIUS now** option button, and then click **Next**.

14. Click **Finish**. A dialog box opens, indicating that you will need to configure the DHCP Relay Agent to support the relaying of DHCP server (which is not necessary for this lab). Click **OK**. The computer saves your settings and starts the Routing and Remote Access Server service.

6. Why do most remote clients (for example, those that dial into a RRAS server) use DHCP and not static IP addressing? (Choose all that apply.)

    a. because using DHCP allows more efficient use of a limited number of IP addresses

    b. because using DHCP ensures that the client is authorized to access the network

    c. because using DHCP ensures that the client is assigned a valid IP address

    d. because using DHCP allows the client to use the same IP address each time he or she dials into the LAN

LAB 7.5 CREATING A VPN WITH THE POINT-TO-POINT TUNNELING PROTOCOL

Objectives

While a remote access server allows users to dial in and use network resources, dialing into a remote access server can be quite expensive if many of the users have to dial long distance. One way to reduce the cost of using a remote access server is to create a virtual private network (VPN). In a VPN, users connect to the remote access server over an encrypted channel through a public network, typically the Internet. Remote users have the same access that they had when dialing in directly to the remote access server. However, instead of paying long distance fees per minute, an organization pays for its users' Internet connections and the Internet connectivity of its remote access server. One type of VPN used on the Internet is made using the Point-to-Point Tunneling Protocol (PPTP).

After completing this lab, you will be able to:

➤ Configure a VPN with PPTP between a client computer and a Windows 2000 server

Materials Required

This lab will require the following:

➤ A Windows 2000 Server computer that has TCP/IP as the only installed protocol, an IP address of 172.30.12.2, and a netmask of 255.255.255.0

➤ Routing and Remote Access disabled on the Windows 2000 server

➤ A client computer running Windows 2000 Server or Professional, with TCP/IP as the only installed network protocol, an IP address of 172.30.12.5, and a netmask of 255.255.255.0

➤ No network connections (besides Local Area Connections) configured in Network and Dial-up Connections

➤ Access as an administrator to both computers

➤ An account on the Windows 2000 server with the name of netplus, a known password, and sufficient rights configured to dial into the Windows 2000 Server

> ➤ The two computers connected in a network by an Ethernet hub and two Category 5 (or higher) cables

Estimated completion time: **20 minutes**

ACTIVITY

1. Power on both computers.

2. Log on to the Windows 2000 Server as an administrator.

3. Click **Start**, point to **Programs**, point to **Administrative Tools**, and then click **Routing and Remote Access**. The Routing and Remote Access window appears.

4. Click **Action**, and then click **Configure and Enable Routing and Remote Access**. The Routing and Remote Access Server Setup Wizard appears.

5. Click **Next**. The Common Configurations window appears.

6. Click the **Virtual private network (VPN) server** option button. Click **Next**. The Remote Client Protocols window opens.

7. Click **Next**. The Internet Connection window opens.

8. Click the **Local Area Connection** icon, and then click **Next**. The IP Address Assignment window appears.

9. Click the **From a specified range of addresses** option button, and then click **Next**. The Address Range Assignment window appears.

10. Click **New**. The New Address Range dialog box opens. In the **Start IP address:** text box, type **172.30.12.100**. In the Number of addresses: text box, type **100**. Click **OK**. This assigns 100 IP addresses to incoming dial-up clients, beginning with 172.30.12.100. The dialog box completes the End IP address: text box.

11. Click **Next**. The Managing Multiple Remote Access Server window appears.

12. Click the **No, I don't want to set up this server to use RADIUS now** option button, and then click **Next**.

13. Click **Finish**. A dialog box opens, indicating that you will need to configure the DHCP Relay Agent to support the relaying of DHCP server (which is not necessary for this lab). Click **OK**. The computer saves your settings and starts the Routing and Remote Access Server service.

14. Log on to the client computer as an administrator.

15. Right-click **My Network Places**, and then click **Properties**.

16. Double-click the **Make New Connection** icon. The Network Connection Wizard appears.

17. Click **Next**. The Network Connection Type window appears.

18. Click the **Connect to a private network through the Internet** option button, and then click **Next**. The Destination Address window appears.

19. Type **172.30.12.2** in the Host name or IP address (such as microsoft.com or 123.45.6.78): text box, and then click **Next**. The Connection Availability window appears.

20. Click **Next**.

21. If the Internet Connection Sharing window opens, click **Next**. Otherwise, go to Step 22.

22. The Completing the Network Connection Wizard window appears. Type **NetPlus VPN** as the name of the connection, and then click **Finish**.

23. The Connect NetPlus VPN dialog box opens. Type **netplus** in the User name: text box and type the password for this account in the Password: text box, and then click **Connect**.

24. The Connecting NetPlus VPN dialog box opens momentarily as the connection is made, and then the Connection Complete dialog box opens once the connection is complete. Click **OK** to close it. You have now made a PPTP connection to the Window 2000 Server.

25. Log off both computers.

Certification Objectives

Objectives for the Network+ Exam:

➤ Define the function of the following remote access protocols and services: RAS, PPP, PPTP, ICA

➤ Given a remote connectivity scenario (e.g., IP, IPX, dial-up, PPPoE, authentication, physical connectivity, etc.), configure the connection

➤ Given a troubleshooting scenario involving a remote connectivity problem (e.g., authentication failure, protocol configuration, physical connectivity), identify the cause of the problem

➤ Identify the basic capabilities (i.e., client support, interoperability, authentication, file and print services, application support, and security) of the following server operating systems: UNIX/Linux, NetWare, Windows, Macintosh

Review Questions

1. What is one reason an organization might employ a VPN rather than simply allow users to dial directly into their remote access server?
   a. VPNs provide better performance than direct-dial connections.
   b. VPNs allow more users to connect to the LAN simultaneously.
   c. VPNs are less expensive for connecting a large number of remote users.
   d. VPNs prevent the need for firewalls between access servers and the Internet.

2. What does "RADIUS" stand for?
    a. Remote Authentication Dial-In UNIX Server
    b. Remote Access Dial-In Uniform Sessions
    c. Remote Access Dial-In Universal Service
    d. Remote Authentication Dial-In User Service

3. Which of the following transmission methods is most apt to be used by VPN clients?
    a. PSTN
    b. T-1
    c. Frame Relay
    d. SONET

4. What does the "T" in PPTP stand for?
    a. tunneling
    b. transmission
    c. transport
    d. telecommunications

7

5. Which of the following protocol suites could be used to transmit data over a VPN that relies on PPTP? (Choose all that apply.)
    a. IPX/SPX
    b. TCP/IP
    c. NetBEUI
    d. AppleTalk

LAB 8.1 CONVERTING FROM A FAT FILE SYSTEM TO AN NTFS FILE SYSTEM

Objectives

In this lab, you will convert a file system from File Allocation Table (FAT) to New Technology File System (NTFS). FAT file systems can be used by other operating systems, including Linux and older versions of Windows. However, you cannot use many of the security features of Windows 2000 on a disk formatted with the FAT file system, nor can you install Active Directory on a FAT file system. In order to use these features, you must convert the system to NTFS.

After completing this lab, you will be able to:

➤ Describe the purpose of the Windows 2000 convert command

➤ Convert a file system from FAT to NTFS

Materials Required

This lab will require the following:

➤ A computer running Windows 2000 Server or Windows 2000 Professional, with drive D: formatted as FAT and Windows installed on the C: drive formatted as NTFS

➤ Administrator access to this computer

Estimated completion time: **10 minutes**

ACTIVITY

1. Log on as an administrator.

2. Double-click the **My Computer** icon. The My Computer window appears, displaying the drives and folders on your computer.

3. Right-click the **D:** drive icon, and then click **Properties**.

4. At the top, record the file system type listed. _____

5. Click **OK** to close the dialog box.

6. Click **Start**, point to **Programs**, point to Accessories, and then click **Command Prompt**. The Command Prompt window appears.

7. Type **convert /?**. The computer displays information about the use of the convert command.

8. Type **convert d: /fs:ntfs**. A message appears, indicating the current file system for drive D:. When prompted, type **ntfs** and then press **Enter**. A series of messages appears, indicating that the computer is calculating the disk space needed to make the conversion, is making the conversion, and that the conversion is complete.

9. Repeat Steps 2 through 4. Record the file system type of the D: drive.

Certification Objectives

Objectives for the Network+ Exam:

➤ Identify the basic capabilities (i.e., client support, interoperability, authentication, file and print services, application support, and security) of the following server operating systems: UNIX/Linux, NetWare, Windows, Macintosh

Review Questions

1. What file system was designed for use with IBM's OS/2 operating system?
   a. NTFS
   b. HPFS
   c. FAT16
   d. FAT32

2. Which of the following is true about partition file systems and their interoperability on a Windows 2000 server? (Choose all that apply.)
   a. NTFS partitions can read FAT32 partitions.
   b. FAT32 partitions can read NTFS partitions.
   c. FAT16 partitions can read NTFS partitions.
   d. NTFS partitions can read HPFS partitions.

3. Which of the following best describes a file system?
   a. a method of organizing and managing files through logical structures
   b. a method of assigning user and group permissions to files and directories
   c. a method of organizing and managing objects in an NOS
   d. a method of converting files from one NOS into a format that can be accessed by another NOS

4. Why would a network administrator choose NTFS over FAT32 for her Windows 2000 server? (Choose all that apply.)
   a. NTFS is more fault-tolerant than FAT32.
   b. NTFS is more secure than FAT32.
   c. NTFS is easier to manage than FAT32.
   d. NTFS is more accessible to other platforms than FAT32.

8

5. What file system must a Windows server use in order to support Macintosh clients?
   a. HPFS
   b. FAT16
   c. FAT32
   d. NTFS

6. What file system is used for CD-ROMs?
   a. CHFS
   b. CTDS
   c. CFSS
   d. CDFS

7. Theoretically, an NTFS partition on a Windows 2000 server can be as large as
   _____.

   a. 16 Terabytes
   b. 16 Exabytes
   c. 16 Nanobytes
   d. 16 Gigabytes

Lab 8.2 Establishing an Explicit One-Way Trust Relationship

Objectives

With Windows 2000 domains, domains in the same tree or forest can share network resources. However, by default, users and computers in one forest cannot access resources in another forest. This prevents users from outside your organization (who would not have accounts in a domain in your tree) from accessing your network resources. In contrast, users in different domains in different trees within the same forest do have a transitive trust relationship and can share resources.

In some situations you may want to allow users in another domain limited access to your network resources. For example, employees of a vendor working on a project for your organization may spend time in your building. They may need to use your organization's printers and share files with your employees. At the same time, you and the vendor do not want your users to have access to resources within the vendor's domain. Instead of creating accounts for them within your domain, you could create an explicit one-way trust between your domain and the vendor's domain. This would allow the vendor's employees to use your network resources as necessary, while preventing your employees from accessing the vendor's domain.

After completing this lab, you will be able to:

➤ Establish a one-way nontransitive trust relationship between two domains in different forests

Materials Required

This lab will require the following:

➤ One Windows 2000 Server computer acting as domain controller in a domain called domain1.com, with an IP address of 172.30.12.2

➤ One Windows 2000 Server computer acting as a domain controller in a domain called domain2.com, with an IP address of 172.30.12.3

➤ DNS server installed on both machines and configured so that both machines have DNS entries for domain2.com pointing to 172.30.12.3 and domain1.com pointing to 172.30.12.2 (The DNS server can be installed automatically at the same time as the domain with the dcpromo command, which brings up the Active Directory Installation wizard.)

➤ Both machines configured to use themselves to resolve DNS queries

➤ Administrator access to both computers

➤ NICs in both computers connected with Category 5 (or higher) cables to a hub

8

Estimated completion time: **30 minutes**

ACTIVITY

1. Power on both computers.

2. Log on to the domain1 domain controller as an administrator.

3. Click **Start**, point to **Programs**, point to **Administrative Tools**, and then click **Active Directory Domains and Trust**. The Active Directory Domains and Trust window appears.

4. In the right pane of the window, right-click the icon for the **domain1.com** domain, and then click **Properties**.

5. Click the **Trusts** tab.

6. Click the **Add** button next to the pane at the top of the dialog box that says Domains trusted by this domain:. The Add Trusted Domain dialog box opens.

7. In the Trusted domain: text box, type **DOMAIN2**. This is the NetBIOS name of the other domain. In the Password: and Confirm password: text boxes, type **netplus**, and then click **OK**. A dialog box opens indicating that Active Directory cannot verify the trust. You must create the other side of the trust relationship. Click **OK**.

8. Log on to the domain2 domain controller as an administrator.

9. Click **Start**, point to **Programs**, point to **Administrative Tools**, and then click **Active Directory Domains and Trust**. The Active Directory Domains and Trust window appears.

LAB 8.3 ADDING DOMAIN AND LOCAL ACCOUNTS IN WINDOWS 2000

Objectives

The goal of this lab is to help you understand Active Directory, the database used by Windows 2000 to organize and manage objects. With Active Directory, you can manage users and groups of users throughout a domain. However, you can also create local users and local groups on individual machines (excluding domain controllers). For example, a local machine also has an administrator account, which you could use to make changes. Often a regular user might not have knowledge of this account; thus, the network administrator can centrally manage the computer. Using domain accounts and passwords make central administration easier.

After completing this lab, you will be able to:

➤ Create a local group

➤ Create a domain group

➤ Add a user to a domain group

➤ Add a domain group to a local group

Materials Required

In this lab, you will need the following:

➤ One Windows 2000 Server computer installed as a domain controller in domain1.com

➤ One Windows 2000 Server or Windows 2000 Professional computer in domain1.com

Estimated completion time: **20 minutes**

ACTIVITY

1. Log on to the domain controller as an administrator.

2. Click **Start**, point to **Programs**, point to **Administrative Tools**, and then click **Active Directory Users and Computers**. The Active Directory Users and Computers window appears.

3. In the left pane of the window, right-click the **Users** folder, point to **New**, and then select **User**. The New Object – User window appears.

4. Enter your first name in the First name: text box. Enter your middle initial in the Initials: text box. Enter your last name in the Last name: text box. As you type, the computer enters your full name in the Full name: text box.

5. Enter your last name in the User logon name: text box, and then click **Next**. In the Password: text box, type **netplus**. Enter **netplus** a second time in the Confirm password: text box, and then click **Next**. The window summarizes the new user you are about to create.

6. Click **Finish**. The user is created, and in the right pane of the Active Directory Users and Computers window, a new user with your name displays.

7. To create a global group, right-click the **Users** folder in the left pane, point to **New**, and then select **Group**. The New Object – Group window appears.

8. In the Group name: text box, type **Laboratory**, and then click **OK**. The new group is created.

9. In the right pane of the Active Directory Users and Computers window, right-click the **Laboratories** group, and then click **Properties**. The Laboratories Properties window appears.

10. Click the Members tab. The Members tab appears.

11. Click **Add**. A list of the users in the domain displays in the top pane of the window.

12. Click the user you created in Step 7, and then click **Add**. The user name appears in the lower pane of the window. Click **OK**.

13. Click **OK**. The computer adds the user you created earlier to the Laboratory group.

14. Log on to the Windows 2000 Professional computer (but not on to the domain) as an administrator.

15. Click **Start**, point to **Settings**, and then click **Control Panel**. The Control Panel opens.

16. Double-click the **Administrative Tools** icon. A list of icons you can use to manage this computer displays. Note that there is no Active Directory Users and Computers icon.

17. Double-click the **Computer Management** icon. The Computer Management window appears.

18. In the tree in the left pane of the Computer Management window, click the **+** next to Local Users and Groups to expand the tree. A list of folders named Users and Groups displays.

19. Right-click the **Group** folder, and then select **New Group**.

20. Type **local_group** in the Group name: text box, and then click **Add**. The Select Users or Groups window appears.

8

21. Click the **Look in**: drop-down arrow, and then click **domain1.com**. A dialog box opens, indicating that you do not have sufficient rights to log into the domain.

22. Log on using the account information for the administrator account of the Windows 2000 Server computer. A list of the user accounts and groups on the Windows 2000 Server displays.

23. Click the **Laboratory** group, and then click **Add**. The Laboratory group appears in the bottom pane of the window.

24. Click **OK**, and then click **Create**. The new group is created.

25. Click **Close**. You have just added a local group on the computer, containing as a member the group you created on the domain controller.

26. Close the Computer Management window.

27. Log off both computers.

Certification Objectives

Objectives for the Network+ Exam:

➤ Identify the basic capabilities (i.e., client support, interoperability, authentication, file and print services, application support, and security) of the following server operating systems: UNIX/Linux, NetWare, Windows, Macintosh

Review Questions

1. Which of the following best describes a group?
   a. a collection of users who are authenticated by the same server
   b. a collection of users, groups, or computers that share the same security privileges and restrictions
   c. a collection of users or objects that are located in the same building
   d. a collection of users with some part of their fully distinguished name in common

2. Which of the following is a group that is predefined in Windows 2000 Server (in other words, it exists after you install the operating system)?
   a. Guests
   b. Remote_Users
   c. Servers
   d. Printers

3. In the context of Windows 2000, what is the difference between a local and a global group?

   a. A local group is used to manage resources within one LAN, while a global group is used to manage resources across several LANs or WANs.

   b. A local group is used to manage resources on a single server, while a global group is used to manage resources on all servers within an organization.

   c. A local group is used to manage resources within a single domain, while a global group is used to manage resources on all domains within a forest.

   d. A local group is used to manage resources on a computer, while a global group is used to manage resources within a domain.

4. What are nested groups?

   a. groups that belong to more than one domain

   b. groups that share the same permissions as other groups in the same domain

   c. groups created within another group

   d. groups that contain objects that are owned by other objects

5. If the user named "JaneY" belongs to the group called "STUDENTS," and the group called "STUDENTS" has been assigned "Full Control" permissions to the folder called "GRADES," which of the following is true? (Choose all that apply.)

   a. JaneY can modify the files in the folder called "GRADES."

   b. JaneY can read, but cannot modify, the files in the folder called "GRADES."

   c. JaneY can delete, but cannot read, the files in the folder called "GRADES."

   d. JaneY can prevent other users who don't belong to the STUDENTS group from reading the files in the folder called "GRADES."

6. What is the term for the database that contains information about Windows 2000 objects and their attributes?

   a. NDS

   b. Master Domain

   c. NFS

   d. Active Directory

LAB 8.4 SHARING FOLDERS AND SETTING PERMISSIONS ON AN NTFS FILE SYSTEM

Objectives

The goal of this lab is to help you understand how to share folders and set permissions in Windows 2000. You can give users permissions based not only on their role in their department but also on their role within the organization. For instance, you can put a salesperson in the Sales group so that he or she can access the same files and network resources as the other salespeople. You can also put individual salespeople in different groups depending on the product they sell, so that they can access the same files as the groups that make those products. Furthermore, you can determine how much control over each file that each user has.

After completing this lab, you will be able to:

➤ Share folders

➤ Understand NTFS share permissions

Materials Required

In this lab, you will need the following:

➤ Completion of Lab 8.3

➤ One Windows 2000 Server computer installed as the domain controller in domain1.com

➤ One Windows 2000 Professional computer in domain1 with a local group named local_group containing the user you created in Lab 8.3

➤ Drive D: on the Windows 2000 Professional computer formatted with the NTFS file system

---

Estimated completion time: **20 minutes**

ACTIVITY

1. Log on to the Windows 2000 Professional as an administrator.

2. Double-click the **My Computer** icon. The My Computer window appears.

3. Double-click the **D:** drive icon. The D: Properties dialog box opens.

4. Click **File**, point to **New**, and then click **Folder**. A new folder is created and you are prompted to enter a folder name.

5. Type **FolderR** for the folder name.

6. Right-click the **FolderR** icon, and then click **Sharing**. The Properties window for FolderR appears.

7. Click **Share this folder**. The name of the folder appears in the Share Name box. Do not change the share name.

8. Click **Permissions**. The Share Permissions dialog box opens with the Everyone group highlighted.

9. Record the permissions for the Everyone group.

10. Click the **Everyone** group, if necessary, and then click **Remove**.

11. Click **Add**. The Select Users, Computers, or Groups dialog box opens.

12. Click the **Look in:** drop-down arrow, and then click the name of the computer, if necessary. The list of groups on the workstation displays in the Name box.

13. Click **local_group**, and then click **Add**. The entry appears in the box at the bottom of the screen. Click **OK**.

14. In the Permissions: window, note that only the Read box in the Allow column is checked. Record the permissions of the FolderR folder.

_____

15. Click **OK** twice to finish sharing the folder.

16. To verify that the user created in Lab 8.3 only has read access over the network to FolderR, log off as administrator. Log on to the domain as the user you created in Lab 8.3. The Windows 2000 desktop appears.

17. To simulate accessing the share from another computer, use My Network Places to access the files. Because you are on the local computer, you could access the files directly through Windows Explorer. Double-click **My Network Places**, and then double-click the **Entire Network** icon. If the Microsoft Windows Network icon does not appear, click the link that indicates that you may also view the entire contents of the network. Double-click the **Microsoft Windows Network** icon.

18. Double-click the **Domain1** icon, and then double-click the icon for the name of the computer. The shares active on the computer appear.

19. Double-click the **FolderR** folder. The FolderR window opens.

20. Click **File**, point to **New**, and then click **Folder**. A dialog box opens indicating that you do not have sufficient permission to do this.

21. Repeat Steps 2 through 16. This time, create a folder named **FolderF** and give the local group Full Control access.

22. Repeat Steps 17 through 23 for the FolderF folder. Now you are able to create a folder within FolderF.

Certification Objectives

Objectives for the Network+ Exam:

➤ Identify the basic capabilities (i.e., client support, interoperability, authentication, file and print services, application support, and security) of the following server operating systems: UNIX/Linux, NetWare, Windows, Macintosh

➤ Given a scenario, predict the impact of a particular security implementation on network functionality (e.g., blocking port numbers, encryption, etc.)

6. Right-click the WSA icon. Select **Manage**. After a brief wait, the Computer Management window appears.

7. A tree of system tools and other utilities on the WSA computer appears in the left pane of the window. Double-click the **Device Manager**. A dialog box opens, indicating that Device Manager is running in read-only mode because it is on a remote computer.

8. Click **OK**. In the right pane of the window, a list of the devices on the WSA computer displays.

9. In the left pane of the window, click the **+** sign next to Services and Applications. Further options appear in the tree underneath it, including the Services icon.

10. Click the **Services** icon. A list of services running on the remote computer displays.

11. Right-click the **ClipBook** icon, and then click **Start**. A dialog box opens, stating that Windows is attempting to start the following service on WSA… ClipBook. The ClipBook service starts on the remote computer.

12. Log on to the WSA computer as an administrator. The Windows 2000 desktop appears.

13. Double-click **My Computer**, and then double-click **Control Panel**. The Control Panel opens.

14. Double-click **Administrative Tools**. The Administrative Tools window appears.

15. Double-click the **Services** icon. The Services icon appears, and the service starts.

16. Back in the Services window on the Windows 2000 Server, right-click the **ClipBook** icon, and then click **Stop**. The service stops.

17. Back in the Services window on the client computer, click **Action,** and then click **Refresh**. The screen is refreshed and the status of each service is updated. The ClipBook service is now stopped.

18. Close all open windows on both computers. Log off both computers.

Certification Objectives

Objectives for the Network+ Exam:

➤ Identify the basic capabilities (i.e., client support, interoperability, authentication, file and print services, application support, and security) of the following server operating systems: UNIX/Linux, NetWare, Windows, Macintosh

➤ Given a troubleshooting scenario involving a remote connectivity problem (e.g., authentication failure, protocol configuration, physical connectivity), identify the cause of the problem

Review Questions

1. Which of the following Windows 2000 tools would you use to determine whether your server is using more than 50 percent of its available RAM?
   a. Device Manager
   b. Event Viewer
   c. System Monitor
   d. Network Monitor

2. If you are a busy network administrator who enlists the help of some of your employees to create new user accounts on the server, how would you enable these employees to do this?
   a. provide your employees with the password to the Administrator account
   b. log on to a specific workstation as Administrator, and then let the employees add user accounts from that workstation
   c. limit access for the Administrator account to only certain hours, during which your employees could use the account to add new users
   d. create a group containing the employees' user names and enable that group to create new user accounts

3. What options would you choose to add a shared printer to your Windows 2000 domain?
   a. click Start, point to Settings, click Printers, and then double-click Add Printer
   b. click Start, point to Programs, point to Administrative Tools, and then click Printer Management
   c. click Start, point to Settings, click Control Panel, and then double-click Printers
   d. click Start, point to Programs, and then click Printer Setup

4. What options would you choose to add a new group to a Windows 2000 domain?
   a. click Start, point to Programs, point to Administrative Tools, and then click Active Directory Users and Computers
   b. click Start, point to Settings, point to Control Panel, and then click Users and Groups
   c. click Start, point to Settings, and then click Active Directory Users and Groups
   d. click Start, point to Programs, point to Administrative Tools, point to Resource Management, and then click Users and Groups

8

5. When you select Services from the Administrative Tools menu on a Windows 2000 server, what will you see?

a. all services currently available on the Windows 2000 server

b. all services currently running on the Windows 2000 server

c. all services currently running on the Windows 2000 server and its clients

d. all services currently running on the Windows 2000 server and other servers in the same domain

CHAPTER NINE

NETWARE-BASED NETWORKING

Labs included in this chapter

➤ Lab 9.1 Starting and Shutting Down a Novell NetWare 5.x Server

➤ Lab 9.2 Understanding NetWare Volumes

➤ Lab 9.3 Understanding Drive Mappings

➤ Lab 9.4 Understanding NDS Objects

➤ Lab 9.5 Understanding NDS Contexts

Net+ Exam Objectives	
Objective	**Lab**
Identify the basic capabilities (i.e., client support, interoperability, authentication, file and print services, application support, and security) of the following server operating systems: UNIX/Linux, NetWare, Windows, Macintosh	9.1, 9.2, 9.3, 9.4, 9.5
Identify the basic capabilities (i.e., client connectivity, local security mechanisms, and authentication) of the following clients: UNIX/Linux, Windows, Macintosh	9.1, 9.3, 9.4, 9.5
Given specific parameters, configure a client to connect to the following servers: UNIX/Linux, NetWare, Windows, Macintosh	9.1, 9.3, 9.4, 9.5

13. At the C:\NWSERVER> prompt, type **server**, and then press **Enter**. The Novell NetWare Server kernel, SERVER.EXE, loads into the computer's RAM. The server prompt changes to NW5:, indicating that the server (named NW5) is up and running.

14. Now you will reboot the NetWare 5.x server. Press **Ctrl+Esc**. A list of options display. Type **1**, and then press **Enter**. The NW5: prompt appears. Type **reset server**, and then press **Enter**.

Certification Objectives

Objectives for the Network+ Exam:

➤ Identify the basic capabilities (i.e., client support, interoperability, authentication, file and print services, application support, and security) of the following server operating systems: UNIX/Linux, NetWare, Windows, Macintosh

➤ Identify the basic capabilities (i.e., client connectivity, local security mechanisms, and authentication) of the following clients: UNIX/Linux, Windows, Macintosh

➤ Given specific parameters, configure a client to connect to the following servers: UNIX/Linux, NetWare, Windows, Macintosh

Review Questions

1. What is the purpose of the NetWare 5.x kernel?
   a. to organize the server's file system
   b. to arbitrate task priority in multiprocessing
   c. to oversee all critical server functions
   d. to act as a gateway with other network operating systems

2. What command starts the NetWare network operating system?
   a. KERNEL.EXE
   b. NOS.EXE
   c. SERVER.EXE
   d. START.EXE

3. What DOS file automatically starts a Novell server?
   a. AUTOEXEC.EXE
   b. CONFIG.SYS
   c. START.EXE
   d. AUTOEXEC.BAT

4. What does "NLM" stand for?
   a. Novell Layered Management
   b. NetWare Loadable Module
   c. Novell Licensed Memory
   d. NetWare Logical Master

5. What is the name of the graphical interface that runs on a Novell NetWare 5.x server?
    a. MONITOR
    b. ConsoleOne
    c. NetView
    d. WinNovell

6. If your server is named SERVER1 and you have installed the NetWare 5.1 software in a directory called "C:\NWSERVER," what will your server's System Console prompt look like?
    a. SERVER1:
    b. NW>
    c. NetWare51>
    d. NWSERVER:

LAB 9.2 UNDERSTANDING NETWARE VOLUMES

9

Objectives

The goal of this lab is to help you understand Novell NetWare volumes. With any network operating system, you will often need to add disk space as you add users or as your users need to share more or larger files. In NetWare, a partition is made of two parts. The area where data is actually stored is known as the data area. Another area of the disk, known as the redirection area or the "hot fix," is reserved for redirecting bad disk blocks. The default size for the "hot fix" depends on the partition size, but usually takes between 5 percent and 10 percent of the total partition size.

After completing this lab, you will be able to:

➤ Create a NetWare partition from free space on a disk

➤ Create a NetWare volume from the partition

➤ View volume properties such as compression and block suballocation

Materials Required

This lab will require the following:

➤ A computer named NW5 running Novell NetWare 5.x

➤ At least 500 MB of free, unpartitioned disk space on the Novell NetWare 5.x computer's hard disk

➤ The NDS organization named NetPlus, with the Admin user in this container

Estimated completion time: **30 minutes**

ACTIVITY

1. At the Novell NetWare 5.x server console, press **Ctrl+Esc**. A list of screens from which to choose displays.

2. Type **1**, and then press **Enter**. The System Console screen appears with the NW5: prompt.

3. Type **nwconfig**, and then press **Enter**.

4. Use the arrow keys to select **Standard Disk Options**, and then press **Enter**. The Available Disk Options dialog box opens.

5. Use the arrow keys to select **Modify disk partitions and Hot Fix**, and then press **Enter**. A table showing the disk partitions and their sizes appears.

6. Use the arrow keys to select **Create NetWare disk partition**, and then press **Enter**. The Disk Partition Information dialog box opens.

7. In the Partition size text box, type **500**, and then press **Enter**.

8. Press **F10** to save your changes. The Create NetWare partition? dialog box opens.

9. Use the arrow keys to select **Yes**, and then press **Enter**. Novell adds the new partition.

10. Press the **Esc** key. The Available Disk Options window reappears.

11. Use the arrow keys to select **NetWare Volume Options**, and then press **Enter**. The volume names and sizes appear. Record the volume names and sizes that appear.

_____

12. Now you will create a new volume. The first step in this process is to determine the amount of free space available. Press the **Insert** key. The Volume Disk Segment List dialog box opens. Record the amount of free space.

_____

13. Next you will make a volume assignment from the free space. Use the arrow keys to select (**free space**), and then press **Enter**. The What would you like to do with this free segment? dialog box opens.

14. Use the arrow keys to select **Make this segment a new volume**, and then press **Enter**. The Disk segment parameters dialog box opens.

15. In the Disk segment volume name text box, type **DATA**, and then press **Enter**. The cursor highlights the Disk segment size text box. Do not change the size.

16. Press **F10** to add the new volume. The Volume Disk Segment List reappears.

17. Press **Esc** twice. The Save volume changes? dialog box opens.

18. Use the arrow keys to select **Yes**, and then press **Enter**. The Directory Services Login/Authentication dialog box opens.

19. In the Administrator name text box, type .**CN=admin.O=NW5_O**, and then press **Enter**. In the Password text box, type the password for the admin user and then press **Enter**. The For your information dialog box opens, indicating that the volume has been installed.

20. Press **Enter** to continue. The Select an action dialog box opens.

21. Use the arrow keys to select **Mount all volumes**, and then press **Enter**. The Available Disk Options window reappears.

22. Press **Esc** twice. The Exit nwconfig? dialog box opens.

23. Use the arrow keys to select **Yes**, and then press **Enter**. The NW5: server prompt appears. You have added a NetWare partition created from free space on the server's hard disk, and you have added a volume within that NetWare partition. Next you will verify the volume's properties.

24. At the server console NW5: prompt, type **nwconfig**, and then press **Enter**.

25. Use the arrow keys to select **Standard Disk Options**, and then press **Enter**. The Available Disk Options screen appears.

26. Use the arrow keys to select **NetWare Volume Options**, and then press **Enter**. The volume names and sizes appear.

27. Use the arrow keys to select the volume named **DATA**, which you created earlier in this lab, and then press **Enter**. The Volume information for the DATA volume appears. Record the status of the DATA volume.

_____

28. Record whether file compression and block suballocation are turned on or off.

_____

29. Press **Esc** four times. The Exit nwconfig? dialog box opens.

30. Use the arrow keys to select **Yes**, and then press **Enter**. The NW5: server prompt appears.

Certification Objectives

Objectives for the Network+ Exam:

➤ Identify the basic capabilities (i.e., client support, interoperability, authentication, file and print services, application support, and security) of the following server operating systems: UNIX/Linux, NetWare, Windows, Macintosh

➤ Access to the admin account on the NetWare server

➤ An ordinary user account on the Windows 2000 Professional computer

➤ A functioning network connection between the two computers

Estimated completion time: **25 minutes**

ACTIVITY

1. Power on the NetWare 5.x server. If the DOS prompt appears, type **cd C:\nwserver**, and then press **Enter**. Type **server**, and then press **Enter**. If the DOS prompt does not appear, go to Step 2.

2. Power on the Windows 2000 client computer. Press **Ctrl + Alt + Del**. The Novell Login dialog box opens. Type **admin** into the Username: text box and the password for this account into the Password: text box.

3. The computer logs you on to the NetWare server and the Windows NT/2000 Workstation dialog box opens. This dialog box will allow you to log on to the Windows 2000 Professional computer in addition to the NetWare server. Often users will synchronize accounts between their workstation and the NetWare server so that they don't have to log on twice. Enter the name of the ordinary account in the Name: text box and the password in the Password: text box, and then click **OK**.

4. Click Start, point to **Programs**, point to **Accessories**, and then click **Command Prompt**. The Command Prompt window appears.

5. At the prompt, type **map**, and then press Enter to display the current drive mappings. Record the current mappings.

_____

6. Type **map H:= NW5\DATA:**, and then press **Enter** to set a drive mapping. The new drive mapping returns.

7. Type **map**, and then press **Ente**r to display a list of the new drive mappings. Record the new drive mappings.

_____

8. Type **H:**, and then press **Enter** to change to the newly mapped drive. The new prompt H:\DATA appears.

9. Type **dir**, and then press **Enter**. A list of the current files and directories on this drive displays.

10. Type **md newdir**, and then press **Enter** to create a new directory. The command prompt returns. If you receive an error indicating the directory already exists, proceed to the next step.

11. Type **map next nw5\data:\newdir**, and then press **Enter** to create a drive mapping to this newly created directory for the next available drive letter.

12. Type **map**, and then press **Enter** to display a list of the current drive mappings. Record the drive letter mapped to the newdir directory.

---

13. Type **map .del H:**, and then press **Enter** to delete the H: mapped drive. A message appears indicating that the drive mapping has been deleted.

14. Type **exit**, and then press **Enter** to exit the Command Prompt window. The Windows desktop appears.

15. Double-click **My Computer**, double-click **Z:**, double-click the **WIN32** folder, and then double-click **nwadmn32**, (which may appear as nwadmn32.exe if the computer is configured to show file extensions). NetWare Administrator opens.

16. In the left screen is a tree consisting of all the objects in the NDS tree. Right-click the **admin** object, and then click **Details**. The User: admin window appears.

17. In the right part of the screen, click the **Login Script** button.

18. In the Login Script box, type **map H:=NW5\DATA:**, and then press **Enter**. This saves a login script thatl maps drive H: to the data volume on NW5.

19. On the next line, type **map L:=NW5\SYS:**, and then press **Enter**.

20. On the next line, type **PATH=%PATH%;L:\public**, and then press **Enter**.

21. Click **OK**.

22. Reboot the Windows 2000 Professional computer. Log on to the computer as you did in Steps 2 and 3.

23. Double-click **My Computer**. The H: and L: network drives appear, just as if they were file systems on your computer. Click the **Close** button, if necessary.

Certification Objectives

Objectives for the Network+ Exam:

➤ Identify the basic capabilities (i.e., client support, interoperability, authentication, file and print services, application support, and security) of the following server operating systems: UNIX/Linux, NetWare, Windows, Macintosh

➤ Identify the basic capabilities (i.e., client connectivity, local security mechanisms, and authentication) of the following clients: UNIX/Linux, Windows, Macintosh

➤ Given specific parameters, configure a client to connect to the following servers: UNIX/Linux, NetWare, Windows, Macintosh

Review Questions

1. What is the purpose of the map command?
   a. to display a graphical representation of a NetWare server's directory
   b. to load a portion of the NetWare kernel on a client workstation
   c. to format a subdirectory according to a different file system than its parent directory
   d. to associate a NetWare directory with a drive letter for easier client access

2. Where on a Windows 2000 Professional client would a user find his or her drive mappings?
   a. through the Control Panel, Drive Mappings options
   b. through the Network and Dial-up Connections, LAN Connection options
   c. through the My Network Places option
   d. through the My Computer option

3. What is one advantage to establishing drive mappings through the login script on a NetWare server?
   a. prevents users from being able to create their own drive mappings
   b. simplifies the process of mapping drives according to users and groups
   c. enables more drive letters to be used for mapping
   d. prevents the mapping of secured data directories

4. Which of the following commands would delete an existing drive mapping, when typed from the client's command prompt?
   a. map del H:
   b. delete mapping H:
   c. del map H:
   d. map −H:

5. As a network administrator, what program would you launch to modify a NetWare 5.x server's login script to add a drive mapping for all users on your network?
   a. nds.exe
   b. admin.exe
   c. nwconfig.exe
   d. nwadmn32.exe

LAB 9.4 UNDERSTANDING NDS OBJECTS

Objectives

In this lab, you will create and manipulate objects in the NetWare Directory Services (NDS) tree. Each user, group, volume, and other device or entity controlled by NDS is called an object. NDS allows you to have fine-grained control over access to any of the objects in the tree. For example, you can allow the sales group to have read-only access to the files used by the engineering group.

You can also delegate some of the ability to administer the NDS tree. For instance, you can allow one of the users in the accounting group to be able to add and delete other users in that group without having the ability to modify objects in other parts of the NDS tree. You would do this by making that user a trustee for the sales group. This can be particularly useful in organizations that are too large to be administered by one person.

After completing this lab, you will be able to:

➤ Create Organizational Unit objects

➤ Create User objects

➤ Create Group objects

➤ Add User objects to Group objects

➤ Make trustee assignments

Materials Required

This lab will require the following:

➤ A computer named NW5 running Novell NetWare 5.x Server

➤ Access to the admin account on the NetWare server

➤ An NDS organization named NetPlus

➤ A computer running Windows 2000 Professional and the Novell Client for NT/2000 4.81 software

➤ Access to an ordinary user account on the Windows 2000 Professional computer

➤ A functioning network connection between the two computers

Estimated completion time: **40 minutes**

ACTIVITY

1. Power on the NetWare 5.x server. If the DOS prompt appears, type **cd C:\nwserver**, and then press **Enter**. Type **server**, and then press **Enter**. If the DOS prompt does not appear, proceed to Step 2.

2. Power on the Windows 2000 Professional client and log on to the admin account. When the Windows NT/2000 Workstation dialog box opens, log on to the Windows 2000 Professional client with the ordinary user account.

3. Double-click **My Network Places**. The My Network Places window appears.

4. Double-click the **Novell Connections** icon.

Certification Objectives

Objectives for the Network+ Exam:

➤ Identify the basic capabilities (i.e., client support, interoperability, authentication, file and print services, application support, and security) of the following server operating systems: UNIX/Linux, NetWare, Windows, Macintosh

➤ Identify the basic capabilities (i.e., client connectivity, local security mechanisms, and authentication) of the following clients: UNIX/Linux, Windows, Macintosh

➤ Given specific parameters, configure a client to connect to the following servers: UNIX/Linux, NetWare, Windows, Macintosh

Review Questions

1. What does "NDS" stand for?
   a. Novell Drive System
   b. NetWare Directory Services
   c. Novell Distribution Services
   d. NetWare Dynamic Sessions

2. What is the purpose of an organizational unit?
   a. to represent an organization's hierarchy in the schema
   b. to group files with similar permissions
   c. to group objects with similar security requirements
   d. to facilitate faster e-mail gateway operation

3. Which of the following are examples of leaf objects? (Choose all that apply.)
   a. user
   b. printer
   c. organizational unit
   d. container

4. What is the uppermost level of the NDS tree called?
   a. leaf
   b. branch
   c. twig
   d. root

5. What is the difference between a group member and a group trustee?
   a. A member belongs to a group while a trustee can modify the properties of that group.
   b. A member belongs to a group and can modify the properties of that group, while a trustee can modify the properties of the group, but does not necessarily belong to the group.
   c. A member belongs to a group all the time, while a trustee belongs to that group only according to certain time restrictions.
   d. A member can be any object (such as user or printer) that belongs to a group, while a trustee is only a user object that belongs to a group.

6. What NetWare program allows you to create new users and groups within the NDS tree?
   a. ndsconfig.exe
   b. nwconfig.exe
   c. nwadmn32.exe
   d. ndscreate.exe

9

LAB 9.5 UNDERSTANDING NDS CONTEXTS

Objectives

The goal of this lab is to increase your knowledge of NDS contexts. The context identifies in which part of the NDS tree you are currently navigating.

In NDS, Novell uses two forms of names. A typeful name is longer and specifically identifies the organization (with the abbreviation 0) and organizational units (with the abbreviation OU). For instance, OU=sales.O=netplus is a typeful name with an organization of sales and an organizational unit of netplus. A typeless name is shorter and does not use O or OU to identify the organization or organizational units. For instance, sales.netplus is a typeless name.

Most of the time, you will use NDS typeless names. The context does not matter for typeless names. However, for some NDS activities, you must enter the typeful names. For example, to save changes to a volume, you must enter the typeful name of the admin user.

The use of NDS contexts also allows you to have multiple users with the same name. For instance, on a server named NW5, you might have two users named davis. However, each user must be in a different context. One davis user might be in the Accounting organizational unit, while the other user named davis might be in the Sales organizational unit within the NW5 directory tree. As a network administrator, you must understand how to create, identify and locate users within their contexts.

3. Which of the following commands will change to a container called PROD?
   a. cd PROD
   b. md PROD
   c. cx /r/PROD
   d. cx PROD

4. Which of the following are examples of NDS typeless names? (Choose all that apply.)
   a. OU=PROD.OU=USA.O=FIRM_A
   b. PROD.USA.FIRM_A
   c. O=FIRM_B
   d. KEVIN.FIRM_B.USA

5. Which of the following are examples of NDS typeful names? (Choose all that apply.)
   a. PROD.USA.FIRM_A
   b. OU=PROD.OU=USA.O=FIRM_A
   c. O=FIRM_B
   d. FIRM_B

6. A container object could be created in which of the following? (Choose all that apply.)
   a. leaf object
   b. organizational unit
   c. [root]
   d. group

NETWORKING WITH UNIX

Labs included in this chapter

➤ Lab 10.1 User and Group Management

➤ Lab 10.2 Managing Directories and Files

➤ Lab 10.3 Understanding UNIX Help

➤ Lab 10.4 Understanding Wildcard Symbols, Redirection Symbols, and the Pipe Symbol

➤ Lab 10.5 Navigating the UNIX File System

Net+ Exam Objectives	
Objective	Lab
Identify the basic capabilities (i.e., client support, interoperability, authentication, file and print services, application support, and security) of the following server operating systems: UNIX/Linux, NetWare, Windows, Macintosh	10.1, 10.2, 10.3, 10.4, 10.5
Identify the basic capabilities (i.e., client connectivity, local security mechanisms, and authentication) of the following clients: UNIX/Linux, Windows, Macintosh	10.3, 10.4, 10.5

LAB 10.1 USER AND GROUP MANAGEMENT

Objectives

The goal of this lab is to help you learn how to manage users and groups within UNIX. While most versions of UNIX, including Linux, have a GUI with which you can manage the computer and add users, quite often it is not installed on servers. Unlike in Windows, the GUI is not required, and removing it frees up resources which can be better used elsewhere. Many UNIX servers are rarely administered from the console.

In UNIX, just as with Windows and NetWare, you can place users in groups to restrict their access to files. You can also change a user's shell, which interprets the user's commands. In UNIX, user names (as well as commands) are case-sensitive. If you add a user named "anthony" and another user named "Anthony," the computer would consider these different users.

After completing this lab, you will be able to:

➤ Add, modify, and delete user accounts

➤ Add, modify, and delete group accounts

➤ Log in using new usernames

Materials Required

This lab will require the following:

➤ A computer, with a host name of UNIX1, running a server installation of Linux Red Hat 7.x (this lab assumes that the GUI is not installed, which is the default for a server installation)

➤ The root user's password

Estimated completion time: **20 minutes**

ACTIVITY

1. Power on the computer. At the UNIX1 login prompt, type **root**, and then press **Enter**. The Password prompt appears on the next line.

2. At the Password prompt, type the correct password for the root user, and then press **Enter**. A prompt similar to [root@UNIX1 /root]# appears.

3. At the prompt, type **cd /**, and then press **Enter**. The prompt changes to [root@UNIX1 /]#. The / in the prompt indicates that this is the root, or top-level, directory.

4. To create a user, type **useradd zac**, and then press **Enter**. The prompt appears, indicating that the command was successfully executed.

5. To create a group, type **groupadd managers**, and then press **Enter**. The prompt returns.

6. To create another group, type **groupadd employees**, and then press **Enter**. The prompt returns.

7. To designate the managers group as the primary group and the employees groups as a secondary group for the zac user, type **usermod –g managers –G employees zac**, and then press **Enter**. The prompt returns. The zac user account has been added to both groups.

8. To verify that zac has been added to both groups, type **groups zac**, and then press **Enter**. A list of groups to which zac belongs displays on the screen.

9. To change the default shell for zac to the Bourne shell (/bin/sh), type **usermod –s /bin/sh zac**, and then press **Enter**.

10. To change the password for zac, type **passwd zac**, and then press **Enter**. The message "Changing password for user zac" appears, followed by the prompt New UNIX password.

11. At the New UNIX password prompt, type a password, and then press **Enter**. The message New UNIX password appears. You may receive an error if the password is less than six characters or if the password resembles a dictionary word (and hence could be easily guessed). If so, repeat this step with a password longer than six characters or with a password that does not occur in the dictionary.

12. At the New UNIX password prompt, confirm the password by typing it a second time, and then press **Enter**. At the prompt, the message "passwd: all authentication tokens updated successfully" appears.

13. To log off as the root user, type **exit**, and then press **Enter**. The UNIX1 login prompt appears.

14. At the UNIX1 login prompt, type **zac**, and then press **Enter**.

15. At the Password prompt, type the password you entered for the zac user in Steps 12 and 13, and then press **Enter**. The sh-2.05$ prompt (or a similar prompt) appears. The prompt is different because you changed the login shell in Step 10.

16. To display information about the user zac, type **finger zac**, and then press **Enter**.

17. Read the output of the finger command, and record how long zac has been logged on.

18. Type **exit** to log off.

19. Log back on as root, as you did in Steps 2 and 3.

20. To prevent zac from logging on, type **usermod –L zac**, and then press **Enter** to lock the account. You use the –U option to unlock the account.

21. To delete the user zac, type **userdel zac**, and then press **Enter**.

22. To delete the group Managers, type **groupdel managers**, and then press **Enter**.

23. Using useradd, create a new user account for yourself. For the user name, use your first initial followed by your last name. For example, if your name is "Todd Meadors," then your username would be tmeadors. Record your username.

---

24. Log off as the root user.

Certification Objectives

Objectives for the Network+ Exam:

➤ Identify the basic capabilities (i.e., client support, interoperability, authentication, file and print services, application support, and security) of the following server operating systems: UNIX/Linux, NetWare, Windows, Macintosh

Review Questions

1. Bob has a Linux user account. He is going on vacation for two weeks. As a UNIX system administrator, you need to make sure no one uses his account during his absence. What is the best way to keep his user information intact, while at the same time preventing others from logging in with Bob's username?
   a. delete Bob's primary group
   b. use the usermod command to change the password for his account
   c. use the usermod command to lock his account
   d. use the finger command to delete his account

2. Which of the following commands would allow you to add a user named "carruthers" on a UNIX system?
   a. usermod −A carruthers
   b. useradd Carruthers
   c. useradd carruthers
   d. add user carruthers

3. Which of the following commands would allow you to add a group named "designers" on a UNIX system?
   a. groupadd designers
   b. groupadd "designers"
   c. add group designers
   d. groupmod +G designers

4. On a UNIX system, what command could you use to determine the groups to which the user named "carruthers" belongs?
   a. carruthers -?
   b. carruthers −groups
   c. group "carruthers"
   d. groups carruthers

5. What is the purpose of having a new user change his password the first time he logs on to a network?

   a. It allows the user to use a more secure password.

   b. It ensures greater security because no one but the user will know the password.

   c. It allows the user to synchronize all his passwords on all systems.

   d. It allows the user to choose a password that will never expire.

6. Which of the following commands gives information about a user?

   a. groupdel

   b. mkdir

   c. ls

   d. finger

LAB 10.2 MANAGING DIRECTORIES AND FILES

Objectives

The goal of this lab is to help you understand how to manage UNIX directories and files. Although graphical file managers are available for most versions of UNIX, files can be manipulated on the command line in all versions. In UNIX, the file extension or name does not have the same meaning that it does in Windows. For instance, in UNIX, an executable program may be named "program," "program.exe," "program.txt," or any other name. Windows programs, however, typically have an extension of .com or .exe.

You can create a "hidden" file in UNIX by creating it with a name that begins with a dot. However, these hidden files may be written to and deleted just like any other file (although they are slightly harder to find).

After completing this lab, you will be able to:

> Create and remove a directory

> Create, view, and remove a file

Materials Required

This lab will require the following:

> A computer, with a host name of UNIX1, running Linux Red Hat 7.x or another version of UNIX

> The root user's password

> An ordinary user account, such as the one you created in Lab 10.1

10

Estimated completion time: **25 minutes**

ACTIVITY

1. Power on the computer.

2. Log on using the ordinary user account.

3. At the prompt, type **pwd**, and then press **Enter**. Record the output of the pwd command.

   _____

4. To create a directory called payroll, type **mkdir payroll**. The prompt returns, indicating that the command was successfully executed.

5. To view files and folders in the current directory, type **ls**, and then press **Enter**. Record the output of the ls command.

   _____

6. To create a file called file2.txt, type **echo "Hello" > file2.txt**, and then press **Enter**. The prompt returns. (Note that the > symbol is known as a redirection symbol. You learn more about it in Lab 10.4.)

7. To view the contents of the file, type **cat file2.txt**, and then press **Enter**. The computer prints "Hello" and the prompt returns.

8. To append the text "The end" to file2.txt, type **echo "The end" >> file2.txt**, and then press **Enter**. (The >> symbol is another redirection symbol and is explained in Lab 10.4.)

9. Repeat Step 7 and record the output.

   _____

10. To copy file2.txt to a file called file3.txt, type **cp file2.txt file3.txt**, and then press **Enter**.

11. Type **ls –l**, and then press **Enter**. A long list of files and directories displays.

12. To create another directory, type **mkdir prod**, and then press **Enter**. The prompt returns, indicating that the command was successfully executed.

13. To delete the directory called prod, type **rmdir prod**, and then press **Enter**. The prompt returns, indicating that the command was successfully executed.

14. To change the payroll directory, created in Step 4, type **cd payroll**, and then press **Enter**. Record the text that is displayed in the prompt.

   _____

15. Enter **pwd**, and then press **Enter**. Record the output.

   _____

16. To create a hidden file, type **echo "Hidden file" > .file-is-hidden**, and then press **Enter**. The prompt returns, indicating that the command was successfully executed.

17. Type **ls**, and then press **Enter**. The file .file-is-hidden is not included in the list.

18. Type **ls −a**, and then press **Enter**. The file .file-is-hidden is now included in the output.

19. Type **cd ..**, and then press **Enter**. This moves your current directory up one level.

20. To rename file2.txt as file7.txt, type **mv file2.txt file7.txt**, and then press **Enter**. The prompt returns, indicating that the command was successfully executed.

21. Type **ls**, and then press **Enter**. Record whether you see either file2.txt or file7.txt in the output.

_____

22. To remove file7.txt, type **rm file7.txt**, and then press **Enter**. The prompt returns, indicating that the command was successfully executed.

23. Type **ls**, and then press **Enter**. Record whether you see file7.txt in the output.

_____

10

24. Log off.

Certification Objectives

Objectives for the Network+ Exam:

➤ Identify the basic capabilities (i.e., client support, interoperability, authentication, file and print services, application support, and security) of the following server operating systems: UNIX/Linux, NetWare, Windows, Macintosh

Review Questions

1. What command would you use to list the contents of a directory called "temporary" on a UNIX system?
   a. list temporary
   b. ls temporary
   c. ls dir temporary
   d. ? temporary

2. On a UNIX system, what command would allow you to view a listing of files in the directory called "temporary," including hidden files?
   a. list temporary −all
   b. ls −a temporary
   c. ls dir −all temporary
   d. ? /a temporary

3. In a UNIX system, a hidden file begins with what character?

    a. comma

    b. pound sign

    c. colon

    d. period

4. What command would allow you to move your current position within a UNIX directory system up one level?

    a. cd\

    b. cd /

    c. cd ..

    d. cd root

5. What command would you use to create a directory called "orders" on a UNIX system?

    a. mkdir orders

    b. mdir orders

    c. crdir orders

    d. create dir orders

6. What command would you use to delete a directory called "orders" on a UNIX system?

    a. rm orders

    b. remdir orders

    c. rdir orders

    d. rmdir orders

7. What command would you use to rename a file from "questions" to "answers?"

    a. ren questions answers

    b. mv questions answers

    c. del questions mk answers

    d. paste questions answers

LAB 10.3 UNDERSTANDING UNIX HELP

Objectives

The goal of this lab is to help you learn about UNIX Help by executing the man command, in conjunction with another command, to learn more about the latter. The man command is an abbreviation for manual. With the man command, you can read information contained in a man page. The man command is available on all versions of UNIX.

You can use the apropos command to search for a command whose name you do not know or cannot remember. The apropos command works by searching through an index of all the man pages on the computer and displaying a summary of each command that matches a particular keyword.

After completing this lab, you will be able to:

➤ Find help on any known UNIX command

➤ Execute the man command

➤ Find out how to search for the name of a command

Materials Required

This lab will require the following:

➤ A computer with a host name of UNIX1, running Linux Red Hat 7.x

➤ The user you created in Lab 10.1

Estimated completion time: **15 minutes**

ACTIVITY

10

1. Power on the computer and log on as the user you created in Step 4 of Lab 10.1.

2. To display information about the cp command, type **man cp**, and then press **Enter**. Information for the cp command appears. Read the man page and then record the purpose of the cp command.

   _____

3. Press **q** to quit the man page and return to the prompt.

4. Type **man ls**, and then press **Enter**. The man pages for the ls command appear. Record the purpose of the −a option.

   _____

5. Press **q** to quit the man page and return to the prompt.

6. Type **man rm**, and then press **Enter**. The Help pages for the rm command appear.

7. Press the **spacebar** to scroll down one page at a time until you locate the option for removing the contents of directories recursively. Record that option here.

   _____

8. Press **q** to quit the man page and return to the prompt. To search for text within a man page, type **man ls**, and then press **Enter**. The man pages for the ls command appear.

Materials Required

This lab will require the following:

> ➤ A computer with a host name of UNIX1 running Linux Red Hat 7.x
>
> ➤ A user account on UNIX1
>
> ➤ A directory named /payroll
>
> ➤ Completion of Lab 10.2

Estimated completion time: **25 minutes**

ACTIVITY

1. Log on to a user account.

2. To change to the payroll directory, type **cd payroll**, and then press **Enter**. The prompt changes to reflect the current directory (\payroll).

3. To demonstrate how wildcards work in this lab, you need to create 10 files. To do this, you will create one file and then copy it to create the other nine files. To create the first file, type **echo "Hi" > Jan01.txt**, and then press **Enter**. The prompt returns. The redirection symbol > is used to redirect output to a newly created file.

4. To copy the contents of the file to a new file, type **cp Jan01.txt Jun05.txt**, and then press **Enter**. The prompt returns, indicating that the command was successfully executed.

5. Use the cp command to create files with the following names: **Jul01.txt**, **Jan14.dat**, **Jul14.dat**, **Feb14.txt**, **Jan06.txt**, **Feb07.txt**, **Apr28.txt**, and **Oct27.dat**. For example, to create the file called Feb07.txt, type **cp Jan01.txt Feb07.txt**, and then press **Enter**.

6. Wildcarding is the process of using two special symbols, * and ?, to display a subset of the file and directories in a given directory. To wildcard multiple characters, use the * symbol. To wildcard a single character, use the ? symbol. To see the files that begin with the letter A, type **ls A***, and then press **Enter**. Record the result.

_____

7. To see the files for February, type **ls Feb***, and then press **Enter**. Record the result.

_____

8. To see the files for the 14th of the month, type **ls ???14***, and then press **Enter**. Record the result.

_____

9. To see the files for January that end in txt, type **ls Jan*.txt**, and then press **Enter**. Record the result.

10. To see the files with a 7 in the fifth position, type **ls ????7***, and then press **Enter**. Record the result.

_____

11. To see who is logged on to the computer, type **who**, and then press **Enter**.

12. You can count the number of users on the computer using the pipe symbol and the wc command. Type **who | wc –l**, and then press **Enter**. The pipe symbol redirects the output of the who command to the wc command, which with the –l option actually counts the number of lines generated by the who command. Record the result.

_____

13. Now you will use the pipe symbol to find your user name in the list of users currently logged on. For example, if your user name is zac, then you would type **who | grep zac**, and then press **Enter**. Type the correct command for your user name, and then press **Enter**. The output of the who command is redirected to the grep command, which filters out all the lines except those that contain your user name.

14. To gain a greater understanding of the pipe symbol, you will need to create a file with multiple lines of text. In the next few steps, you will create a file of five lines, with each line containing a single number. Initially, the numbers will be arranged in random order. In a later step, you will sort the numbers in the file using the | symbol. To create the file, type **echo "5" > unsort.dat**, and then press **Enter**.

15. The redirection symbol >> is used to append data to an existing file. Text already in the file will be left intact. To append text to the file unsort.dat, type **echo "3" >> unsort.dat**, and then press **Enter**.

16. To append text to the file unsort.dat, type **echo "1" >> unsort.dat**, and then press **Enter**.

17. To append text to the file unsort.dat, type **echo "4" >> unsort.dat**, and then press **Enter**.

18. To append text to the file unsort.dat, type **echo "2" >> unsort.dat**, and then press **Enter**.

19. To view the contents of the unsort.dat file, type **cat unsort.dat**, and then press **Enter**. Record the result.

_____

20. Now that you have created the file, you can sort it. To sort the file, type **cat unsort.dat | sort**, and then press **Enter**. The pipe symbol redirects the output from the command on the left side of the pipe symbol to the command on the right side of the pipe symbol. (Note that you could also sort the file without using the pipe symbol, as follows: sort unsort.dat.)

10

21. To sort the file and place the sorted output into a new file, type **sort unsort.dat >
sort.dat**, and then press **Enter**.

22. To see the contents of the new file, type **cat sort.dat**, and then press **Enter**.
Record the result, and the difference between this result and the file you displayed in Step 19.

23. Next, you will use the pipe symbol for one of its most common uses, displaying
a lot of output one screen at a time. First, type **ps –auxw**, and then press **Enter**
to display all the processes currently running on the computer.

24. Now type **ps –auxw | more**, and then press **Enter**. The pipe symbol redirects
the output of the ps command to the more command, which displays the output
one screen at a time. Press the **spacebar** until the prompt returns or until the
bottom of your screen displays (END). If the bottom of your screen displays
(END), press **q** to quit.

25. Next type **ps –auxw | head**, and then press **Enter**. The pipe symbol redirects
the output of the ps command to the head command, which displays the first
ten lines of the output. The column description and 11 columns of information
display. The fourth column of information is %MEM, the amount of
memory used by each process.

26. To see which programs are using the most memory, type **ps –auxw | sort –r
–k 4 | head**, and then press **Enter**. The pipe symbol sends the output of the
ps command to sort. The sort command sorts the output in reverse order with
the –r flag based on the fourth column with the –k 4 flag. Then the next pipe
symbol sends its output to the head command, which displays the processes
that are using the most memory on the computer.

27. Log off the computer.

Certification Objectives

Objectives for the Network+ Exam:

> ➤ Identify the basic capabilities (i.e., client support, interoperability, authentication, file and print services, application support, and security) of the following
server operating systems: UNIX/Linux, NetWare, Windows, Macintosh

> ➤ Identify the basic capabilities (i.e., client connectivity, local security mechanisms,
and authentication) of the following clients: UNIX/Linux, Windows, Macintosh

Review Questions

1. What is the purpose of a wildcard symbol?
    a. to allow you to use any character or string of characters in the syntax of a
command, instead of only the proper character(s)
    b. to represent any character or string of characters in the object of a command
    c. to modify the meaning of the command as is appropriate for the directory
context
    d. to represent an unknown value in the equation part of a command

2. Which of the following symbols represents only one wildcard character?
   a. *
   b. **
   c. ?
   d. ::

3. Which of the following is the pipe symbol?
   a. |
   b. >
   c. >>
   d. **

4. Which of the following commands would redirect the output of the directory listing for a directory called "tables" into a file called "tables.txt?" on a UNIX system?
   a. echo tables >> tables.txt
   b. dir tables > tables.txt
   c. list tables >> "tables.txt"
   d. ls tables > tables.txt

5. Which of the following commands would append "table 1 belongs to Mary" to the file called "tables.txt?" on a UNIX system?
   a. echo "table 1 belongs to Mary" >> tables.txt
   b. add "table 1 belongs to Mary" to "tables.txt"
   c. table 1 belongs to Mary | tables.txt
   d. "table 1 belongs to Mary" >> tables.txt

6. What command would allow you to view only the files that ended with the ".txt" extension in a directory on a UNIX system? (Choose all that apply.)
   a. dir *.txt
   b. ls *.txt
   c. ls | grep tables
   d. ls −a | echo tables

7. What command would allow you to view the contents of the "table.txt" file on a UNIX system?
   a. ls table.txt
   b. cat table.txt
   c. view table.txt
   d. list table.txt

8. What command will allow you to view the users logged on to a UNIX system?
   a. whois *
   b. ls users
   c. users ?
   d. who

10

LAB 10.5 NAVIGATING THE UNIX FILE SYSTEM

Objectives

The goal of this lab is to teach you how to navigate the UNIX file system. UNIX does not have the concept of drive letters. A file system in UNIX is assigned a directory name just like any other directory. As a result, you may have as many file systems as you need on a computer.

You use the mount command to view the file systems currently available on a UNIX system. These file systems are often called the mounted file systems. You can refer to a UNIX file or directory by its full path (which begins with a forward slash, or /, such as /home/zac), or you can refer to it by a partial or relative path (which does not begin with a slash). A partial or relative path is relative to the directory in which you are currently navigating.

After completing this lab, you will be able to:

➤ Create directories

➤ Change directories

➤ Explain how to change directory locations using the full pathname and the partial pathname

➤ View the currently mounted file systems

Materials Required

This lab will require the following:

➤ A computer with a host name of UNIX1 running Linux Red Hat 7.x

➤ An ordinary user account on UNIX1 using the bash shell

Estimated completion time: **25 minutes**

ACTIVITY

1. Log on to the ordinary user account.

2. To create a directory named sales, type **mkdir sales**, and then press **Enter**. The prompt returns.

3. To change to the sales directory, type **cd sales**, and then press **Enter**. The prompt changes to reflect the current directory (sales). This is a relative path. To verify your current directory, type **pwd**, and then press **Enter**.

4. Create a directory named monthly. Write the full command you used.

5. Create a directory named yearly. Write the full command you used.

   _____

6. To view a list of files and directories, type **ls**, and then press **Enter**. Two directories appear.

7. To change to the monthly directory, type **cd monthly**, and then press **Enter**.
   The prompt changes to reflect the current directory (monthly), and output
   appears on the screen. Record the output.

   _____

8. To verify your current directory, type **pwd**, and then press **Enter**.

9. Draw the file system hierarchy beginning with your home directory. Draw
   lines extending down from one directory level to the next directory level.
   Write the name of each directory.

   _____

   _____

   _____

10. To change to the root directory, type **cd /**, and then press **Enter**. The prompt
    changes to reflect the root; or top, of the file system.

11. To change to your home directory, you need to type **/home** followed by your
    username. For example, if your username is tmeadors, you would type
    cd /home/tmeadors, and then press **Enter**. This is a full path name. Use the
    appropriate command now to change to your home directory. The prompt
    changes to reflect your new directory location. Write the full command you
    used to change to your home directory.

    _____

12. Change to the sales directory, which you created in Step 2. The prompt changes
    to reflect the current directory (sales). Write the full command you used.

    _____

13. Change to the yearly directory, which you created in Step 5. The prompt
    changes to reflect the new directory location. Write the full command you used.

    _____

14. To change to the monthly directory from within the yearly directory, type
    cd ../monthly, and then press **Enter**. The directories monthly and yearly
    are peer, or sibling, directories. Peer, or sibling, directories are directories that
    exist on the same level in the hierarchy; they have the same parent directory.
    This is another form of a relative path name. The prompt changes to reflect
    the new directory location.

15. To verify your current directory, type **pwd**, and then press **Enter**.

10

16. To change back to the yearly directory from within the monthly directory, type **cd ../yearly**, and then press **Enter**. The prompt changes to reflect the new directory location.

17. To verify your current directory, type **pwd**, and then press **Enter**. What output do you see?

_____

18. To change to the parent directory, type **cd ..**, and then press **Enter**. The prompt changes to reflect the new directory location. (The two dots represent the parent directory.)

19. To verify your current directory, type **pwd**, and then press **Enter**.

20. Type **mount** at the prompt, and then press **Enter**. You see one or more lines of output such as /dev/hda1 on / type ext2 (rw). The /dev/hda1 is the computer's name for the partition, on / tells you that it is mounted on / (the root file system), type ext2 tells you the type of file system, and (rw) tells you that it is read-write. Record the number of file systems mounted on the computer.

_____

21. Log off the computer.

Certification Objectives

Objectives for the Network+ Exam:

➤ Identify the basic capabilities (i.e., client support, interoperability, authentication, file and print services, application support, and security) of the following server operating systems: UNIX/Linux, NetWare, Windows, Macintosh

➤ Identify the basic capabilities (i.e., client connectivity, local security mechanisms, and authentication) of the following clients: UNIX/Linux, Windows, Macintosh

Review Questions

1. What command will reveal what directory you're currently in as you navigate a UNIX system?
   a. dir ?
   b. cd
   c. pwd
   d. namedir

2. What command will allow you to change your current position from the "/data" directory to the "/programs" directory on a UNIX system?
   a. cd ..
   b. cd data / programs
   c. cd \programs
   d. cd /programs

3. What command will allow you to change to the root directory from the "/programs" directory on a UNIX system, if the programs directory were one level down from the root directory? (Choose all that apply.)

   a. cd /

   b. cd [root]

   c. cd ..

   d. cd \\

4. On a UNIX system, what symbol represents the parent directory?

   a. .

   b. ..

   c. /

   d. //

5. What will typing the "mount" command, with no switches or parameters, accomplish on a UNIX system?

   a. It will mount a newly added file system.

   b. It will reveal the currently mounted file systems.

   c. It will mount all unmounted file systems.

   d. It will make a file system available to all users.

10

NETWORKING WITH TCP/IP AND THE INTERNET

Labs included in this chapter

➤ Lab 11.1 Understanding the Purpose of the Default Gateway

➤ Lab 11.2 Understanding the TCP/IP Hosts File

➤ Lab 11.3 Configuring Dynamic Host Configuration Protocol (DHCP)

➤ Lab 11.4 Configuring Domain Name System (DNS) Properties

➤ Lab 11.5 Using FTP

➤ Lab 11.6 Understanding Port Numbers

Net+ Exam Objectives	
Objective	Lab
Identify the purpose, features, and functions of the following network components: hubs, switches, bridges, routers, gateways, CSU/DSU, Network Interface Cards/ISDN adapters/system area network cards, wireless access points, modems	11.1
Identify the purpose of subnetting and default gateways	11.1
Given a network configuration, select the appropriate NIC and network configuration settings (DHCP, DNS, WINS, protocols, NetBIOS/host name, etc.)	11.1, 11.2, 11.3, 11.4
Identify the purpose of the following network services: DHCP/bootp, DNS, NAT/ICS, WINS, and SNMP	11.2
Given output from a diagnostic utility (e.g., tracert, ping, ipconfig, etc.), identify the utility and interpret the output	11.1, 11.2, 11.3
Given a scenario, predict the impact of modifying, adding, or removing network services (e.g., DHCP, DNS, WINS, etc.) on network resources and users	11.2, 11.3, 11.4
Given a troubleshooting scenario, select the appropriate TCP/IP utility from among the following: tracert, ping, arp, netstat, nbtstat, ipconfig/ifconfig, winipcfg, nslookup	11.1, 11.3, 11.4

Net+ Exam Objectives (continued)	
Objective	Lab
Identify the basic capabilities (i.e., client support, interoperability, authentication, file and print services, application support, and security) of the following server operating systems: UNIX/Linux, NetWare, Windows, Macintosh	11.4, 11.5, 11.6
Define the purpose, function and/or use of the following protocols within TCP/IP: IP, TCP, UDP, FTP, TFTP, SMTP, HTTP, HTTPS, POP3/IMAP4, TELNET, ICMP, ARP, NTP	11.5, 11.6
Given a scenario, predict the impact of a particular security implementation on network functionality (e.g., blocking port numbers, encryption, etc.)	11.5
Define the function of TCP/UDP ports. Identify well-known ports	11.6

LAB 11.1 UNDERSTANDING THE PURPOSE OF THE DEFAULT GATEWAY

Objectives

To send packets from a computer on one network to a computer on another network, a computer must know where to send the packets. Routers often do this by having large routing tables with lists of networks and where they need to send packets to reach those networks.

Many times a router does not need to know exactly where to send a packet. It just must know how to send it to another router that does know. To tell a computer where to send packets outside of its own network, you can configure a default gateway. The default gateway is the computer (or router) associated with a LAN or LAN segment that knows where to send packets so that they will reach their destination.

After completing this lab, you will be able to:

➤ Identify the purpose of the default gateway

➤ Configure a default gateway

Materials Required

This lab will require the following:

➤ Two computers running Windows 2000 Server or Windows 2000 Professional with NICs and TCP/IP as the only network protocol installed

➤ Computer 1 configured with an IP address of 192.168.1.1 with a subnet mask of 255.255.255.0 and no default gateway

➤ Computer 2 configured with an IP address of 192.168.1.2 with a subnet mask of 255.255.255.0 and no default gateway

➤ Administrator access to both computers

➤ The computers networked together with an Ethernet hub and two Category 5 UTP cables

Estimated completion time: **20 minutes**

ACTIVITY

1. Log on to Computer 1 as an administrator. Click **Start**, point to **Programs**, point to **Accessories**, and then click **Command Prompt**. The Command Prompt window appears.

2. At the command prompt, type **ping 192.168.1.2**. On the screen, the computer prints out the following text four times: Reply from 192.168.1.2: bytes=32 *time* (where *time* is the time it took to receive the reply and other information).

3. Repeat Steps 1 and 2 on Computer 2. However, ping the address **192.168.1.1** instead.

4. Now you will add a secondary IP address to one of the computers. On Computer 1, right-click **My Network Places**, and then click **Properties**. The Network and Dial-up Connections window appears.

5. Right-click **Local Area Connection**, and then click **Properties**. The Local Area Connection Properties window appears.

6. Click **Internet Protocol (TCP/IP)**, and then click **Properties**. The Internet Protocol TCP/IP Properties window appears.

7. Click **Advanced**. The Advanced TCP/IP Settings window appears.

8. Click **Add**. The TCP/IP Address window appears. In the IP address: text box, type **172.16.1.1**. In the Subnet mask: text box, type **255.255.0.0**, if necessary.

9. Click **Add**. Click **OK** three times to finish configuring the secondary IP address.

10. On Computer 2, type **ping 172.16.1.1** at the command prompt. The computer prints out the following text four times: Destination host unreachable. Computer 2 does not know where to send packets destined for 172.16.1.1.

11. Type **netstat −r** to list the routing table on Computer 2. Record the information in the routing table.

_____

_____

_____

_____

11

12. You will now add a default gateway to Computer 2. Repeat Steps 4 through 6 on Computer 2 to open the Internet Protocol (TCP/IP) Properties window.

13. In the Default gateway: text box, type **192.168.1.1**. This tells Computer 2 to send packets to 192.168.1.1 whenever it does not have another route for them. Click **OK** twice to exit.

14. At the command prompt on Computer 2, type **ping 172.16.1.1**. This time the computer prints the following text four times: Reply from 172.16.1.1: bytes=32 *time* (where *time* is the time it took to receive the reply and other information).

15. Type **netstat −r** to show the routing table again on Computer 2. Look at the routing table you recorded in Step 11 before adding the default gateway, and record the difference between the two routing tables.

_____

_____

16. Close the Command Prompt window and all open windows on both computers.

Certification Objectives

Objectives for the Network+ Exam:

➤ Identify the purpose, features, and functions of the following network components: hubs, switches, bridges, routers, gateways, CSU/DSU, Network Interface Cards/ISDN adapters/system area network cards, wireless access points, modems

➤ Identify the purpose of subnetting and default gateways

➤ Given a network configuration, select the appropriate NIC and network configuration settings (DHCP, DNS, WINS, protocols, NetBIOS/host name, etc.)

➤ Given a troubleshooting scenario, select the appropriate TCP/IP utility from among the following: tracert, ping, arp, netstat, nbtstat, ipconfig/ifconfig, winipcfg, nslookup

➤ Given output from a diagnostic utility (e.g., tracert, ping, ipconfig, etc.), identify the utility and interpret the output

Review Questions

1. What is the purpose of the default gateway?

   a. to assign IP addresses to clients as soon as they log on to the network

   b. to ensure that no two nodes on the same subnet have identical TCP/IP addresses

   c. to accept and relay packets from nodes on one network destined for nodes on another network

   d. to advertise the best, current routing paths between networks from one router to another

2. Which of the following is most likely to act as a default gateway?
   a. modem
   b. hub
   c. switch
   d. router

3. On a Windows 2000 Professional computer, what options would you choose to modify the client's default gateway address?
   a. Start, Settings, Control Panel, and TCP/IP Properties
   b. My Network Places Properties, Local Area Connection Properties, and Internet Protocol (TCP/IP) Properties
   c. Start, Local and Dial-up Connections, LAN Connection Properties, TCP/IP Properties, and then the Gateways tab
   d. My Network Places Properties, Protocol Properties, Internet Protocol (TCP/IP) Properties, and then the Gateways tab

4. What type of information would the netstat –r command yield, when typed at the command prompt of a networked client?
   a. a list of all routers to which that client might connect
   b. a list of the client's NIC adapter IP address(es)
   c. the client's routing table
   d. the client's TCP/IP settings

5. What is the default subnet mask for a Class B network in the IP version 4 addressing scheme?
   a. 255.255.0.0
   b. 255.255.255.0
   c. 255.255.255.255
   d. 0.0.0.0

6. Which of the following utilities can show the routers a packet traverses between its source node and destination node on a network?
   a. ping
   b. nbtstat
   c. netstat
   d. tracert

11

LAB 11.2 UNDERSTANDING THE TCP/IP HOSTS FILE

Objectives

To use host names instead of IP addresses to reach remote computers, a computer must have some way to find the IP address that corresponds to each remote computer. One of the simplest ways to do this is to use the hosts file. The hosts file is a file that contains a list of IP addresses and the names of the computers at those addresses. When the computer recognizes the name of another computer in its hosts file, it will use the IP address associated with it when it tries to communicate with that computer.

Because it is impossible to distribute hosts files to thousands or millions of computers, computers typically use the Domain Name System (DNS) to associate host names with IP addresses. However, the hosts file is often useful as a temporary measure or where you cannot make a DNS entry.

After completing this lab, you will be able to:

➤ Identify the purpose of the hosts file

➤ Modify a computer's hosts file

➤ Connect to another computer using its host name

Materials Required

This lab will require the following:

➤ A computer running Windows 2000 Server or Windows 2000 Professional with a NIC installed and an IP address of 192.168.1.1

➤ Administrator access to the Windows 2000 computer

➤ A computer running Linux Redhat 7.x with an IP address of 192.168.1.2

➤ The Linux computer's root password

➤ The computers networked together with an Ethernet hub and two Category 5 UTP cables

Estimated completion time: **25 minutes**

ACTIVITY

1. Log on to the Windows 2000 computer as an administrator.

2. Click **Start**, point to **Programs**, point to **Accessories**, and then click **Command Prompt**. The Command Prompt window opens.

3. Type **cd C:\winnt\system32\drivers\etc**. Press **Enter**. The prompt changes to reflect the new directory location. On a Windows 2000 Server or Windows 2000 Professional computer, this directory contains the hosts file.

4. To modify the hosts file, type **notepad hosts**, and then press **Enter**. Notepad opens with the text of the hosts file.

5. At the bottom of the file, type **192.168.1.2 unixbox**. Make sure the entry is on a line by itself and that there is no pound sign (#) in front of the entry. (A pound sign at the beginning of a line indicates a comment.) Also, make sure

there is at least one space before the word unixbox. Click **File**, and then click **Save**. Exit Notepad.

6. At the command prompt, type **ping unixbox**, and then press **Enter**. You should see four successful replies.

7. Now log on to the Linux computer as **root**. The prompt appears.

8. At the prompt, type **cd/etc**. The prompt changes to reflect the new directory.

9. Type **echo "192.168.1.1 windowsbox" >> hosts** at the prompt. Be careful to use two greater than symbols and to leave a space between the IP address and the host name. The computer appends the IP address and the host name between the parentheses into the hosts file.

10. To see what the hosts file contains, type **cat hosts**.

11. Type **ping windowsbox**. Lines display indicating that the computer has received 64 bytes from windowbox, followed by additional information. Press **Ctrl+C** to stop the ping command.

Certification Objectives

Objectives for the Network+ Exam:

➤ Identify the purpose of the following network services: DHCP/bootp, DNS, NAT/ICS, WINS, and SNMP

➤ Given a network configuration, select the appropriate NIC and network configuration settings (DHCP, DNS, WINS, protocols, NetBIOS/host name, etc.)

➤ Given output from a diagnostic utility (e.g., tracert, ping, ipconfig, etc.), identify the utility and interpret the output

➤ Given a scenario, predict the impact of modifying, adding, or removing network services (e.g., DHCP, DNS, WINS, etc.) on network resources and users

11

Review Questions

1. What is the purpose of a host name?
   a. to uniquely identify a node on a network
   b. to associate a node with a particular domain
   c. to indicate which domain a node belongs to
   d. to identify the IP address of a host

2. What is the purpose of a hosts file?
   a. to help determine the best route for packets between gateways
   b. to make it easier for network administrators to remember a computer's IP address
   c. to map IP addresses to host names
   d. to indicate which hosts on a network are available to a client

3. What is the hosts file on a Windows 2000 Professional computer called?
   a. hosts
   b. lmhosts
   c. hostfile
   d. hostsfile

4. What file on a UNIX system holds information about host names and their IP addresses?
   a. /etc/hosts
   b. /bin/hosts
   c. /lib/users/hostfile
   d. /root/hostfile

5. Which of the following symbols indicates a comment in the hosts file?
   a. >
   b. >>
   c. :
   d. #

6. On a UNIX computer, what key(s) would you type to stop the ping utility after it has been started?
   a. Shift [P]
   b. Ctrl [C]
   c. Ctrl [P]
   d. Shift [X]

7. What is the alias of the computer whose host name is "C2" in the following hosts file?

   ```
   160.12.122.13   C1C2.gameco.com canasta
   156.11.21.145   Comp2.gameco.com chess
   123.14.11.214   C2.gameco.com checkers
   44.112.133.15   CIC2.gameco.com backgammon
   ```
   a. canasta
   b. chess
   c. checkers
   d. backgammon

LAB 11.3 CONFIGURING DYNAMIC HOST CONFIGURATION PROTOCOL (DHCP)

Objectives

In very small networks, network administrators often start out by manually assigning the IP address of each machine. However, they must keep track of each IP address they assign. Later, if the network administrator needed to change any of the IP addresses, she would need to visit each computer and modify that computer's TCP/IP parameters.

The Dynamic Host Configuration Protocol (DHCP) was developed to allow network administrators to administer IP addresses from a central server. A DHCP server can assign an IP address, a subnet mask, a default gateway, and other information to all the computers on its local network and to computers on other networks as well. This way a network administrator can change IP addressing information once on the DHCP server without having to manually change it on any other computers.

With most DHCP servers, network administrators enjoy a great deal of flexibility in IP addressing. For example, you can restrict ranges of IP addresses so that the DHCP server doesn't assign them. You also can configure the DHCP server to always assign a certain address to a particular client.

However, you should not attempt to add a DHCP server to a production network without careful planning. An extra DHCP server on a network could cause serious problems for most or all the users on the network.

11

After completing this lab, you will be able to:

➤ Configure DHCP to automatically distribute the IP addresses and subnet masks to other computers

➤ Renew the IP address on a DHCP client

Materials Required

This lab will require the following:

➤ A computer running Windows 2000 Server with a NIC, configured as a domain controller for a domain named domain1.com, with an IP address of 192.168.1.1, TCP/IP installed as the only network protocol, and a DNS server installed with entries for domain1.com

➤ Dynamic Host Configuration Protocol installed on the server

➤ A computer running Windows 2000 Server or Windows 2000 Professional that contains a NIC that does not have a specific IP address and that is configured as a member of domain1

➤ Administrator access to both computers

➤ The computers networked together with an Ethernet hub and two Category 5 UTP cables

Estimated completion time: **30 minutes**

ACTIVITY

1. Log on to the Windows 2000 server as an administrator.

2. Click **Start**, point to **Programs**, point to **Administrative Tools**, and then click **DHCP**. The DHCP window opens.

3. In the tree in the left pane of the DHCP window, right-click the name of the server and then click **New Scope**. The New Scope Wizard appears.

4. Click **Next**. The Scope Name window appears.

5. Type **NetPlus** in the Name: text box. Type **Computer lab DHCP scope** in the Description: text box, and then click **Next**. The IP Address Range window appears.

6. In this window, you add the range of IP addresses that the DHCP server will assign to clients. In the Start IP address: text box, type **192.168.1.50**. In the End IP address: text box, type **192.168.1.200**. The computer automatically fills in the Length: and Subnet mask: text boxes with the default values for the number of bits in the subnet mask and the subnet mask. Click **Next**. The Add Exclusions window appears.

7. In this window, you can add a range of IP addresses which will not be assigned by DHCP. In the Start IP address: text box, type **192.168.1.100**. In the End IP address: text box, type **192.168.1.110**, click **Add**, and then click **Next**. The Lease Duration window appears.

8. In this window, you can configure the amount of time a client computer can keep its address before it has to check with the DHCP server again. Click **Next** to accept the default time. The Configure DHCP Options window appears.

9. Click **Next** to configure DHCP options such as default gateways and DNS servers. The Router (Default Gateway) window appears.

10. In the IP address text box, type **192.168.1.1**, and then click **Add**. Clients assigned DHCP addresses by this computer will now also use this computer as their default gateway. Click **Next**. The Domain Name and DNS Servers window appears.

11. In the Parent domain: text box, type **domain1.com**. This configures each client assigned an IP address by this DHCP server to use the domain1.com name when a domain name has not been specified. In the IP address: box, type **192.168.1.1**, and then click **Add**. Each client will now use this server as the DNS server. Click **Next**. The WINS Servers window appears.

12. In this window, you can assign a WINS server to each client computer. In the IP address: box, type **192.168.1.1**, click **Add**, and then click **Next**. The Activate Scope window appears.

13. Click **Next**. A folder named Scope [192.168.1.0] NetPlus appears in the tree in the left pane of the window.

14. Now you must authorize the server in Active Directory so that it can assign IP addresses. Click **Action**, and then click **Authorize**.

15. Now log on to the client computer as an administrator.

16. Right-click **My Network Places**, and then click **Properties**. The Network and Dial-up Connections window appears. Right-click the **Local Area Connection** icon and click **Properties**.

17. Click the **Internet Protocol (TCP/IP)** icon to highlight it and then click **Properties**. The Internet Protocol (TCP/IP) Properties window opens.

18. The Obtain an IP address automatically and Obtain DNS Server Address automatically options are selected. Click **OK** twice to exit.

19. Click **Start**, point to **Programs**, point to **Accessories**, and then click **Command Prompt**. The Command Prompt window appears.

20. At the command prompt, type **ipconfig**, and then press **Enter**. The new IP address of the computer displays, which is the beginning of the IP address range you specified earlier.

21. Now you will release and renew the leased IP address from the DHCP server. Type **ipconfig/release**. The output confirms the IP address was successfully released for adapter "Local Area Connection 3."

22. Type **ipconfig**, and then press **Enter**. The output indicates the IP address and subnet mask of the computer are both 0.0.0.0.

23. Type **ipconfig/renew**, and then press **Enter**. The computer renews the DHCP lease from the DHCP server.

24. Type **ipconfig**, and then press **Enter**. The computer displays IP address information.

25. Type **ipconfig/all**. The computer displays all the IP address information. The output shows all IP addressing information, including the default gateway and the DNS server you specified earlier in this lab.

26. On the Windows 2000 server, double-click the folder named **Scope [192.168.1.0] NetPlus** in the left pane of the DHCP window. The tree expands underneath the folder named Scope [192.168.1.0] NetPlus.

27. Click the **Address Leases** folder. The name of the Windows 2000 client computer appears in the right pane in a list of computers whose IP addresses have been assigned by this DHCP server.

28. Exit the DHCP server window. Close all open windows on both computers.

11

Certification Objectives

Objectives for the Network+ Exam:

➤ Given a network configuration, select the appropriate NIC and network configuration settings (DHCP, DNS, WINS, protocols, NetBIOS/host name, etc.)

➤ Given a troubleshooting scenario, select the appropriate TCP/IP utility from among the following: tracert, ping, arp, netstat, nbtstat, ipconfig/ifconfig, winipcfg, nslookup

➤ Given output from a diagnostic utility (e.g., tracert, ping, ipconfig, etc.), identify the utility and interpret the output

➤ Given a scenario, predict the impact of modifying, adding, or removing network services (e.g., DHCP, DNS, WINS, etc.) on network resources and users

Review Questions

1. What is the purpose of DHCP?
   a. to automatically track and record changes in the TCP/IP settings for clients on a network
   b. to automatically assign TCP/IP addressing information to clients on a network
   c. to request TCP/IP addressing information from authoritative addressing servers across the Internet
   d. to continually update and broadcast a network's TCP/IP addressing information to public networks

2. Which of the following parameters would not be automatically assigned to clients by their DHCP server?
   a. subnet mask
   b. IP address
   c. nameserver address
   d. hostname

3. On a Windows 2000 Professional computer, what command would release a DHCP lease?
   a. winipcfg dhcp -release
   b. ipconfig release all
   c. dhcp release -a
   d. ipconfig /release

4. On a UNIX-based computer, what command would release a DHCP lease?
   a. dhcp -release
   b. ifconfig auto-dhcp release
   c. ipconfig dhcp -release
   d. ifconfig release all

5. Which of the following services was a precursor to DHCP, and performs many of the same functions as DHCP?

   a. SNMP

   b. BOOTP

   c. ICMP

   d. WINS

6. What options would you choose on a Windows 2000 Server to establish it as a DHCP server?

   a. Start, Programs, Administrative Tools, and then DHCP

   b. Start, Settings, Control Panel, and then DHCP Server

   c. My Network Places Properties, Local Area Connection Properties, Internet Protocol (TCP/IP) Properties, and then DHCP tab

   d. My Network Places Properties, Local Area Connection Properties, Programs, and then DHCP Services

LAB 11.4 CONFIGURING DOMAIN NAME SYSTEM (DNS) PROPERTIES

Objectives

The Domain Name System (DNS) is another method of associating an IP address with a host name. Unlike a hosts file, however, DNS is easier to manage and maintain over many servers. For instance, DNS is used throughout the Internet, which consists of millions of computers. When you open a Web browser and attempt to connect to *www.comptia.com*, for example, the web browser first queries a DNS server to find the IP address of the Web site. If the DNS server (or nameserver) your computer is configured to use does not know the IP address associated with *www.comptia.com*, it queries the authoritative nameserver for the comptia.com domain (or zone). The authoritative nameserver is the DNS server with the definitive DNS information for that domain. When the authoritative DNS server responds with the IP address to your DNS server, your DNS server sends that information to your computer. The Web browser on your computer then uses that IP address to connect to the web site.

DNS queries can be quite complicated. In addition to finding the IP address belonging to a particular host name (known as a forward DNS lookup), DNS is also used to find the host name belonging to a particular IP address. This is known as a reverse DNS lookup.

One tool you can use to find DNS information directly is the nslookup command. This command will allow you to find out the IP address associated with a particular host name and other information.

After completing this lab, you will be able to:

➤ Add a DNS server to DNS

➤ Add a DNS zone

11

➤ Add a DNS host

➤ Configure a computer to refer to the DNS server

➤ Access a computer using its DNS name

Materials Required

This lab will require the following:

➤ A computer running Windows 2000 Server with a NIC configured with an IP address of 192.168.1.1

➤ The Windows 2000 Server computer configured as a domain controller with the DNS server installed (you can automatically configure both with the dcpromo command, which brings up the Active Directory wizard)

➤ A client computer running Windows 2000 Server or Windows 2000 Professional configured with an IP address of 192.168.1.2 and without any DNS servers configured

➤ Administrator access to both computers

➤ A functioning network connection between the two computers

Estimated completion time: **30 minutes**

ACTIVITY

1. Log on to the Windows 2000 server as an administrator.

2. Click **Start**, point to **Programs**, point to **Administrative Tools**, and then click **DNS**. The DNS window appears.

3. In the left pane of the window, right-click the name of the server. Click **New Zone**. The New Zone Wizard appears.

4. Click **Next**. The Zone Type window appears.

5. The Standard primary option is clicked by default. Click **Next** to accept the default option. The Forward or Reverse Lookup Zone window appears.

6. The Forward lookup zone option is clicked by default. Click **Next** to accept the default option. The Zone Name window appears.

7. In the Name: text box, type **netplus.com**, and then click **Next**. The Zone File window appears.

8. The Create a new file with this file name: option is clicked by default. Click **Next** to accept the default option.

9. Click **Finish**.

10. In the right pane of the DNS window, double-click the **Forward Lookup Zones** folder. A list of domains for which this DNS server is authoritative displays, including the new netplus.com domain.

11. Right-click the **netplus.com** domain icon. Click **New Host**. The New Host dialog box opens.

12. In the Name (uses parent domain name if box): text box, type **www**. In the IP address: text box, type **192.168.1.1**.

13. Click the **Add Host**. The DNS dialog box opens, indicating that the host record www.netplus.com was successfully created. Click **OK**, and then click **Done**.

14. Log on to the client computer as an administrator.

15. Right-click **My Network Places**. Click **Properties**. The Network and Dial-up Connections window appears.

16. Right-click **Local Area Connection** and click **Properties**. The Local Area Connection Properties window appears.

17. Click **Internet Protocol (TCP/IP)**. Click **Properties**.

18. Click the **Use the following DNS server addresses:** option button, if necessary. In the Preferred DNS server: text box, type **192.168.1.1**.

19. Click **OK** twice to exit the Local Area Connection Properties window.

20. Click **Start**, point to **Programs**, point to **Accessories**, and click **Command Prompt**. The Command Prompt window appears.

21. Type **nslookup** at the command prompt. The > prompt appears.

22. Type **www.netplus.com**. The nslookup command displays the name and IP address of www.netplus.com.

23. Type **Ctrl+C**. The computer exits the nslookup command and returns to the command prompt.

24. Type **ping www.netplus.com**. The computer indicates that it is pinging www.netplus.com by its numeric number, and that it has received four responses.

25. Close the Command Prompt window and all open windows on both computers.

Certification Objectives

Objectives for the Network+ Exam:

➤ Identify the basic capabilities (i.e., client support, interoperability, authentication, file and print services, application support, and security) of the following server operating systems: UNIX/Linux, NetWare, Windows, Macintosh

➤ Given a network configuration, select the appropriate NIC and network configuration settings (DHCP, DNS, WINS, protocols, NetBIOS/host name, etc.)

➤ Given a troubleshooting scenario, select the appropriate TCP/IP utility from among the following: tracert, ping, arp, netstat, nbtstat, ipconfig/ifconfig, winipcfg, nslookup

➤ Given a scenario, predict the impact of modifying, adding, or removing network services (e.g., DHCP, DNS, WINS, etc.) on network resources and users

Review Questions

1. What is the purpose of a nameserver?
   a. to maintain the DNS database for an entire zone
   b. to supply clients with IP address resolution for requested hosts
   c. to track and record all TCP/IP host name information for a network
   d. to track and record all NetBIOS naming information for a network

2. What is the term for the group of devices that a nameserver manages?
   a. hierarchy
   b. tree
   c. zone
   d. directory

3. Which of the following are examples of top-level domains? (Choose all that apply.)
   a. .net
   b. .com
   c. .uk
   d. .aut

4. When a DNS server retrieves the host name associated with an IP address, what type of lookup is it accomplishing?
   a. forward
   b. adjacent
   c. backward
   d. reverse

5. What is one advantage of using DNS instead of hosts files?
   a. DNS does not require manual updating of files on multiple networked nodes.
   b. DNS is more compatible with UNIX systems.
   c. DNS will map both NetBIOS and TCP/IP host names to IP addresses, while hosts files will map only TCP/IP host names to IP addresses.
   d. Using DNS is more secure than using hosts files.

6. What options would you choose to configure DNS services on a
   Windows 2000 server?

   a. Start, Settings, Control Panel, and then DNS Services

   b. Start, LAN and Dial-up Connections, Local Area Connection Properties,
      and then DNS tab

   c. Start, Programs, Administrative Tools, and then DNS

   d. Start, Programs, and then DNS Services

Lab 11.5 Using FTP

Objective

In this lab, you will connect to a File Transfer Protocol (FTP) server on a remote host.
FTP is used throughout the Internet to make files available for downloading. If a network
administrator would like to make files available to the general public, he may create an
anonymous FTP server.

Users can log on to an anonymous FTP server by using a special account named anonymous without knowing the password. FTP servers are available on nearly all platforms. If
you run an anonymous FTP server, you should not allow users to upload (or transfer to
the server) files because a malicious user could fill up your server's disk drive with their
files. Another potential problem with FTP is that it sends passwords in unencrypted text,
so they could be captured by a malicious user.

You will use the command line Windows FTP client and manually run the FTP commands. The many GUI FTP programs available automate these same commands for you.

After completing this lab, you will be able to:

➤ Log on to an FTP site

➤ Download files from an FTP site

➤ Copy files to an FTP site

➤ Define security policies for an FTP site

Materials Required

This lab will require the following:

➤ A computer running Windows 2000 Server, with a NIC configured as a
  domain controller with an IP address of 192.168.1.1

➤ Internet Information Service (IIS) installed and running on the Windows 2000
  server with the FTP site installed and with the default configuration and sample
  files in place

➤ A domain account for an ordinary user

➤ A client computer running Windows 2000 Server or Windows 2000
  Professional, with a NIC and an IP address of 192.168.1.2

11

Estimated completion time: **35 minutes**

ACTIVITY

1. On the Windows 2000 Server computer, create a text file named **netplus.txt** containing a small amount of random text. Save the file in the \inetpub\ ftproot folder.

2. Click **Start**, point to **Programs**, point to **Accessories**, and then click **Command Prompt**. The Command Prompt window appears.

3. At the prompt, type **copy \inetpub\wwwroot\win2000.gif \inetpub\ ftproot**. The computer copies the file from one directory to the other. This image file now will be available on the FTP site configured on this computer.

4. On the client computer, click **Start**, point to **Programs**, point to **Accessories**, and then click **Command Prompt**. The Command Prompt window appears.

5. At the command prompt, type **ftp 192.168.1.1**, and then press **Enter**. The output indicates that the computer has connected to 192.168.1.1 and that the remote FTP server is running the Microsoft FTP Service.

6. At the User (192.168.1.1:(none)): prompt, type **anonymous**. The Anonymous access allowed, send identity (e-mail name) as password output displays. Type an e-mail address or a brief phrase, and then press the **Enter** key. The 230 Anonymous user logged in output displays, and the prompt changes to ftp>.

7. Type **dir**. The files found on the remote computer, including win2000.gif and netplus.txt, displays.

8. Type **ls**. The files found on the remote computer display. This is a UNIX-style command.

9. At the prompt, type **get netplus.txt**. The computer indicates that it is opening ASCII mode data connection to transfer the file, and the ftp> prompt returns when the transfer is completed. ASCII mode file transfers are only suitable for text files.

10. To transfer the image file, type **binary** at the prompt, and then press **Enter**. The computer will now transfer files using binary mode.

11. Type **get win2000.gif** at the prompt, and then press **Enter**. The output indicates that the computer is using BINARY mode data connection to transfer the file. The ftp> prompt returns when the transfer is complete.

12. Type **!copy netplus.txt upload.txt**. The 1 file(s) copied output displays. The ! tells the ftp program that you wish to run a command in the command prompt, which copies the file netplus.txt to upload.txt.

13. To try to put a file onto the remote server, type **put upload.txt**. The 550 upload.txt: Access is denied output displays.

14. Type **quit**, and then press **Enter** to exit the FTP site.

15. Now you will remove anonymous FTP access to the server. On the Windows 2000 Server computer, click **Start**, point to **Programs**, point to **Administrative Tools**, and then click **Internet Services Manager**. The Internet Information Services window appears.

16. Click the icon with the name of the Windows 2000 Server in the left pane of the window. Icons for services run by IIS appear in the right pane of the window, including an icon for Default FTP Site.

17. Right-click **Default FTP Site** and click **Properties**. The Default FTP Site Properties window appears.

18. Click the **Security Accounts** tab. Uncheck the **Allow Anonymous Connections** check box. The Internet Services Manager dialog box opens.

19. Click **Yes** to close the Internet Services Manager dialog box.

20. Click the **Home Directory** tab. Check the **Write** check box. You will now be able to upload files. Click **OK**.

21. Right-click the name of the Windows 2000 Server computer in the left pane of the window. Click **Restart IIS**. The Stop/Start/Reboot... window dialog box opens with the Restart Internet Services option chosen in the What do you want IIS to do? drop-down menu.

22. Click **OK**. The Shutting Down... dialog box opens, indicating that the computer is shutting down IIS. An hourglass appears briefly and then the Internet Information Services window reappears.

23. Now you will configure the user account to be able to log on to the FTP server. Click **Start**, point to **Programs**, point to **Administrative Tools**, and then click **Domain Security Policy**. The Active Directory Users and Computers window appears. The Domain Security Policy window appears.

24. In the tree in the left pane of the window, double-click the **Security Settings** icon to expand the tree underneath it. Double-click the **Local Policies** icon. The tree expands.

25. Click the **User Rights Assignment** icon in the tree in the left pane of the window. Numerous options appear in the right pane. Right-click the **Access this computer from the network** icon, and then click **Security**. The Security Policy Setting window appears.

26. Check the **Define these policy settings:** check box, and then click **Add**. The Add user or group names dialog box opens.

27. Click **Browse**. Click the name of the user account in the top pane of the window, and then click **Add**. The account name appears in the bottom pane of the window.

28. Click **OK** three times to return to the Domain Security Policy window. Exit the Domain Security Policy window.

11

29. In the Command Prompt window on the client computer, type **ftp 192.168.1.1** and then press **Enter**. The login prompt appears. Type **anonymous** and then press **Enter**. Type a password and then press **Enter**. The ftp command indicates that User anonymous cannot log on and that the login failed.

30. Type **quit**, press **Enter**, type **ftp 192.168.1.1**, and then press **Enter**. The login prompt appears. Enter the name of the user account. At the Password: prompt, type the password. You are now logged on to the remote server.

31. At the ftp> prompt, type **put upload.txt**. The computer indicates that the file is being uploaded onto the remote computer in ASCII mode data connection.

32. Type **quit**, and then press **Enter**. Close the Command Prompt window and all open windows on both computers.

Certification Objectives

Objectives for the Network+ Exam:

➤ Define the purpose, function and/or use of the following protocols within TCP/IP: IP, TCP, UDP, FTP, TFTP, SMTP, HTTP, HTTPS, POP3/IMAP4, TELNET, ICMP, ARP, NTP

➤ Identify the basic capabilities (i.e., client support, interoperability, authentication, file and print services, application support, and security) of the following server operating systems: UNIX/Linux, NetWare, Windows, Macintosh

➤ Given a scenario, predict the impact of a particular security implementation on network functionality (e.g., blocking port numbers, encryption, etc.)

Review Questions

1. Which of the following commands would you type at the ftp> prompt to copy a file named "textfile.doc" from your C:\ directory to an FTP server?
   a. copy "textfile.doc"
   b. put C:\textfile.doc
   c. get C:\textfile.doc
   d. move C:\textfile.doc

2. On what Transport layer protocol does FTP rely?
   a. TCP
   b. UDP
   c. ICMP
   d. NTP

3. What is the term for an FTP site that allows any user to access its directories?
   a. anonymous
   b. restricted
   c. private
   d. unlimited

URL *www.microsoft.com*. To look for a Web server at the same site on port 7777, you would use the URL *www.microsoft.com*:7777 instead. Port numbers in UDP work the same way as port numbers in TCP.

After completing this lab, you will be able to:

> ➤ Identify default port numbers for several services

> ➤ Modify a service's default port numbers

> ➤ Connect to a service using a non-default port number

Materials Required

This lab will require the following:

> ➤ A computer running Windows 2000 Server, with a NIC and an IP address of 192.168.1.1

> ➤ IIS installed and running on the Windows 2000 server with the default configuration (you may ensure that the default configuration is enabled by removing and reinstalling the software)

> ➤ A text file in the web root of the Windows 2000 server (/inetpub/wwwroot) named default.htm and containing the text "This is a test page"

> ➤ Administrator access to the Windows 2000 server

> ➤ A client computer running Windows 2000 Server or Windows 2000 Professional

> ➤ Access with an ordinary user account to the client computer

---

Estimated completion time: **20 minutes**

ACTIVITY

1. On the client computer, click **Start**, point to **Programs**, and click **Internet Explorer**. Internet Explorer opens.

2. In the **Address** bar, type **http://192.168.1.1**, and then press **Enter**. The web page says "This is a test page."

3. Log on to the Windows 2000 Server computer as an administrator.

4. Click **Start**, point to **Programs**, point to **Administrative Tools**, and then click **Internet Services Manager**. The Internet Information Services window appears.

5. In the left pane of the window, double-click the name of the server. The tree underneath it expands to show a number of services, including the Default Web Site.

4. What command allows you to list the contents of a directory on an FTP serv
   a. list
   b. lf
   c. ls
   d. la

5. What would you type at the ftp> prompt to view a list of available FTP con
   mands? (Choose all that apply.)
   a. list
   b. ?
   c. help
   d. commands

6. At what layer of the OSI Model does FTP operate?
   a. Session
   b. Network
   c. Application
   d. Transport

7. What two file types can you specify when transferring files via FTP?
   a. text and binary
   b. alphabetical and numeric
   c. program and data
   d. dynamic and static

LAB 11.6 UNDERSTANDING PORT NUMBERS

Objectives

In TCP/IP, servers use port numbers to identify processes associated with different services. For instance, a server might run several different services over TCP, including HTTP and FTP. Based only on the IP address, there is no way to distinguish between the two services. However, requests from client computers can connect to different port numbers. The default port number for the HTTP service, for example, is 80, while the default port number for the FTP control service is 21.

Most client software is designed to look for the default port number when you connect to a service. For example, by default, Web browsers attempt to find web servers at port 80. However, you can usually configure a service to run on another port and configure the client software to look for that service on the new port.

You can tell a Web browser to look for a Web server at a non-default port by adding a colon and the port number after the web site name or IP address in the URL. For instance, to go to the Microsoft web site using the default port (80), you would use the

6. Right-click the **Default Web Site** icon, and then click **Properties**. The Default Web Site properties window appears.

7. In the TCP Port: text box, change the number from 80 to **8880**. This will tell IIS to run the WWW on port 8880 instead of on port 80. Press **OK**.

8. In the tree in the left pane of the window, right-click the name of the server. Click **Restart IIS**. The Stop/Start/Reboot... dialog box opens, with Restart Internet Services clicked in the What do you want IIS to do? drop-down menu.

9. Click **OK**. The Shutting Down... dialog box opens, indicating that the computer is attempting to shut down IIS. An hour glass appears briefly, and then the computer restarts IIS.

10. Close the Internet Services Manager.

11. On the client computer, close Internet Explorer. This will ensure that Internet Explorer does not use its disk cache of the web page when you try to load the web page again.

12. Click **Start**, point to **Programs**, and then click **Internet Explorer**. Internet Explorer opens.

13. In the Address bar, type **http://192.168.1.1**, and then press **Enter**. An error message appears indicating that the page cannot be displayed.

14. In the Address bar, type **http://192.168.1.1:8880**, and then press **Enter**. A web page displays "This is a test page."

15. Close Internet Explorer.

Certification Objectives

Objectives for the Network+ Exam:

➤ Define the purpose, function and/or use of the following protocols within TCP/IP: IP, TCP, UDP, FTP, TFTP, SMTP, HTTP, HTTPS, POP3/IMAP4, TELNET, ICMP, ARP, NTP

➤ Define the function of TCP/UDP ports. Identify well-known ports

➤ Identify the basic capabilities (i.e., client support, interoperability, authentication, file and print services, application support, and security) of the following server operating systems: UNIX/Linux, NetWare, Windows, Macintosh

Review Questions

1. What symbol is used to separate the computer name from the port number in a URL (assuming that IP version 4 is in use)?

   a. ;
   b. :
   c. #
   d. .

11

2. What is the default port number for the Telnet service?
   a. 20
   b. 21
   c. 22
   d. 23

3. What is the default port number for the HTTP service?
   a. 40
   b. 44
   c. 60
   d. 80

4. What range of port numbers comprises the well-known port numbers?
   a. 0 to 64
   b. 0 to 128
   c. 0 to 1023
   d. 0 to 8800

5. What is a socket?
   a. a virtual connector that associates a URL with its IP address
   b. a method of identifying the IP addresses belonging to clients as they connect to servers
   c. a logical address assigned to a specific process running on a computer
   d. a discreet unit of data

6. Which of the following addresses could represent the SMTP service using its default port on a mail server?
   a. 188.65.79.80:25
   b. 188.65.79.80...24
   c. 188.65.79.80$24
   d. 188.65.79.80;25

CHAPTER TWELVE

TROUBLESHOOTING NETWORK PROBLEMS

Labs included in this chapter

➤ Lab 12.1 Using the Ping Utility to Troubleshoot a TCP/IP Network
➤ Lab 12.2 Using the Traceroute Command to Troubleshoot a TCP/IP Network
➤ Lab 12.3 Troubleshooting Client Logon Problems
➤ Lab 12.4 Troubleshooting Web Client Problems

Net+ Exam Objectives	
Objective	**Lab**
Given a troubleshooting scenario, select the appropriate TCP/IP utility from among the following: tracert, ping, arp, netstat, nbtstat, ipconfig/ifconfig, winipcfg, nslookup	12.1, 12.2, 12.3, 12.4
Given output from a diagnostic utility (e.g., tracert, ping, ipconfig, etc.), identify the utility and interpret the output	12.1, 12.2, 12.3, 12.4
Given a network problem scenario, select an appropriate course of action based on a general troubleshooting strategy. This strategy includes the following steps: 1. Establish the symptoms, 2. Identify the affected area, 3. Establish what has changed, 4. Select the most probable cause, 5. Implement a solution, 6. Test the result, 7. Recognize the potential effects of the solution, 8. Document the solution	12.1, 12.2, 12.3, 12.4
Given a network troubleshooting scenario involving a wiring/infrastructure problem, identify the cause of the problem (e.g., bad media, interference, network hardware)	12.1, 12.2, 12.3, 12.4
Given a scenario, predict the impact of modifying, adding, or removing network services (e.g., DHCP, DNS, WINS, etc.) on network resources and users	12.3, 12.4
Given a network scenario, interpret visual indicators (e.g., link lights, collision lights, etc.) to determine the nature of the problem	12.3, 12.4
Given a network troubleshooting scenario involving a client connectivity problem (e.g., incorrect protocol/client software/authentication configuration, or insufficient rights/permissions), identify the cause of the problem	12.3, 12.4

6. Click **Start**, point to **Programs**, point to **Accessories**, and then click **Command Prompt**. The Command Prompt window appears.

7. To determine if the local computer's NIC is operating correctly, type **ping 127.0.0.1**, and then press **Enter**. Record the output of the ping command and indicate whether it was successful.

_____

8. To determine if TCP/IP is operating properly, type **ping 192.168.1.2**, and then press **Enter**. Record the output of the ping command and indicate whether it was successful.

_____

9. To determine if the connection to the near side of the router is operating properly, type **ping 192.168.1.1**, and then press **Enter**. Record the output of the ping command and indicate whether it was successful.

_____

10. To determine if the router is operating properly, type **ping 172.16.1.1**, and then press **Enter**. Record the output of the ping command and indicate whether it was successful.

_____

11. To determine if a computer on the network segment on the far side of the router is operating properly, type **ping 172.16.1.2**, and then press **Enter**. Record the output of the ping command and indicate whether it was successful.

_____

12. Unplug the cable that is connected to the NIC with the IP address of 172.16.1.1.

13. Repeat Steps 7 through 11. Record the step that failed.

_____

14. Plug in the cable you unplugged in Step 12.

Certification Objectives

Objectives for the Network+ Exam:

➤ Given a troubleshooting scenario, select the appropriate TCP/IP utility from among the following: tracert, ping, arp, netstat, nbtstat, ipconfig/ifconfig, winipcfg, nslookup

➤ Given output from a diagnostic utility (e.g., tracert, ping, ipconfig, etc.), identify the utility and interpret the output

➤ Given a network problem scenario, select an appropriate course of action based on a general troubleshooting strategy. This strategy includes the following steps: 1. Establish the symptoms, 2. Identify the affected area, 3. Establish what has changed, 4. Select the most probable cause, 5. Implement a solution, 6. Test the result, 7. Recognize the potential effects of the solution, 8. Document the solution

➤ Given a network troubleshooting scenario involving a wiring/infrastructure problem, identify the cause of the problem (e.g., bad media, interference, network hardware)

Review Questions

1. What would you ping to determine whether your own computer's TCP/IP services and NIC were available?
   a. the gateway address
   b. the near side of the router
   c. the loopback address
   d. the far side of the router

2. Which of the following, when found in the response of a ping command that was issued on a Windows-based computer, indicates that the ping test was successful?
   a. Packets: Sent = 4, Received = 4, Loss = 0 (0%)
   b. Packets: Sent = 0, Received = 0, Loss = 0 (0%)
   c. Packets: Sent = 0, Received = 0, Loss = 4 (100%)
   d. Packets: Sent = 4, Received = 4, Loss = 4 (100%)

3. When you issue a ping command, what Application layer protocol sends a message to the destination host?
   a. ARP
   b. RARP
   c. SNMP
   d. ICMP

4. Suppose you were troubleshooting a network connectivity problem between a server on a private LAN and a server on the Internet. As part of a logical troubleshooting methodology, what address would you ping first?
   a. the server's loopback address
   b. the server's default gateway
   c. the private LAN's Internet nameserver
   d. the Internet server you're trying to reach

5. In the scenario described in Question 4, as part of a logical troubleshooting methodology, what address would you ping second?
   a. the server's loopback address
   b. the server's default gateway
   c. the private LAN's Internet nameserver
   d. the Internet server

12

6. Which of the following is the loopback address in IP version 4 addressing?
   a. 127.0.0.1
   b. 1.1.1.1
   c. 127.0.0.0
   d. 10.0.0.0

7. What type of message would you receive if you were trying to ping www.comptia.org and misspelled the host's name as "wwv.comptia.org" in the ping command syntax?
   a. Host wwv.comptia.org not responding.
   b. Unknown host wwv.comptia.org.
   c. Reply from wwv.comptia.org: bytes= 0.
   d. The host wwv.comptia.org does not exist.

LAB 12.2 USING THE TRACEROUTE COMMAND TO TROUBLESHOOT A TCP/IP NETWORK

Objectives

Another useful troubleshooting command in a TCP/IP network is the traceroute command. Although this command is usually called by its name on UNIX systems, traceroute, the name of the command on Windows-based systems is tracert.

The traceroute command traces the path that a packet travels as it goes over the network from a source to a destination node. This is particularly useful on large networks (including the Internet), as it can indicate at which hop along the route between two computers a problem exists. In smaller networks where you already know the network path, you can use the ping command instead. Note that on the Internet, firewalls and packet filtering can restrict the usefulness of the traceroute and tracert commands.

After completing this lab, you will be able to:

➤ Use the traceroute command to trace the path to a destination

➤ Interpret both successful and unsuccessful traceroute responses

Materials Required

This lab will require the following:

➤ A Windows 2000 Server computer with two NICs configured as a router, one NIC configured with an IP address of 192.168.1.1 and a subnet mask of 255.255.255.0, and the other NIC configured with an IP address of 172.16.1.1 and a subnet mask of 255.255.0.0

➤ Two Ethernet hubs, each connected to a different NIC on the router

➤ A client computer (Client 1) running Windows 2000 Server or Windows 2000 Professional with a NIC configured with an IP address of 192.168.1.2 and a subnet mask of 255.255.255.0, connected to one of the hubs with a Category 5 UTP cable

➤ A client computer (Client 2) running Windows 2000 Server or Windows 2000 Professional with a NIC configured with an IP address of 172.16.1.2 and a subnet mask of 255.255.0.0, connected to the other hub with a Category 5 UTP cable

➤ Access to Client 1 as an ordinary user

Estimated completion time: **15 minutes**

ACTIVITY

1. Log on to Client 1.

2. Click **Start**, point to **Programs**, point to **Accessories**, and then click **Command Prompt**. The Command Prompt window appears.

3. At the command prompt, type **tracert 172.16.1.2**, and then press **Enter**. The tracert command traces the path to the computer with the IP address of 172.16.1.2, showing the number of each hop, three response times, and the name or IP address for each hop. (Note that you can also use a domain name, such as microsoft.com). Figure 12-2 shows an example of the output of the tracert command.

12

Figure 12-2   Output of the tracert command

4. Remove the cable from the NIC attached to Client 2.

5. Repeat Step 3. Instead of recording two hops and stopping, the tracert command continues. However, after the first hop, the response times are replaced by asterisks and the IP address is replaced by Request timed out. This indicates that the tracert command could not determine the path to the destination address after the first hop.

establishing that physical connectivity is not the problem, determine if the user's computer has network connectivity. Can you ping the server from the user's computer? After you have determined that network connectivity is not the problem, try to determine if the application is functioning properly.

In this lab, you will first verify that the network, the client computers, and the server are all functioning properly by logging on to two client computers. Then your instructor or another set of lab partners will do something to prevent at least one of the computers from logging on to the server. Your mission will be to identify and solve the problem.

After completing this lab, you will be able to:

> ➤ Follow a logical troubleshooting methodology to determine the nature of client connectivity problems

> ➤ Interpret the results of diagnostic utilities such as ping and ipconfig to identify a network problem

Materials Required

This lab will require the following:

> ➤ A computer running Windows 2000 Server with a NIC, configured as a domain controller for the domain1.com domain with an IP address of 192.168.1.1

> ➤ A DHCP server running on the Windows 2000 server, assigning DHCP addresses in the range from 192.168.1.50 to 192.168.1.100

> ➤ A shared folder named NetPlus on the Windows 2000 server

> ➤ Administrator access to the Windows 2000 server computer

> ➤ Two client computers, Client 1 and Client 2, running Windows 2000 Server or Windows 2000 Professional with NICs configured to obtain a DHCP address

> ➤ Domain accounts client1 and client2 with known passwords to log on to the client computers

> ➤ An Ethernet hub

> ➤ Three Category 5 UTP cables connecting the hub to each computer's NIC, as shown in Figure 12-3

> ➤ A faulty or improperly made cable the same color as at least one of the working Category 5 cables

> ➤ An instructor or classmate to cause a problem in the network

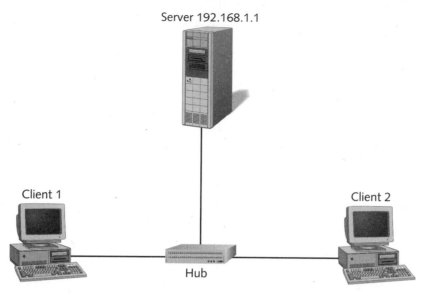

Figure 12-3   Network layout of Lab 12.3

Estimated completion time: **45 minutes**

ACTIVITY

12

1. Log on to the client1 account on the Client 1 computer.

2. Double-click **My Network Places**. The My Network Places window appears. Double-click **Entire Network**. If the Microsoft Windows Network icon does not appear, click the link in the left pane that says you may view the entire contents of the network. Double-click **Microsoft Windows Network**. Double-click **Domain1**. The NetPlus shared folder appears.

3. Repeat Steps 1 and 2 in the client2 account on the Client 2 computer. You have now verified that you can log on to the Windows 2000 server with both client computers.

4. At this point, you will leave the room. Your instructor or another set of lab partners will cause a network problem by performing one of the following actions:

   - Replace the network cable connecting Client 1 to the hub with the faulty network cable (task to be performed by the instructor or classmate).

   - Replace the network cable connecting the Windows 2000 Server computer to the hub with the faulty network cable (task to be performed by the instructor or classmate).

   - Pull the cable far enough out of Client 1's NIC so that the link light turns off but not so far that it falls completely out of the NIC (task to be performed by the instructor or classmate).

- Reconfigure the IP address on Client 1 (steps to be performed by the instructor or classmate):
    a. Right-click **My Network Places**, and click **Properties**. The Network and Dial-up Connections window appears.
    b. Right-click **Local Area Connection**, click **Properties**, click **Internet Protocol (TCP/IP)**, and then click **Properties**.
    c. Click the **Use the following IP address** option button. In the IP address: text box, type **192.68.1.51**. In the Subnet mask: text box, type **255.255.255.0**.
    d. Click **OK** twice. Then close the My Network Places window.

- Reconfigure the IP address on the Windows 2000 server (steps to be performed by the instructor or classmate):
    a. Right-click **My Network Places**, and then click **Properties**. The Network and Dial-up Connections window appears.
    b. Right-click **Local Area Connection**, click **Properties**, click **Internet Protocol (TCP/IP)**, and then click **Properties**.
    c. Click the **Use the following IP address** option button. In the IP address: text box, type **172.16.1.1**. In the Subnet mask: text box, type **255.255.255.0**.
    d. Click **OK** twice, then close the My Network Places window.

- Reconfigure the subnet mask on Client 1 (steps to be performed by instructor or classmate):
    a. Right-click **My Network Places**, and click **Properties**. The Network and Dial-up Connections window appears.
    b. Right-click **Local Area Connection**, click **Properties**, click **Internet Protocol (TCP/IP)**, and then click **Properties**.
    c. Click the **Use the following IP address** option button. In the IP address: text box, type **192.168.1.50**. In the Subnet mask: text box, type **255.255.255.248**.
    d. Click **OK** twice, then close the My Network Places window.

5. When you return to the room, reboot both client computers.

6. Attempt to repeat Steps 1 and 2 on Client 1. You are unable to browse to the NetPlus folder. You will now attempt to solve the problem using the following steps. If you identify the problem before completing all the steps, proceed to Step 13.

7. Now begin to determine the scope of the problem by attempting to log on to Client 2. If you are able to log on and browse the NetPlus folder, the problem is local to the Client 1 computer and you may concentrate on potential problems that affect only Client 1. Otherwise, the problem is common to all clients and you should concentrate on potential problems which affect all clients.

8. To determine the state of physical connectivity in the network, check the status of the link lights on the hub and in the NICs for each computer.

9. To determine the state of network connectivity in the network, on Client 1, click **Start**, point to **Programs**, point to **Accessories**, and click **Command Prompt**. The Command Prompt window appears. Type **ping 127.0.0.1**, and then press **Enter**. Success indicates that the TCP/IP stack on Client 1 is working. Depending on the scope of the problem, repeat this step for Client 2.

10. At the command prompt on Client 1, type **ping 192.168.1.1**, and then press **Enter**. If the output indicates success, then network connectivity exists between Client 1 and the server. Depending on the scope of the problem, repeat this step for Client 2.

11. If there is no network connectivity, at the command prompt on Client 1, type **ipconfig**, and then press **Enter**. IP addressing information displays on the computer. If this is correct, then there may be a problem with the network configuration on the server. Depending on the scope of the problem, repeat for Client 2.

12. On the Windows 2000 Server computer, repeat Steps 9 through 11. However, in Step 10 ping the IP addresses of the client computers.

13. By this time, you should have identified the problem. Fix it, and repeat Steps 4 through 13 two more times using another of the problem scenarios in Step 4.

Certification Objectives

12

Objectives for the Network+ Exam:

➤ Given a troubleshooting scenario, select the appropriate TCP/IP utility from among the following: tracert, ping, arp, netstat, nbtstat, ipconfig/ifconfig, winipcfg, nslookup

➤ Given output from a diagnostic utility (e.g., tracert, ping, ipconfig, etc.), identify the utility and interpret the output

➤ Given a network problem scenario, select an appropriate course of action based on a general troubleshooting strategy. This strategy includes the following steps: 1. Establish the symptoms, 2. Identify the affected area, 3. Establish what has changed, 4. Select the most probable cause, 5. Implement a solution, 6. Test the result, 7. Recognize the potential effects of the solution, 8. Document the solution

➤ Given a scenario, predict the impact of modifying, adding, or removing network services (e.g., DHCP, DNS, WINS, etc.) on network resources and users

➤ Given a network scenario, interpret visual indicators (e.g., link lights, collision lights, etc.) to determine the nature of the problem

➤ Given a network troubleshooting scenario involving a wiring/infrastructure problem, identify the cause of the problem (e.g., bad media, interference, network hardware)

➤ IIS installed and configured on the Windows 2000 server with the IP address of 172.16.1.2, with a text file in \inetpub\wwwroot named default.asp containing the text "This is a test page"

➤ A client computer running Windows 2000 Server or Windows 2000 Professional with a NIC configured with an IP address of 192.168.1.2 and a subnet mask of 255.255.0.0, connected to the other hub with a Category 5 UTP cable

➤ The client computer configured to use the router 192.168.1.1 as its DNS server

➤ Administrator access to all three computers

➤ A faulty network cable of the same color as the network cables used elsewhere

➤ An instructor or classmate to cause a problem in the network

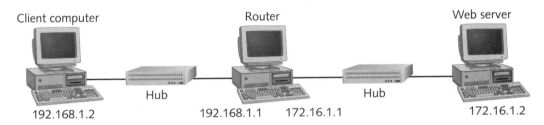

Figure 12-4   Network layout of Lab 12.4

Estimated completion time: **45 minutes**

ACTIVITY

1. Log on to the client computer as an administrator.

2. Click **Start**, point to **Programs**, and then click **Internet Explorer**. Internet Explorer opens.

3. In the Address bar, type **www.netplus.com**, and then press **Enter**. A Web page opens with the text "This is a test page."

4. Close Internet Explorer.

5. At this point, you will leave the room. Your instructor or another set of lab partners will cause a network problem by performing one of the following actions:

   ■ Replace the network cable connecting the Web server to the hub with the faulty network cable (task to be performed by the instructor or classmate).

   ■ Reconfigure the IP address on the Web server (steps to be performed by instructor or classmate):

      a. Log on to the Web server as an administrator.

      b. Right-click **My Network Places**, and click **Properties**. The Network and Dial-up Connections window appears.

    c. Right-click **Local Area Connection**, click **Properties**, click **Internet Protocol (TCP/IP)**, and then click **Properties**.

    d. Click the **Use the following IP address** option button. In the IP address: text box, type **172.16.1.50**. In the Subnet mask: text box, type **255.255.0.0**.

    e. Click **OK** twice, then close the My Network Places window.

- Change the DNS server on the client computer (steps to be performed by instructor or classmate):

    a. Right-click **My Network Places**, and click **Properties**, the Network and Dial-up Connections window appears.

    b. Right-click **Local Area Connection**, click **Properties**, click **Internet Protocol (TCP/IP)**, and then click **Properties**.

    c. Click the **Use the following DNS server addresses** option button. In the Preferred DNS server: text box, type **192.168.1.100**.

    d. Click **OK** twice, then close the My Network Places window.

- Change the DNS entry for www.netplus.com (steps to be performed by instructor or classmate):

    a. Log on to the router computer as an administrator.

    b. Click **Start**, point to **Programs**, point to **Administrative Tools**, and then click **DNS**. The DNS window appears.

    c. In the tree in the left pane of the window, double-click the server name. The tree expands underneath the server name. Double-click **Forward Lookup Zones** in the tree in the left pane. The tree expands underneath Forward Lookup Zones. Click **netplus.com**.

    d. In the left pane, click **netplus.com**. In the right pane, right-click **www**, and then click **Properties**.

    e. Type **172.16.1.200** in the IP address: text box, and then click **OK**.

    f. Close the DNS window.

6. Attempt to repeat Steps 1 through 3 on the client computer. You are unable to open the Web page. Attempt to solve the problem using the following steps. If you solve the problem before completing all the steps, proceed to Step 17.

7. Attempt to determine the state of physical connectivity in the network. Check the status of the link lights on both hubs and the NICs in the client computer, the router, and the Web server.

8. Attempt to determine the state of network connectivity. On the client computer, click **Start**, point to **Programs**, point to **Accessories**, and then click **Command Prompt**. The Command Prompt window appears. Type **ping 127.0.0.1**, and then press **Enter**. Success indicates that the TCP/IP stack on Client 1 is working.

12

9. At the command prompt on Client 1, type **ping 192.168.1.1**, and then press **Enter**. Success indicates that you can connect to the near NIC on the router.

10. Type **ping 172.16.1.1**, and then press **Enter**. Success indicates that you can connect to the far NIC on the router.

11. Type **ping 172.16.1.2**, and then press **Enter**. Success indicates that you can connect to the Web server.

12. If there is no network connectivity, at the command prompt on the client computer, type **ipconfig**, and then press **Enter**. IP addressing information displays, indicating there may be a problem with the network configuration on the server.

13. If you cannot find a problem with the IP addressing information on the client computer, repeat the previous Step 13 on the router and the Web server.

14. If you have verified network connectivity between the client computer and the Web server, at the client computer type **http://172.16.1.2** in the Address bar in Internet Explorer, and then press **Enter**. If you can open the Web page, this indicates that there is a problem with DNS.

15. At the command prompt on the client computer, type **ipconfig /all**, and then press **Enter**. Look through the IP addressing information to verify that the client computer is configured to use the router (at 192.168.1.1) as its DNS server.

16. If the client computer is using the correct DNS server, type **nslookup www.netplus.com**, and then press **Enter**. The IP address of www.netplus.com displays. Check to see if this matches the IP address of the Web server.

17. By this time, you should have been able to identify the problem. Fix it, and repeat Steps 5 through 16 two more times using another of the problem scenarios in Step 5.

Certification Objectives

Objectives for the Network+ Exam:

➤ Given a troubleshooting scenario, select the appropriate TCP/IP utility from among the following: tracert, ping, arp, netstat, nbtstat, ipconfig/ifconfig, winipcfg, nslookup

➤ Given output from a diagnostic utility (e.g., tracert, ping, ipconfig, etc.), identify the utility and interpret the output

➤ Given a network problem scenario, select an appropriate course of action based on a general troubleshooting strategy. This strategy includes the following steps: 1. Establish the symptoms, 2. Identify the affected area, 3. Establish what has changed, 4. Select the most probable cause, 5. Implement a solution, 6. Test the result, 7. Recognize the potential effects of the solution, 8. Document the solution

➤ Given a scenario, predict the impact of modifying, adding, or removing network services (e.g., DHCP, DNS, WINS, etc.) on network resources and users

➤ Given a network scenario, interpret visual indicators (e.g., link lights, collision lights, etc.) to determine the nature of the problem

➤ Given a network troubleshooting scenario involving a wiring/infrastructure problem, identify the cause of the problem (e.g., bad media, interference, network hardware)

➤ Given a network troubleshooting scenario involving a client connectivity problem (e.g., incorrect protocol/client software/authentication configuration, or insufficient rights/permissions), identify the cause of the problem

Review Questions

1. What does the nslookup command reveal?
   a. a client's current connections
   b. a client's routing table entries
   c. the IP address of a given host name or vice versa
   d. the NetBIOS name based on a computer's IP address

2. If the link light on a hub port is not lit, what can you assume about the client connected to that hub's port?
   a. There are no connectivity problems with the client.
   b. The client cannot exchange data with the network.
   c. The client can exchange data only with other nodes on its segment.
   d. The client can exchange Network layer, but not Transport layer data.

3. If a client does not have the correct DNS server address specified in its TCP/IP properties, which of the following will occur?
   a. The client cannot log on to or exchange data with the network.
   b. The client can exchange data with nodes on its local network, but not with nodes on other networks.
   c. The client can exchange data with nodes on external networks, but not with nodes on its local network.
   d. The client can exchange data with most, but not all, nodes on both its local and external networks.

4. What would happen if you assigned your Web server a new IP address that didn't match its DNS entry?
   a. It would be unavailable to clients.
   b. It would be available only to local clients, but not to clients accessing it over the Internet.
   c. It would be available to clients accessing it over the Internet, but not to local clients.
   d. It would still be available to all clients.

12

5. Which of the following tools will issue a simple pass/fail indication for a CAT 5 UTP cable?

   a. cable checker

   b. time domain reflectometer

   c. multimeter

   d. tone generator

6. Suppose you ping the IP address of a known Web server, and the response to your command indicates that the Web server is responding. It then follows that the Web server would successfully respond to HTTP requests from clients. True or False?

CHAPTER THIRTEEN

MAINTAINING AND UPGRADING A NETWORK

Labs included in this chapter

➤ Lab 13.1 Researching Network Solutions

➤ Lab 13.2 Installing and Removing a Service Pack on Windows 2000

➤ Lab 13.3 Upgrading an Ethernet Network to a Fast Ethernet Network

➤ Lab 13.4 Replacing a Web Server

Net+ Exam Objectives	
Objective	**Lab**
Identify the basic capabilities (i.e., client support, interoperability, authentication, file and print services, application support, and security) of the following server operating systems: UNIX/Linux, NetWare, Windows, Macintosh	13.1, 13.2, 13.4
Specify the characteristics (e.g., speed, length, topology, cable type, etc.) of the following: 802.3 (Ethernet) standards, 10BaseT, 100BaseT, 100BaseTX, 10Base2, 10Base5, 100BaseFX, Gigabit Ethernet	13.3
Choose the appropriate media type and connectors to add a client to an existing network	13.3
Given output from a diagnostic utility (e.g., tracert, ping, ipconfig, etc.), identify the utility and interpret the output	13.3
Given a network scenario, interpret visual indicators (e.g., link lights, collision lights, etc.) to determine the nature of the problem	13.3

Lab 13.1 Researching Network Solutions

Objectives

In this lab, you will research network solutions by examining business case studies on vendor Web sites. By examining these case studies, you can get an idea of how each vendor uses its product line to help customers solve problems. It is important to keep in mind, however, that few vendors are objective about their products. When considering a solution, you should look for information from multiple sources. Additionally, you may find it helpful to talk to someone who has attempted to implement a solution such as the one you are considering

After completing this lab, you will be able to:

➤ Review case studies of networking companies

➤ Identify the needs of the customer in a case study

➤ Identify the solutions provided by the networking companies

Materials Required

This lab will require the following:

➤ Pencil and paper

➤ A computer with Internet access and a Web browser, such as Internet Explorer

➤ An ordinary user account on the computer

Estimated completion time: **25 minutes**

Activity

1. If necessary, power on the computer.

2. Log on to the computer and open Internet Explorer.

3. To review case studies for Novell, type **www.novell.com/success/** into the Address bar. You see a list of case studies that demonstrate how Novell products have helped Novell customers.

4. Review a case study of your choice. Record the name of the customer and type of business in the case study.

_____

5. Record background information on the company in the case study. This information might include the type of business, the size, and what networking hardware or software it used.

_____

6. Record the business need or challenge for the company that was the customer in the case study.

   _____

7. Record the Novell solution. Be sure to identify the software or hardware solution that was implemented.

   _____

8. Record the results of the solution.

   _____

9. To review case studies for Microsoft, type **www.microsoft.com** into the Address bar.

10. Locate the Search text box on the Microsoft Web page. (Begin by looking at the upper-left side of the page.) In the text box, type **case study**, and then press **Enter**. A list of links for this search term displays. Click the **Case Study Index** link.

11. Select a case study by clicking the case study's title. The case study's page appears. Scroll through the page and read the details of the study. Record the name of the customer and the type of business you reviewed.

   _____

12. Record background information on the company in the case study. This information might include the type of business, the size, and what networking hardware or software it used.

   _____

13. Record the business need or challenge for the company that was the customer in the case study.

   _____

14. Record the Microsoft solution. Be sure to identify the software or hardware solution that was used.

   _____

15. Record the results of the solution.

   _____

16. Close your Web browser.

Certification Objectives

Objectives for the Network+ Exam:

➤ Identify the basic capabilities (i.e., client support, interoperability, authentication, file and print services, application support, and security) of the following server operating systems: UNIX/Linux, NetWare, Windows, Macintosh

13

Review Questions

1. If you were the network manager for a large healthcare provider whose network depended on NetWare 5.0 servers, which of the following Novell products would be the best choice to provide centralized desktop management?

    a. BorderManager

    b. GroupWise

    c. ZENworks

    d. eDirectory

2. Which of the following networking trends would increase a network administrator's concerns about network security? (Choose all that apply.)

    a. More and more users have access to public networks.

    b. Costs of complex networking equipment continue to fall.

    c. Standards for key encryption are being managed by government bodies.

    d. The most popular protocol in use today is open source, not proprietary.

    e. Network providers are investing in more fiber-optic media.

3. If you were a network administrator for a network that ran exclusively NetWare 5.0 servers, what proxy server software would you probably choose?

    a. BorderManager

    b. GroupWise

    c. ZENworks

    d. eDirectory

4. Which of the following products would you run on your NetWare 5.0 servers to allow Windows 2000 Active Directory objects to be managed on those NetWare servers?

    a. BorderManager

    b. GroupWise

    c. ZENworks

    d. eDirectory

5. As a network administrator, which of the following networking trends would help you save time in managing accounts and shared resources on the network?

    a. The Ethernet network access method is becoming more popular than its counterparts.

    b. Costs of complex networking equipment continue to fall.

    c. Vendors are increasingly offering better tools for NOS interoperability on the same network.

    d. Network providers are investing in more fiber-optic media.

    e. NOSs are providing simpler and more consistent GUIs for administration.

6. If you were a network administrator for a network that exclusively used Microsoft Windows 2000 servers, which of the following products would you install on the servers to provide users with centralized discussion lists and online collaboration?

   a. Outlook

   b. PowerPoint

   c. Exchange Server

   d. Transaction Server

7. As a network administrator for a network that used primarily Windows 2000 servers and relied on large amounts of data to supply information to its e-commerce Web sites, which of the following products would you select to store the data and make it easily accessible to the Web pages?

   a. Exchange Server

   b. SQL Server

   c. Transaction Server

   d. MMSQ

LAB 13.2 INSTALLING AND REMOVING A SERVICE PACK ON WINDOWS 2000

Objectives

Keeping software up to date on both servers and network devices is an important part of maintaining and upgrading a network. Usually software updates will consist of patches or other fixes to problems that users and administrators have encountered when using the software. In other cases, a software update might solve a potential security problem, or it might even add a new feature.

Microsoft typically releases its software updates in one of two forms. The first form is a hot fix, which is an update to a specific piece of software. You might use a hot fix to correct a specific problem. For instance, a hot fix might solve a problem with Internet Information Services (IIS), which is its Web server. The second form is a service pack, which is a grouping of numerous software updates. You might use a service pack as part of a server's regular maintenance.

You should be careful when applying any software update; you don't want to cause other problems. For instance, you might run a certain application on your Windows 2000 servers. If this application relies on a piece of software which has been changed in a service pack or hot fix, the application may no longer work after the update has been applied. As a result, you may have to backlevel, or revert to the previous version of the software, after the upgrade. Thus, if at all possible, you should verify that a software upgrade will work in a test environment *prior* to applying it to production machines.

13

After completing this lab, you will be able to:

➤ Install a service pack on a Windows 2000 server

➤ Remove a service pack from a Windows 2000 server

Materials Required

This lab will require the following:

➤ A Windows 2000 Professional computer

➤ A copy of Service Pack 2 saved in a directory called C:\sp

➤ Administrator access to the computer

Estimated completion time: **30 minutes**

ACTIVITY

1. Log on to the computer as an administrator.

2. Click **Start**, point to **Programs**, point to **Accessories**, and click **Command Prompt**. The Command Prompt window appears.

3. Type **cd C:\sp**, and then press **Enter**.

4. Type **w2ksp2**, and then press **Enter**. The Extracting Files dialog box opens. The computer will extract files from the service pack into a temporary directory. The Windows 2000 Service Pack Setup dialog box opens.

5. Click the **Read Me** button. A Web page entitled Microsoft Windows 2000 Service Pack 2 Readme opens in Internet Explorer. This Web page contains information about installing and uninstalling the Service Pack. Close Internet Explorer.

6. In the Windows 2000 Service Pack Setup dialog box, click the **Accept the License Agreement (must accept before installing the Service Pack)** check box. Leave the Backup files necessary to uninstall this Service Pack check box checked.

7. Click the **Install** button. The Windows 2000 Service Pack Setup dialog box opens. The computer prepares the files it will install, backs up the existing files, and then installs the new files.

8. Finally, the Windows 2000 Service Pack Setup dialog box indicates that the installation is complete. Click **Restart** to reboot the computer.

9. Log on to the computer as an administrator.

10. Now you will uninstall the service pack. Double-click **My Computer**, double-click **Control Panel**, and then double-click **Add/Remove Programs**. The Add/Remove Programs window appears.

11. Click **Windows 2000 Service Pack 2**. The Change/Remove button appears.

12. Click the **Change/Remove** button. The Windows 2000 Service Pack Uninstall dialog box opens.

13. Click **Yes** to remove the service pack. The Deleting Files dialog box opens as the computer deletes files installed by Service Pack 2, followed by the Copying Files... dialog box as the computer reinstalls the original files. Finally the Windows 2000 Service Pack Uninstall dialog box opens, indicating that Service Pack 2 has been uninstalled.

14. Click **OK** to reboot the computer.

15. Log on to the computer.

16. The Control Panel opens. Double-click **Add/Remove Programs**. The Add/Remove Programs window appears. Note that Service Pack 2 no longer appears in the list of programs currently installed on the computer.

17. Close the Add/Remove Programs and Control Panel windows.

Certification Objectives

Objectives for the Network+ Exam:

➤ Identify the basic capabilities (i.e., client support, interoperability, authentication, file and print services, application support, and security) of the following server operating systems: UNIX/Linux, NetWare, Windows, Macintosh

Review Questions

1. In which of the following situations would it be wise to backlevel?
   a. You have just performed a complete backup of your server's data directories, and you cannot confirm that the backup was successful.
   b. You have just applied a fix to your NOS and have discovered that the fix resulted in a lack of network access for half of your users.
   c. You have just installed a database program on one of your servers and have discovered that you neglected to install an optional component that your users will need.
   d. You have just installed the Windows 2000 Server NOS on a new computer and you cannot get the operating system to recognize the NIC.

2. Which two of the following may typically be accomplished by applying a patch to a network operating system?
   a. replacing all the NOS's program files
   b. modifying an existing feature
   c. removing an old feature
   d. fixing a known bug
   e. recording specifics about your installation for vendor troubleshooting

13

3. Before installing a major NOS patch, you should _____.
   a. remove all protocols installed on the server
   b. prevent users from logging on
   c. disable Internet services
   d. disable network connectivity

4. When installing a Microsoft Service Pack, which of the following occurs first?
   a. old files are moved into a temporary directory for later deletion
   b. the computer reboots
   c. new files are copied to the server
   d. temporary files are deleted

5. In Microsoft terminology, what is a hot fix?
   a. a patch that replaces an entire portion, or all, of the NOS
   b. a patch that requires that the server be connected to Microsoft's Web site as it is installed
   c. a patch that updates a specific type of software, often the operating system
   d. a patch that can be installed while users are logged on without causing adverse effects

6. What is the primary difference between a software upgrade and a patch?
   a. The software manufacturer issues a patch, and an upgrade may be issued by any organization that has the software's source code.
   b. A patch fixes a specific part of a piece of software, and an upgrade typically replaces the entire software program.
   c. A patch typically does not require that the network administrator test its changes before applying it to a server; an upgrade does.
   d. A patch typically is not supported by the software manufacturer; an upgrade is.

7. When planning significant NOS software changes, which of the following steps should you undertake first?
   a. install the new or updated software on a test server
   b. research the steps involved in the software change through the vendor's Web site
   c. inform users that you intend to make software changes and let them know how their network access might be affected
   d. determine whether the software update is really necessary

LAB 13.3 UPGRADING AN ETHERNET NETWORK TO A FAST ETHERNET NETWORK

Objectives

In this lab, you will upgrade the cabling and network devices in a small LAN. Although this lab is relatively simple, performing this sort of upgrade in a larger network can be a complex and potentially troublesome undertaking. To begin with, most users will be unable to use the network while you replace their cabling. Thus, to perform this upgrade in a large LAN, you would typically perform it in stages so that few users at a time are affected. You would also have to perform each stage at a time when few users (if any) will be logged onto the network. At each step in a network upgrade, you should also verify that the network works as expected or otherwise meets your specifications. Obviously, if the upgrade does not turn out as planned, you must troubleshoot and solve the problem.

After completing this lab, you will be able to:

> ➤ Upgrade a LAN from 10BaseT to 100BaseT

Materials Required

This lab will require the following:

> ➤ Computer A running Windows 2000 Server or Windows 2000 Professional, with a 10/100 NIC configured with an IP address of 192.168.1.1

> ➤ Computer B running Windows 2000 Server or Windows 2000 Professional, with a 10/100 NIC configured with an IP address of 192.168.1.2

> ➤ Access to both computers as a user

> ➤ A 10-Mbps Ethernet hub and a 100-Mbps Ethernet hub, or a 10/100-Mbps hub

> ➤ Two Category 3 UTP cables connecting the hub to the NICs in both computers

> ➤ Two Category 5 UTP cables for the upgrade

> ➤ A cable tester

Estimated completion time: **20 minutes**

13

ACTIVITY

1. Power on both computers.

2. Log on to Computer A as a user.

3. Click **Start**, point to **Programs**, point to **Accessories**, and click **Command Prompt**. The Command Prompt window appears.

4. At the command prompt, type **ping 192.168.1.2**, and then press **Enter**. You see four successful replies from Computer B.

5. If you are using a 10/100 Ethernet hub, look at the NIC in the back of the computer. 10/100 NICs typically have a link light indicating whether the computer is connecting at 10 Mbps or 100 Mbps. Note the speed of the connection.

6. Now you will upgrade the cabling in the network from Category 3 UTP cable to Category 5 UTP cable. Shut down both computers and power them off.

7. If you are using a 10-Mbps Ethernet hub, power off the hub and set it aside. Replace it with the 100-Mbps Ethernet hub. If you are using a 10/100 Ethernet hub, proceed on to the next step.

8. Remove the Category 3 UTP cables from each NIC and each port on the hub.

9. Plug both ends of one of the cables into the cable tester. The lights on the cable tester should go on. Repeat with the other cable.

10. Connect one Category 5 UTP cable from a port in the hub to the NIC in the back of one of the computers. Plug the other Category 5 UTP cable from a port in the hub to the NIC in the back of the other computer.

11. Power on both computers and the hub (if necessary).

12. Look at the link lights on the NIC in the back of one of the computers. Compare the connection speed indicated by the light to the connection speed you saw in Step 5.

---

13. Repeat Steps 2 through 4 to confirm that you still have network connectivity between the two computers.

Certification Objectives

Objectives for the Network+ Exam:

➤ Specify the characteristics (e.g., speed, length, topology, cable type, etc.) of the following: 802.3 (Ethernet) standards, 10BaseT, 100BaseT, 100BaseTX, 10Base2, 10Base5, 100BaseFX, Gigabit Ethernet

➤ Choose the appropriate media type and connectors to add a client to an existing network

➤ Given output from a diagnostic utility (e.g., tracert, ping, ipconfig, etc.), identify the utility and interpret the output

➤ Given a network scenario, interpret visual indicators (e.g., link lights, collision lights, etc.) to determine the nature of the problem

Review Questions

1. Why is it necessary to upgrade a network's cabling in stages?
   a. because users will take a while to adjust to the changes
   b. because the upgrade will require downtime, and limiting the scope of the change will limit the number of users affected
   c. because you cannot rely on obtaining all your necessary cabling by one date
   d. because during the change, traffic on the network will increase and making changes in stages will reduce the potential for network congestion in parts of the network

2. Which of the following would be the most complex and potentially trouble-some type of network upgrade?

   a. client software version upgrade

   b. NOS version upgrade

   c. router replacement

   d. backbone upgrade

3. Which of the following network changes have the potential to halt network access for all users on a LAN that consists of one server, one gateway, one router, 12 hubs, and 100 users, should the change go awry? (Choose all that apply.)

   a. NOS upgrade

   b. hub upgrade

   c. work area wiring upgrade

   d. workstation OS upgrade

   e. backbone upgrade

4. If you were the network administrator for a network that relied on a combination of CAT3 and CAT 5 cabling to run 10BaseT Ethernet and you were planning an upgrade to 100BaseTX Ethernet within the next six months, what could you do at present that would prepare for the upgrade but that would not impair current functionality? (Choose all that apply.)

   a. upgrade the client software to a 100BaseTX-compatible version

   b. upgrade all the workgroup hubs to 100BaseTX

   c. install 10/100 BaseT-NICs in each new workstation that's added to the network

   d. replace CAT3 wiring with CAT5 or higher wiring

   e. replace CAT5 wiring with fiber-optic cabling

5. Why is baselining important prior to upgrading a network?

   a. It allows you to measure the benefits of an upgrade, once the upgrade is complete.

   b. It ensures that you have not inadvertently forgotten a segment or work-group while planning the upgrade.

   c. It prevents upgrade errors from causing a network outage.

   d. It is helpful in predicting how complex the network upgrade will be.

6. In planning a backbone upgrade, which of the following steps would you take first?

   a. purchase new NICs for workstations, servers, and connectivity devices

   b. develop a project plan for implementing the upgrade

   c. hire consultants to help with the upgrade

   d. justify the upgrade

13

Lab 13.4 Replacing a Web Server

Objectives

Upgrading network devices and servers happens frequently in a network of any size. As a network administrator, a significant part of your job will be managing these changes to minimize their effect on your users.

Some changes may be performed with little or no effect on users. For instance, replacing a NIC on a domain controller will have little effect on users if the network has multiple domain controllers. Other changes, especially in networks without redundant servers or network devices, will affect users and must be scheduled for times when as few users as possible might need to use services on the network. After the changes, you must be very careful to verify that everything works as expected.

On the job, you might need to replace or upgrade hardware on Web servers. In this lab, you will simulate replacing a Web server. To swap out the Web server, you will add a new Web server to the network, copy the Web site files onto the new server, and then replace the existing Web server with a third Web server. Note that there are many ways to upgrade a Web server. For instance, you could also add the Web server to the network with a different IP address. Then you could change the DNS entry for the Web server to point to the new IP address. However, on the Internet, many clients will not see the new DNS entry for several hours or even days.

After completing this lab, you will be able to:

➤ Replace a Web server with a minimum of down time

Materials Required

This lab will require the following:

➤ A computer running Windows 2000 Server, called Web Server A, with a NIC and configured with a workgroup of NetPlus, an IP address of 192.168.1.1, and a netmask of 255.255.255.0

➤ IIS installed on Web Server A, and the Default Web Site configured with a home directory of C:\inetpub\wwwroot

➤ A text file named default.htm in C:\inetpub\wwwroot containing the text "Web site home page"

➤ A computer running Windows 2000 Server, called Web Server B, with a NIC and a workgroup of NetPlus, but without an IP address configured

➤ IIS installed on Web Server B, and the Default Web Site configured with a home directory of C:\inetpub\wwwroot

➤ Administrator access to both Windows 2000 Server computers

➤ A computer running Windows 2000 Server or Windows 2000 Professional, called Client A, with a NIC and configured with an IP address of 192.168.1.2

➤ Access as an ordinary user to the client computer

➤ An Ethernet hub

➤ Three category 5 UTP cables

Estimated completion time: **30 minutes**

ACTIVITY

1. Power on all three computers and the hub. Using two of the Category 5 cables, connect the NICs in the back of Web Server A and Client A to the hub.

2. Log on to Client A as an ordinary user.

3. On Client A, click **Start**, point to **Programs**, and then click **Internet Explorer**. The Internet Explorer window appears.

4. In the Address bar, type **http://192.168.1.1**, and then press **Enter**. A Web page containing the text "Web site home page" appears in the Internet Explorer window, showing that the Web server is working properly.

5. Using the third Category 5 cable, connect the NIC in the back of Web Server B to the hub.

6. Log on to Web Server B as an administrator.

7. Right-click **My Network Places** and select **Properties**. The Network and Dial-up Connections window appears.

8. Right-click **Local Area Connection** and select **Properties**. The Local Area Connection Properties window appears.

9. Click **Internet Protocol (TCP/IP)**. Click the **Properties** button.

10. Now you will give Web Server B an IP address on the same network. This will allow you to verify that Web Server B works properly before completing the upgrade. Click the **Use the following IP address:** option button. In the IP address: text box, type **192.168.1.3**. In the Subnet mask: text box, type **255.255.255.0**, and then click the **OK** button twice.

11. Close the Network and Dial-up Connection Properties window on the Web Server B.

12. Log on to Web Server A as an administrator.

13. Double-click the **My Computer** icon, double-click the **Local Disk (C:)** icon, and then double-click the **inetpub** folder. Right-click the **wwwroot** folder, and then click **Sharing**. The wwwroot properties window appears.

14. Click the **Share this folder** option button, and then click **OK** to close the wwwroot properties window. Close the inetpub window.

13

15. On Web Server B, double-click **My Network Places**. Double-click **Entire Network**. If the Microsoft Windows Network icon does not appear, click the link that indicates that you may also view the entire contents of the network. Double-click the **Microsoft Windows Network** icon.

16. Double-click the **NetPlus** workgroup. Double-click the **Web Server A** icon. Log on as administrator if prompted to do so. The wwwroot shared folder appears.

17. Double-click the **wwwroot** shared folder. Right-click the file named **default.htm**, and then click **Copy**. Close the wwwroot window.

18. Double-click **My Computer**, double-click **Local Disk (C:)**, double-click the **inetpub** folder, and then double-click the **wwwroot** folder. Click **Edit**, and then click **Paste**. The file default.htm is pasted into the wwwroot folder on Web Server B. You have now copied the Web page from the current Web server to the new Web server.

19. On Client A, type **http://192.168.1.3** into the Address bar, and then press **Enter**. A Web page appears with the text "Web site home page." You have now verified that the Web server on Web Server B is working properly.

20. Close Internet Explorer. This will help keep Internet Explorer from going to the copy of the Web page it has cached on its hard drive after you have finished swapping the Web servers.

21. On Web Server B, right-click **My Network Places**, and then click **Properties**. The Network and Dial-up Connections window appears.

22. Right-click **Local Area Connection**, and then click **Properties**. The Local Area Connection Properties window appears.

23. Click **Internet Protocol (TCP/IP)**. Click **Properties**.

24. In the IP address: text box, type **192.168.1.1**. In the Subnet mask: text box, type **255.255.255.0**. Do not click OK yet! If you do, Web Server A and Web Server B will have the same IP address. On a production network, this could prevent clients from reaching either server.

25. Remove the cable connecting Web Server A to the hub.

26. On Web Server B, click **OK** twice to finish changing the IP address.

27. On Client A, repeat Steps 3 and 4. You should see the Web page with the text "Web site home page" appear again.

28. Close any open windows on all three computers.

Certification Objectives

Objectives for the Network+ Exam:

➤ Identify the basic capabilities (i.e., client support, interoperability, authentication, file and print services, application support, and security) of the following server operating systems: UNIX/Linux, NetWare, Windows, Macintosh

Review Questions

1. By default, in what folder does IIS store a Web site's home page?
   a. internet
   b. IIS
   c. wwwroot
   d. webfolder

2. What should you do with a server's NIC that you are replacing with a newer NIC?
   a. send it back to its manufacturer
   b. keep it in case you need to reinstall it
   c. throw it away
   d. use it in a workstation

3. What is the term for recording and tracking all modifications to a network, including hardware and software upgrades?
   a. asset management
   b. quality control
   c. change management
   d. network monitoring

4. When adding a new hub to a network, which of the following must you do?
   a. ensure that the length of cabling between the hub and its connected workstations does not exceed 100 meters
   b. notify all users that the network may experience downtime as you add a hub
   c. assign the hub an object name and attributes in at least one of the network's server's NOS
   d. ensure that the hub's workgroup users have privileges to access that hub

5. Which of the following is a common reason for replacing a server on a network?
   a. The network's NOS directory has become too large.
   b. The server's NIC no longer operates at the same speed as the rest of the network.
   c. The server's BIOS needs to be upgraded.
   d. The server has insufficient resources, such as hard disk space, to meet the network's requirements.

6. When adding a new member server to a network that already contains five other Windows 2000 file servers, which of the following must you do?
   a. replicate the domain's Active Directory database on the new server
   b. copy the data files from the domain controller to the new server's hard disk
   c. give the server a name that matches the names of the other servers in the domain
   d. add the new server to the network's Windows 2000 domain

13

CHAPTER FOURTEEN

ENSURING INTEGRITY AND AVAILABILITY

Labs included in this chapter

➤ Lab 14.1 Viruses

➤ Lab 14.2 Uninterruptible Power Supplies (UPSs)

➤ Lab 14.3 Implementing RAID Level 0 (Disk Striping)

➤ Lab 14.4 Implementing RAID Level 1 (Disk Mirroring)

➤ Lab 14.5 Understanding Backups

Net+ Exam Objectives	
Objective	**Lab**
Identify the purpose and characteristics of fault tolerance	14.1, 14.2, 14.3, 14.4, 14.5
Given a scenario, predict the impact of modifying, adding, or removing network services (e.g., DHCP, DNS, WINS, etc.) on network resources and users	14.1
Identify the basic capabilities (i.e., client support, interoperability, authentication, file and print services, application support, and security) of the following server operating systems: UNIX/LInux, NetWare, Windows, Macintosh	14.3, 14.4, 14.5
Identify the purpose and characteristics of disaster recovery	14.5

LAB 14.1 VIRUSES

Objectives

Viruses can infect computers from a variety of sources. For instance, you can infect a client (or a server) with a virus by running an infected executable file, by previewing e-mail with an e-mail client that has not been upgraded with the latest patches, by browsing the Web with a Web browser that has not been upgraded with the latest patches, or even by running certain services on the Internet. Keeping a file server free of viruses can be even more challenging, as your users may try to store infected files on its shared drives. Sometimes users will save infected files to a shared drive, have their computers cleared of viruses, and then re-infect their computers from the files on the shared drive.

Virus scanners will not be helpful if you do not keep them up to date. Many virus scanners require that you periodically update the virus definition files they use to search for viruses. If you do not, the virus scanner will be unable to find newer viruses.

After completing this lab, you will be able to:

➤ Understand different types of viruses

➤ Use virus scanning software

Materials Required

This lab will require the following:

➤ A Windows 2000 Server or Windows 2000 Professional computer with an Internet connection

➤ McAfee VirusScan 6.x software installed (full or evaluation version) or equivalent virus software

> Estimated completion time: **20 minutes**

ACTIVITY

1. Power on the Windows 2000 computer and log on as an administrator.

2. To gain an understanding of virus-related terms, you will access the Webopedia Web site. Click **Start**, point to **Programs**, and click **Internet Explorer**. In the Address bar, type **www.webopedia.com**.

3. Type the term **macro virus** into the SEARCH: text box, and then click **Go!**. Record the definition in your own words.

4. Type the term **virus** into the Enter a keyword… text box, and then click **Go!**. Record the definition of worm (a type of virus) in your own words.

5. Type the term **Trojan horse** into the Enter a keyword… text box, and then click **Go!**. Record the definition of a Trojan horse (which technically is not a virus, but can cause similar damage) in your own words.

_____

6. Now you will try checking for a virus using McAfee VirusScan. Click **Start**, point to **Programs**, point to **McAfee**, and click **VirusScan**. If you are using other anti-virus software, the steps you need to scan for viruses will likely differ from Steps 6 through 9.

7. Under Quick Jump, click **Scan for Viruses Now**.

8. Under Select a location to scan, click **Local Disk (C:)**, and then click **Scan**. The McAfee software scans your hard disk for viruses.

9. After the scan has completed, look for any infected files. If you find any, record the file name, the virus name, and the status.

_____

10. Close McAfee VirusScan and any open windows.

Certification Objectives

Objectives for the Network+ Exam:

➤ Identify the purpose and characteristics of fault tolerance

➤ Given a scenario, predict the impact of modifying, adding, or removing network services (e.g., DHCP, DNS, WINS, etc.) on network resources and users

Review Questions

1. If you receive an infected file as an executable program attached to an e-mail message, which of the following is this program likely to be?
   a. a macro virus
   b. a Trojan horse
   c. a worm
   d. a boot sector virus

2. What is the difference between a Trojan horse and a true virus?
   a. A Trojan horse does not automatically replicate itself, while a true virus does.
   b. A Trojan horse causes harm by simply being on the computer's hard disk, while a true virus file must be executed by the user.
   c. A Trojan horse is often undetectable by a virus scanning program, while a true virus can almost always be detected by such a program.
   d. A Trojan horse will change its binary characteristics to avoid detection, while a true virus's binary characteristics will remain static.

14

3. Which of the following types of virus checking requires frequent database updates to remain effective?

   a. signature scanning

   b. heuristic scanning

   c. rotation checking

   d. integrity checking

4. If a virus is polymorphic, what is it able to do?

   a. replicate itself over a network connection

   b. change its binary characteristics each time it's transferred to a new system

   c. modify the network properties of a client or server

   d. remain inactive until a particular date

5. What is unique about a time-dependent virus?

   a. It changes its binary characteristics at regularly scheduled intervals.

   b. It can only be eradicated by applying a virus fix at certain times of the day.

   c. It is alternately detectable, then undetectable, by virus scanning software, depending on the date.

   d. It remains dormant until a particular date or time.

6. A macro virus is most apt to affect which of the following programs?

   a. Microsoft Client for Networks

   b. Microsoft Outlook

   c. Microsoft Excel

   d. Microsoft SQL Server

LAB 14.2 UNINTERRUPTIBLE POWER SUPPLIES (UPSs)

Objectives

An uninterruptible power supply (UPS) is a power supply that uses a battery to ensure that any device attached to it will be able to function for some length of time despite a power failure. If the power outage lasts only a few seconds, the UPS will prevent the attached devices from losing power. If the power outage lasts more than a few seconds, the UPS affords you (or a software program) the opportunity to gracefully shut down the attached devices.

 A sudden power failure or outage can cause numerous computer problems. If power were interrupted while a computer's files were open, for instance, those files might be corrupted.

Depending on the power requirements of your network devices and servers and the amount of power produced by a UPS, you may be able to use one UPS with multiple devices. However, you should check the power requirements of each device against the specifications of the UPS before attempting to do this. In general, estimating the power consumption of a network device is difficult. You should usually overestimate the power consumption to provide a healthy margin of error.

Some servers come with multiple power supplies. If one power supply fails, the other power supply will continue to power the computer. For truly critical servers or network devices, you may find that attaching multiple power supplies to a single UPS is insufficient. If the UPS failed, the device would also fail during a power outage. However, if you plugged each power supply into a separate UPS, the failure of a single UPS would not cause the computer to lose power in case of an overall power failure. Some data centers might also plug each UPS into a different circuit, and each circuit into a different generator. However, these fault-tolerance measures increase costs considerably.

In addition to the smaller UPSs you will investigate in this lab, you can also purchase large models designed to support many devices in large data centers.

After completing this lab, you will be able to:

➤ Perform a cost comparison of UPSs

➤ Discuss the characteristics of UPSs

Materials Required

This lab will require the following:

➤ Pencil and paper

➤ Access to a retail store that sells UPSs

Estimated completion time: **60 minutes**

14

ACTIVITY

1. Go to a retail computer store that sells UPSs. Examples of stores where you might find a UPS include Best Buy and CompUSA.

2. Choose a model of UPS. Record the vendor name.

   _____

3. Record the model number.

   _____

4. Record the price.

   _____

5. Record the amount of time that a UPS will keep a device running after a power failure.

   _____

6. Record whether the UPS comes with software that will automatically shut down a computer after a power failure.

_____

7. Repeat Step 2 through Step 6 with two other models of UPS.

_____

_____

_____

_____

8. For each model, calculate how much it would cost to buy UPSs for a data center consisting of ten servers, three routers, three switches, and eight hubs. In lieu of calculating the power consumption of each device, assume that each UPS can support three devices.

Certification Objectives

Objectives for the Network+ Exam:

➤ Identify the purpose and characteristics of fault tolerance

Review Questions

1. What is line conditioning?
   a. the regular testing of the integrity of electrical systems
   b. the periodic application of a large amount of voltage to electrical systems to clean the lines
   c. the continuous filtering of an electrical circuit to protect against noise
   d. the intermittent fluctuation of voltage on a circuit, which over time will cause power flaws for connected devices

2. Which of the following devices typically provides even more fault tolerance than UPSs?
   a. surge protector
   b. circuit breaker
   c. generator
   d. circuit mirroring

3. Which of the following power conditions equates to a power failure?
   a. sag
   b. line noise
   c. brownout
   d. blackout
   e. surge

4. Which of the following power conditions would not necessarily cause a power failure, but may adversely affect computer equipment? (Choose all that apply.)

   a. sag

   b. line noise

   c. brownout

   d. blackout

   e. surge

5. What specification is necessary for you to determine the amount of electrical power that your computer devices require?

   a. capacitance

   b. impedance

   c. resistance

   d. wattage

6. What is the difference between a standby UPS and an online UPS?

   a. A standby UPS engages when it detects a power failure, while an online UPS continuously provides power to its connected devices.

   b. A standby UPS requires that the network administrator connect it to key devices when a power failure is detected, while an online UPS can remain connected to devices indefinitely, even when not in use.

   c. A standby UPS continuously provides power to its connected devices, while an online UPS engages when it detects a power failure.

   d. A standby UPS can remain connected to devices indefinitely, even when not in use, while an online UPS requires that the network administrator connect it to the devices when a power failure is detected.

7. If you are working on several documents in Microsoft Word when your Windows 2000 Professional workstation loses power, and you are not relying on a UPS or other alternate power source, which of the following is a significant risk?

   a. The installation of the Word program on your hard disk may become corrupt and require replacing.

   b. Your computer's operating system may fail to recognize the Word program in the future.

   c. The Word documents you were working on when the power failed may become corrupt.

   d. Your computer's power source may become damaged.

14

Review Questions

1. Which of the following levels of RAID offers disk striping? (Choose all that apply.)
   a. 0
   b. 1
   c. 3
   d. 5

2. Why is RAID Level 0 not considered fully fault-tolerant?
   a. because if a hard disk fails, its data will be inaccessible
   b. because it cannot stripe files whose size exceeds 64 MB
   c. because it is incompatible with modern NOSs
   d. because it cannot verify whether its fault-tolerance activities are successful

3. RAID Level 0 achieves performance benefits through using multiple
   _____ .
   a. NICs
   b. hard disks
   c. processors
   d. instances of RAID software

4. Which of the following RAID levels is preferred for use on mission-critical systems?
   a. 0
   b. 1
   c. 3
   d. 5

5. What does the "A" in RAID stand for?
   a. access
   b. authentication
   c. array
   d. arbitration

6. What is the term for units of data written across multiple disks in disk striping?
   a. packets
   b. clusters
   c. blocks
   d. cells

LAB 14.4 IMPLEMENTING RAID LEVEL 1 (DISK MIRRORING)

Objectives

In RAID Level 1, two physical disks contain identical copies of the data for one logical volume. If one disk fails, all the data remains available on the second disk. However, the disadvantage to using RAID Level 1 (as compared to RAID Level 0, for example) is that it requires twice as much disk space, leaving much less space available for storage. This space is known as the overhead.

After completing this lab, you will be able to:

> ➤ Create a stripe set

> ➤ Identify the characteristics of RAID Level 1

Materials Required

This lab will require the following:

> ➤ A computer running Windows 2000 Server with three hard disks installed, with no partitions or logical volumes allocated on two of the disks

> ➤ Administrator access to the computer

Estimated completion time: **25 minutes**

ACTIVITY

1. Power on the Windows 2000 Server computer. Log on as an administrator.

2. Click **Start**, point to **Programs**, point to **Administrative Tools**, and then click **Computer Management**. The Computer Management window appears.

3. In the left pane of the window, click the **Disk Management** folder.

4. If the Write Signature and Upgrade Disk Wizard appears, click **Next >**. The Select Disks to Upgrade window appears. This wizard typically appears after new disks have been added. If the wizard does not appear, go on to Step 6. Make sure that all disks listed contain check marks, click **Next >**, and then click **Finish**. In the right pane of the Computer Management window, the Logical Disk Manager Service appears.

5. If the Write Signature and Upgrade Disk Wizard does not appear, right-click **Disk 1**, and then click **Upgrade to Dynamic Disk**. The Upgrade to Dynamic Disk window appears. Make sure that all disks listed contain check marks. Click **Upgrade**. Click **Yes** when prompted, and then click **OK**.

6. At the top of the right pane of the window, you see a list of the partitions currently configured on the system. At the bottom of the right pane, you see a list of the hard disks installed on the system, along with a bar to the right, roughly

14

indicating the amount of space allocated to partitions or volumes on each disk. Disk 0 contains the C: drive, while Disk 1 and Disk 2 contain only unallocated space. Right-click **Disk 1**, and then click **Create Volume**. The Create Volume Wizard appears.

7. Click **Next >**. The Select Volume Type window appears.

8. Click the **Mirrored Volume** option button, and then click **Next >**. The Select Disks window appears.

9. In the All available dynamic disks: window, click **Disk 2**, click **Add >>**, and then click **Next >**.

10. In the drop-down menu next to the Assign a drive letter: option button, select **K:**, and then click **Next >**. The Format Volume window appears.

11. Click **Next >** to select the defaults and format the volume with the NTFS file system, and then click **Finish**. The Logical Disk Manager Service appears again, and the drive letter K: appears to the right of both Disk 1 and Disk 2. Underneath the size of each volume, the computer indicates that it is formatting each volume.

12. Record the size of the new K: volume.

---

13. If the two disks are the same size, go to Step 18. If the two disks are different sizes, unallocated space appears in one of the drives next to the new mirrored volume. Right-click the unallocated space next to the larger disk, and then click **Create Volume**. The Create Volume Wizard appears.

14. Click **Next >**. The Select Volume Type window appears. The Simple volume option button is the only option button available.

15. Click **Next >**. The Select Disks button appears.

16. Click **Next >** to accept the disk in the Selected dynamic disks: field. The Assign Drive Letter or Path window appears. Click **Next >** to choose the default drive mapping. The Format Volume window appears.

17. Click **Next >** to select the default option and format the volume with the NTFS file system, and then click **Finish**. The new logical volume appears to the right of the mirrored volume you created. Underneath the size of the logical volume, the computer indicates that it is formatting the volume.

18. Close the Computer Management window.

Certification Objectives

Objectives for the Network+ Exam:

➤ Identify the purpose and characteristics of fault tolerance

➤ Identify the basic capabilities (i.e., client support, interoperability, authentication, file and print services, application support, and security) of the following server operating systems: UNIX/Linux, NetWare, Windows, Macintosh

Review Questions

1. What level of RAID is also known as disk mirroring?
   a. 0
   b. 1
   c. 3
   d. 5

2. What is the minimum number of physical hard disks required for disk mirroring?
   a. 1
   b. 2
   c. 4
   d. 5

3. What is one disadvantage of using RAID Level 1 compared to using RAID Level 0?
   a. RAID Level 1 is not fault-tolerant and RAID Level 0 offers at least some fault tolerance.
   b. RAID Level 1 requires a third-party software program, while RAID Level 0 is provided with every NOS.
   c. RAID Level 1 requires more physical hard disks than RAID Level 0.
   d. RAID Level 1 does not supply error correction coding, while RAID Level 0 does.

4. Which of the following best describes the process of disk mirroring?
   a. Data are simultaneously written in small blocks of data across two logical volumes on one server.
   b. Data are written to one physical hard disk on a server, and then periodically copied to a physical hard disk on a second server.
   c. Data are copied from a logical volume on a server to a logical volume on another server.
   d. Data are written to two physical hard disks on a server.

5. Which of the following types of RAID use disk mirroring? (Choose all that apply.)
   a. 0
   b. 1
   c. 3
   d. 5

6. On a Windows 2000 Server computer, what options would you choose to begin to establish RAID on that computer?
   a. Start, Programs, Administrative Tools, and Computer Management
   b. Start, Settings, Control Panel, and then Disk Management
   c. Start, Programs, Accessories, and then System Management
   d. Start, Settings, Control Panel, Computer Manager, and then Disk Manager

14

17. In the left pane of the window, double-click the **File** icon. One or more icons with a name of Media created, followed by the date, appear. Double-click the latest icon, or the only icon, if there is only one. A folder with a question mark followed by C: appears.

18. Double-click the **C:** folder. The Backup File Name dialog box opens with A:\Backup.bkf in the Catalog backup file: text box.

19. Click **OK**. The Operation Status window appears, and the computer builds a list of files backed up on the floppy disk. The NetPlus folder appears in the right pane of the window.

20. Click the box next to the NetPlus folder. A check mark appears in the box. Click **Next >**, and then click **Finish**.

21. The Enter Backup File Name box appears. Click **OK** to accept the name of the file to which you saved the backup earlier—A:\Backup.bkf. The Restore Progress window appears, showing the progress of the backup.

22. Click the **Close** button to close the Restore Progress window. Close the Backup window.

23. Double-click **My Computer**, double-click **Local Disk (C:)**, and then double-click the **NetPlus** folder. The files backup1.txt and backup2.txt are back in the NetPlus folder.

24. Repeat Steps 2 through 23 with files of your own creation.

25. Close any open windows on the computer.

Certification Objectives

Objectives for the Network+ Exam:

➤ Identify the purpose and characteristics of fault tolerance

➤ Identify the basic capabilities (i.e., client support, interoperability, authentication, file and print services, application support, and security) of the following server operating systems: UNIX/Linux, NetWare, Windows, Macintosh

➤ Identify the purpose and characteristics of disaster recovery

Review Questions

1. Assume that a company has 50 users (at a single location), a limited budget, and significant security concerns. What method would it most likely use to back up its server data?

   a. online backup

   b. DASD

   c. RAID Level 5

   d. tape backup

2. Which of the following types of backup requires the most attention to the security of data while it is being backed up?

   a. online backup

   b. DASD

   c. RAID Level 5

   d. tape backup

3. Why do network administrators prefer not to back up every file on their servers everyday?

   a. because it would take too much time

   b. because it would be less accurate than periodic backups

   c. because it would be more costly

   d. because this type of backup is not simple to configure in a backup software program

4. Which of the following methods will back up only data that has been changed since the last backup?

   a. full

   b. incremental

   c. differential

   d. interval

5. Which backup method will back up data regardless of whether the data has been changed?

   a. full

   b. incremental

   c. differential

   d. interval

6. On a Windows 2000 Server computer, what options would you choose to initiate the Backup utility?

   a. Start, Programs, Administrative Tools, Computer Management, and then Backup

   b. Start, Settings, Control Panel, Disk Management, and then Backup

   c. Start, Programs, Accessories, System Tools, and then Backup

   d. Start, Settings, Control Panel, Computer Manager, Disk Manager, and then Backup

14

NETWORK SECURITY

Labs included in this chapter

➤ Lab 15.1 Auditing

➤ Lab 15.2 Checking for Vulnerable Software

➤ Lab 15.3 Implementing Password Restrictions in Novell NetWare

➤ Lab 15.4 Implementing Network Address Restrictions in a Novell NetWare LAN

➤ Lab 15.5 Implementing Time of Day Restrictions in Novell NetWare

Net+ Exam Objectives	
Objective	**Lab**
Identify the basic capabilities (i.e., client support, interoperability, authentication, file and print services, application support, and security) of the following server operating systems: UNIX/Linux, NetWare, Windows, Macintosh	15.1, 15.2, 15.3, 15.4, 15.5
Identify the basic capabilities (i.e., client connectivity, local security mechanisms, and authentication) of the following clients: UNIX/Linux, Windows, Macintosh	15.1, 15.3, 15.4, 15.5
Given a scenario, predict the impact of a particular security implementation on network functionality (e.g., blocking port numbers, encryption, etc.)	15.1, 15.2, 15.3, 15.4, 15.5
Given specific parameters, configure a client to connect to the following servers: UNIX/Linux, NetWare, Windows, Macintosh	15.5

17. Enter an invalid password in the Password: text box. Click **OK**. The Logon Message window appears, indicating the login attempt failed. Click **OK**.

18. Now log on with the correct password.

19. Click **Start**, point to **Programs**, point to **Administrative Tools**, and then click **Event Viewer**. The Event Viewer window appears.

20. In the left pane of the window, click **Security Log** to select it. The Security Log displays in the right pane of the window and lists the security events that have occurred. In this case, it should include all successful and failed login attempts.

21. Double-click a **Failure Audit icon**. Information about a failed login attempt appears. Figure 15-1 shows an example of a failed login attempt by the administrator.

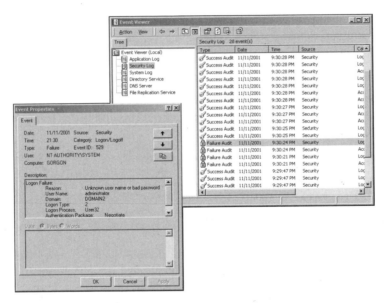

Figure 15-1   Failed login attempt

22. Log on to the client computer as an ordinary user.

23. Double-click **My Network Place**, and then double-click **Entire Network**. If the Microsoft Windows Networks icon is not visible, click the link that indicates you may also view the entire contents of the network. Double-click the name of the domain.

24. Double-click the name of the server. You should be prompted to log on. Enter the name of the ordinary user account in the User name: text box and leave the password blank.

25. On the Windows 2000 Server computer, open the Event Viewer. Click **Security Log** in the left pane of the window. Press **F5**. The Event Browser refreshes.

26. Double-click the **Failure Audit** icon closest to the top of the window. Record the user name and host name of the failed login.

_____

27. Close the Event Viewer and all other open windows on both computers.

Certification Objectives

Objectives for the Network+ Exam:

➤ Identify the basic capabilities (i.e., client support, interoperability, authentication, file and print services, application support, and security) of the following server operating systems: UNIX/Linux, NetWare, Windows, Macintosh

➤ Identify the basic capabilities (i.e., client connectivity, local security mechanisms, and authentication) of the following clients: UNIX/Linux, Windows, Macintosh

➤ Given a scenario, predict the impact of a particular security implementation on network functionality (e.g., blocking port numbers, encryption, etc.)

Review Questions

1. Which of the following best describes authentication?
   a. the process of verifying the precise spelling of a user's user name
   b. the process of accepting and matching a user name with unique account information, such as a password
   c. the process of replicating user login information from one domain controller to the others on a network
   d. the process of tracking a user's login habits and collecting that information in an audit log

2. How does knowing about failed login attempts help a network administrator's security efforts?
   a. The information could help her determine whether stricter password requirements need to be implemented.
   b. The information could help her refine the NOS schema.
   c. The information could help her determine whether an unauthorized user is attempting to log on with that user name.
   d. The information could help her predict the likelihood of future security breaches.

3. Which of the following tools allows you to view security events that have occurred on a Windows 2000 server?
   a. Security Log
   b. Authentication Log
   c. Failure Log
   d. Access Log

15

4. In the context of Windows networking, why must failed login attempts be recorded by a domain controller instead of by any random server on the network?

   a. because only a domain controller will have the resources necessary to record and hold the volume of information that auditing requires

   b. because domain controllers contain a complete set of Windows 2000 Server administrative tools, while other servers do not

   c. because domain controllers typically provide Web and remote access, enabling a network administrator to remotely audit events on a network

   d. because domain controllers authenticate users

5. As a network administrator, what should you do if you notice that a user account has experienced multiple failed login attempts?

   a. revoke the user's login privileges

   b. change the user's password

   c. contact the user to find out whether she is having trouble logging on

   d. limit the times of day during which that user account may log on

LAB 15.2 CHECKING FOR VULNERABLE SOFTWARE

Objectives

A common security risk taken by network administrators is running unpatched software. Frequently, these software patches address security issues. For instance, in 2001, a number of Internet worms affected large numbers of Windows NT and 2000 servers running IIS, even though software patches fixing the vulnerabilities were available. Many administrators simply did not know that they needed to patch their software.

 Any operating system left unpatched also can be a security risk.

In this lab, you will run a utility that can determine which service packs or hot fixes you need to apply on a Windows 2000 Server.

After completing this lab, you will be able to:

➤ Scan a Windows 2000 Server computer to identify whether it is operating with vulnerable software

Materials Required

This lab will require the following:

➤ A computer running Windows 2000 Server or Windows 2000 Professional with Internet access

➤ The Microsoft Network Security Hotfix Checker installed in the C:\security folder

➤ Administrator access to both computers

Estimated completion time: **20 minutes**

ACTIVITY

1. Power on the computer, if necessary. Log on to the computer as an administrator.

2. Click **Start**, point to **Programs**, point to **Accessories**, and then click **Command Prompt**. The Command Prompt window appears.

3. At the command prompt, type **cd C:\security**, and then press **Enter**. The prompt changes to reflect the new directory.

4. Type **hfnetchk –?**, and then press **Enter**. Information displays about the Microsoft Network Security Hotfix Checker command and its syntax. Record whether you can use the hfnetchk program to find patch information about remote computers.

_____

5. Type **hfnetchk –v**, and then press **Enter**. The hfnetchk program attempts to download data files from the Microsoft Web site.

6. If the Security Warning dialog box opens, click **Yes**. This dialog box may not open, depending on the local security settings. The hfnetchk program scans the computer and lists patches not found, as well as information about the patch and the Microsoft Knowledge Base article associated with each hot fix or service pack not yet installed. These article numbers typically begin with Q and end with a string of numbers (such as Q305385). Record an article number listed in the hfnetchk results.

_____

7. Click **Start**, point to **Programs**, and then click **Internet Explorer**. The Internet Explorer window appears.

8. In the Address: text box, type **www.microsoft.com**, and then press **Enter**. The Microsoft Web site opens.

9. Click the **Support page link**. The Microsoft Web site changes frequently, so you may have to search for it.

10. From the Support page, go to the Microsoft Knowledge Base. The Web site changes frequently, but at the time of this writing, you can click the **Specific article ID number** option button to search for specific Knowledge Base articles.

11. In the Command Prompt window, choose a Knowledge Base article number. Write this down. Typically, the number begins with Q and ends with a string of several numbers in a row (such as Q306121). In Internet Explorer, enter the knowledge base article number that you wrote down earlier into the appropriate blank, and then press **Enter**.

15

Estimated completion time: **25 minutes**

ACTIVITY

1. Power on both computers.

2. At the DOS prompt on the Novell server, type **cd nwserver**, and then press **Enter**. Type **server**, and then press **Enter**. The NetWare splash screens appear as NetWare starts.

3. After NetWare is running, log on as Admin from the Windows 2000 client computer. Enter the user name and password for the ordinary user when prompted.

4. Double-click **My Computer**, double-click **Z:**, double-click the **WIN32** folder, and then double-click **nwadmn32** (which may appear as nwadmn32.exe if the computer is configured to show file extensions). NetWare Administrator opens.

5. Double-click the **sales** object.

6. Double-click the **todd** user object. The properties page for the todd user object appears. Various buttons on the right side of the screen allow you to perform activities for this user object. The Password Restrictions button includes settings for requiring a password, setting minimum password length, and allowing the user to change passwords.

7. Click Password Restrictions. The Password Restrictions property page appears for the selected user object.

8. To require a password for this user, check the **Require a password** check box. The Minimum password length: text box is enabled and displays a default value of 5. Leave the default value at 5.

9. To force the user to change passwords periodically, check the **Force Periodic password changes** check box. The Days between forced changes text box is enabled and automatically set to 40 days. This is the minimum number of days that a password will be valid before the user is forced to change it. Leave the default value at 40. Also, the setting in the Date password expires: text box changes to the current date and time by default. This forces the password to expire immediately, thus forcing the user to change his or her password. This is useful when you want to assign a temporary password for a new user account and then force the user to select a new password upon logging on for the first time. Leave the default values.

10. To require a unique password for a user, check the **Require unique passwords** check box. This prevents the user from re-using old passwords as new passwords in the future.

11. To limit the number of grace logins, check the **Limit grace logins** check box. This specifies the number of times that the user can log on incorrectly before

the account is disabled. Once checked, the Grace logins allowed and the Remaining grace logins settings are set to 6 by default. Your properties page should now look similar to Figure 15-2. Click **OK**.

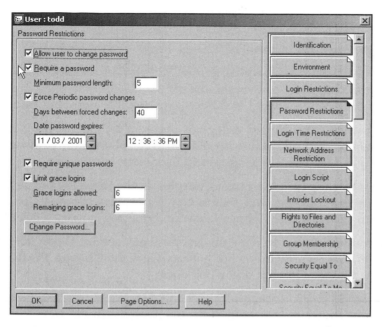

Figure 15-2   Password Restrictions property page for the todd user

12. Now you are ready to test some of these password restriction settings for the user named todd. Close NetWare Administrator.

13. Click **Start**, point to **Programs**, point to **Novell (Common)**, and click **Novell Login**. The Novell Login dialog box opens.

14. Click the **Advanced** button. Type **todd** in the Username: text box. Do not enter any text in the Password: text box; you have not created a password for this account. Type **sales.netplus** in the Context: text box, and then click **OK**. The Confirm… dialog box opens.

15. Click **Yes** to close the dialog box. The Results dialog box opens because you are logged into the Novell server. Another Confirm… dialog box opens, indicating that you have five grace logins left to change your password and asking if you want to change your password.

16. Click **Yes**. The Change Password dialog box opens.

17. To check the password length restrictions, type **foo** in both the Enter new password: and the Retype new password: text boxes, and then click **OK**. The Confirm… dialog box opens, indicating that the new password is too short and asking if you still want to change your password.

15

LAB 15.4 IMPLEMENTING NETWORK ADDRESS RESTRICTIONS IN A NOVELL NETWARE LAN

Objectives

In NetWare, the network address of a machine consists of the network address plus the MAC address of the machine, also known as the node address in NetWare terminology. In this lab, you will set restrictions for a user to log on from only a certain network address.

The potential advantage to requiring users to log on from only certain machines is that you can prevent them from logging on to the network from any workstation but their own. This can help you keep a closer eye on users, as well as entirely prevent users from accessing certain networks. The disadvantage is that this requires more maintenance. If a user changes machines, then you would have to reconfigure the network address restrictions.

To restrict users from logging on from other workstations, you first must find the network address information. In NetWare, a machine's network address consists of the network address plus the machine's MAC address, known in NetWare terminology as the node address. However, address restrictions that you can implement depend on the protocols in use on the network.

After completing this lab, you will be able to:

➤ Determine a node's MAC address in Novell NetWare

➤ Set network address restrictions in Novell NetWare

Materials Required

This lab will require the following:

➤ A computer running Novell NetWare 5.x with the SYS public volume mapped by default to drive Z:

➤ Administrator access to the Novell server

➤ An organization named netplus in the NDS tree, with an organizational unit named sales and a user named todd with a known password

➤ A client computer running Windows 2000 Server or Windows 2000 Professional with the Novell Client for NT/2000 4.8 software installed

➤ Access to the Windows 2000 computer as an ordinary user (with the ability to log on interactively)

➤ A functioning network connection between the two computers

Estimated completion time: **35 minutes**

ACTIVITY

1. Power on both computers.

2. At the DOS prompt on the Novell server, type **cd \nwserver**, and then press **Enter**. Type **server**, and then press **Enter**. The Novell splash screen appears as the Novell server starts.

3. After the Novell server has successfully started, log on as an administrator on the Windows 2000 computer. Enter the user name and password for the ordinary user account on the Windows 2000 computer, if prompted to do so.

4. Click **Start**, point to **Programs**, point to **Accessories**, and then click **Command Prompt**. The Command Prompt window appears.

5. At the command prompt, type **Z:**, and then press **Enter**.

6. At the command prompt, **type nlist user /a**, and then press **Enter**. This command displays the users that are logged in, their network addresses, and their node addresses, as shown in Figure 15-3.

Figure 15-3   Output of the nlist user /a command

7. The asterisk indicates the current login session from your workstation. In Figure 15-3, this is the first entry (*admin). On your computer screen, find and record the network address for the entry with an asterisk next to it.

_____

8. Record the node address for the same entry.

_____

9. Close the Command Prompt window.

15

10. Double-click **My Computer**, double-click **Z:**, double-click the **WIN32** folder, and then double-click **nwadmn32** (which may appear as nwadmn32.exe if the computer is configured to show file extensions). NetWare Administrator appears.

11. In NetWare Administrator, double-click the **Sales** object in the NDS tree in the left side of the window. The tree expands underneath the Sales object.

12. Right-click the **todd** object, and then click **Details**.

13. On the right side of the window, click the **Network Address Restrictions** button. The Network Address Restrictions Property page opens. By default, there are no entries in the Network Address Restrictions box, meaning that the user can log on from any workstation.

14. With the IPX/SPX protocol selected by default, click **Add** to create a network address restriction. The IPX/SPX dialog box opens with two text boxes: Network and Node.

15. In the Network text box, enter the number recorded in Step 6.

16. In the Node text box, enter the number recorded in Step 7, and then click **OK**. The Network Address Restrictions Property page displays with the network address restriction entry.

17. Click **OK**, and then close NetWare Administrator.

18. Click **Start**, point to **Programs**, point to **Novell (Common)**, and then click **Novell Login**. The Novell Login screen opens.

19. Click **Advanced**. More options appear at the bottom of the Novell Login screen.

20. In the Context: text box, type **sales.netplus** to ensure that you log on with the proper context. In the Username: text box, type **todd**. In the Password: text box, enter the password for the todd account, and then click **OK**. The Confirm... dialog box opens. Click **Yes**. You should have logged in successfully.

21. Click **Start**, point to **Programs**, point to **Novell (Common)**, and then click **Novell Login**. The Novell Login screen appears.

22. Log on again as an administrator, and repeat Steps 10 through 17. This time, use 010101010101 as the node address of the workstation (or another node address that does not match the node address you found in Step 6). Because this node address does not match the node address of your workstation, you should be unable to log on.

23. Attempt to log on by repeating Steps 18 through 20.

24. The NetWare Security Message dialog box opens, indicating that you may not log on because the supervisor has restricted the workstations from which you may log on.

25. Click **OK**. Log on as the administrator.

26. Now you will remove the address restrictions on the user. Repeat Steps 10 through 13 to open the Network Address Restrictions window for the todd user.

27. Click the network address restriction that you added in Step 22. Click **Delete** to remove the network address restrictions for the todd user, and then click **OK**.

28. Close NetWare administrator and all open windows.

Certification Objectives

Objectives for the Network+ Exam:

➤ Identify the basic capabilities (i.e., client support, interoperability, authentication, file and print services, application support, and security) of the following server operating systems: UNIX/Linux, NetWare, Windows, Macintosh

➤ Identify the basic capabilities (i.e., client connectivity, local security mechanisms, and authentication) of the following clients: UNIX/Linux, Windows, Macintosh

➤ Given a scenario, predict the impact of a particular security implementation on network functionality (e.g., blocking port numbers, encryption, etc.)

Review Questions

1. What is the function of the nlist command on a NetWare server?
   a. to list the NLMs that are currently loaded on the server
   b. to list the protocols currently bound to the server's NIC
   c. to list the server's network addresses
   d. to list the users currently logged on to the server

2. Which of the following commands on a UNIX server would perform similar functions as the nlist command?
   a. netstat
   b. nbtstat
   c. ifconfig
   d. who

3. Which of the following network security methods provides the greatest resistance to unauthorized external file access on a server?
   a. A central computer room is accessible only to authorized personnel through hand-scanning.
   b. A NOS is configured to allow logins only during the hours of 8 a.m. to 5 p.m.
   c. A NOS requires users' computers to have an address that matches one belonging to their LAN segment in order to log on to the server.
   d. A proxy server disguises transmissions issued from clients on a private LAN.

4. What is the best defense against social engineering?
   a. having a strong security policy and educating users
   b. employing Kerberos authentication for all users
   c. configuring a firewall to accept transmissions only from certain IP addresses
   d. limiting the ports on a server through which client communication may take place

15

➤ Identify the basic capabilities (i.e., client connectivity, local security mechanisms, and authentication) of the following clients: UNIX/Linux, Windows, Macintosh

➤ Given specific parameters, configure a client to connect to the following servers: UNIX/Linux, NetWare, Windows, Macintosh

➤ Given a scenario, predict the impact of a particular security implementation on network functionality (e.g., blocking port numbers, encryption, etc.)

Review Questions

1. You can combine time of day restrictions and network address restrictions for a user. True or False?

2. In which of the following situations would it be most beneficial for a network administrator to restrict the time of day during which the users can log on to the network to improve security?
   a. A salesperson accesses a company's network via a dial-up connection to upload sales data every night.
   b. Groups of customer service representatives enter sales data during three different shifts throughout the day and night.
   c. A corporate executive frequently travels to a company's various locations and requires access to confidential information on the server.
   d. A group of engineers who are establishing an international office in a country several time zones away from the server's location.

3. What is one potential disadvantage to restricting the time of day during which a user can log on to the network?
   a. It prevents the network administrator from imposing other login restrictions such as specifying a valid network address.
   b. It can only be applied to users who log on from an internally connected workstation, and not to users who log on through a dial-up connection.
   c. It works properly only if the time of day setting on each client workstation is synchronized with the time of day setting on the server.
   d. It requires additional maintenance for the network administrator.

4. Which of the following encryption methods is commonly used to secure transmissions over VPNs?
   a. Kerberos
   b. RAS
   c. PGP
   d. IPSec

5. If someone floods your gateway with so much traffic that it cannot respond to or accept valid traffic, what type of security breach has she accomplished?
   a. IP spoofing
   b. social engineering
   c. denial of service
   d. Trojan horse

CHAPTER SIXTEEN

MANAGING NETWORK DESIGN AND IMPLEMENTATION

Labs included in this chapter

➤ Lab 16.1 Creating a Project Plan

➤ Lab 16.2 Planning an Upgrade

➤ Lab 16.3 Observing a Network Upgrade

Net+ Exam Objectives

Objective

The labs in this chapter do not map directly to objectives on the exam. However, each lab teaches a skill that is valuable to networking professionals.

LAB 16.1 CREATING A PROJECT PLAN

Objectives

When planning a project—particularly a large, technical project—you must keep track of details pertaining not only to the hardware and software involved, but also to the people responsible for tasks, the time each task might take, and which tasks rely on other tasks. To track all these details, it's helpful to use project planning software.

Microsoft Project 2000 is one of several project planning software packages available. One of the advantages of using project planning software is the ability to easily create charts and timelines. A Gantt chart, for example, is a chart that displays the timelines of all project tasks and their relationships.

After completing this lab, you will be able to:

➤ Create a project plan using Microsoft Project 2000

Materials Required

This lab will require the following:

➤ A Windows 2000 Server or Windows 2000 Professional computer with Microsoft Project 2000 installed

Estimated completion time: **20 minutes**

ACTIVITY

1. In this lab, you will use Microsoft Project to create a PERT (Program Evaluation and Review Technique) chart. The PERT chart will provide you with a graphical diagram of a project. Review the task list in Table 16-1.

Table 16-1   Project task list

Number	Task Description	Precedence	Duration
1	Order server hardware	None	1 day
2	Order server software	None	1 day
3	Install server hardware	1	1 day
4	Install server software	2 and 3	1 day
5	Add servers to LAN	4	1 day

2. To open Microsoft Project, click **Start**, point to **Programs**, and then click **Microsoft Project**. (You might find Microsoft Project located elsewhere on your Start menu.)

3. On the left side of the window, look for a column labeled Task Name. You can enter task information in this text box. On the right side of the window, look for a chart that marks tasks on the calendar with boxes; this part of the window also shows precedence information. Figure 16-1 shows the window after task information has already been entered. You will enter the same information in the following steps.

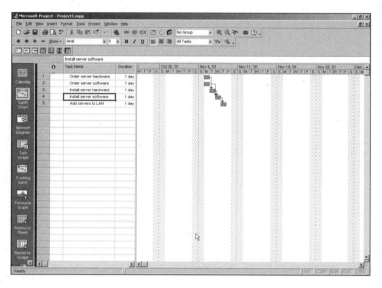

Figure 16-1   Microsoft Project 2000 window

4. In the Task Name column, enter the tasks and their duration, as given in Table 16-1. For now, leave the Precedence information blank.

5. To set the task dependencies for Task 3, right-click **Install server hardware** (Task number 3), and then click **Task Information**. The Task Information dialog box opens with several tabs. You will make the "Order server hardware" task a predecessor to the "Install server hardware" task.

6. Click the **Predecessors** tab.

7. Click the **Task Name** drop-down arrow, and then click **Order server hardware**. The Order server hardware task appears in the list of predecessors.

8. Click **OK**. The Precedence information on the right side of the screen changes to reflect the new dependency. An arrow points from the "Order server hardware" task to the "Install server hardware" task, indicating that the latter is dependent on the former.

9. Repeat Steps 5 through 8 for the remaining tasks with predecessors. Order server software and Install server hardware are predecessors to Install server software, and Add servers to LAN is a predecessor to Load Protocol. The Gantt chart in the right of the screen finishes.

16

10. Click **File**, and then click **Save**. The Save As dialog box appears. Choose a unique name for the file, and then click **Save**. The Planning Wizard dialog box appears. Click the option button to save your file with a baseline, and then click **Save**.

11. Close Microsoft Project 2000.

Certification Objectives

Objectives for the Network+ Exam:

This lab does not map directly to an objective on the exam. However, it does teach a skill that is valuable to networking professionals.

Review Questions

1. The _____ task must be completed before another task is begun.
   a. successor
   b. predecessor
   c. antecedent
   d. dependent

2. In a significant network upgrade project, which of the following tasks takes place first?
   a. identify which tasks are dependent on other tasks
   b. complete a needs assessment survey
   c. test the proposed solution on a pilot network
   d. assign tasks to the most qualified or appropriate individuals on the project team

3. Which of the following best describes contingency planning?
   a. obtaining support from high-level project sponsors before committing resources to the project
   b. installing identical software and hardware, on a smaller scale, as the project's proposed solution will require, to test the feasibility of the solution
   c. identifying a team and assigning roles to that team in case of disaster
   d. identifying steps that will minimize the impact of unforeseen obstacles

4. What is a potential danger in breaking down larger tasks into smaller tasks?
   a. The greater the task breakdown, the less enthusiastic staff may be about accomplishing those tasks.
   b. Some larger tasks cannot be broken down into smaller tasks.
   c. The greater the task breakdown, the less meaningful each separate task may become.
   d. It is more difficult for staff to understand the project's scope when larger tasks are divided into too many smaller tasks.

5. You are a network administrator managing a network backbone upgrade. Your supervisor has scheduled a meeting to discuss the project's status with you. What is the advantage in printing out a Gantt chart to take to the meeting?

   a. A Gantt chart will help the supervisor better understand the project's costs.

   b. A Gantt chart will help the supervisor determine how much of each employee's time is spent on each task.

   c. A Gantt chart will help the supervisor see timelines of each task in addition to the project as a whole.

   d. A Gantt chart will demonstrate why some tasks have taken longer to complete than first anticipated.

6. One way of predicting how long a task might take is by examining the time taken to complete previous similar tasks. True or False?

LAB 16.2 PLANNING AN UPGRADE

Objectives

Even when making relatively minor changes, a project plan can be helpful. The potential benefits include minimizing downtime, creating an efficient implementation, and planning for when something goes wrong. For instance, a project plan for changing the NIC on a server might include contingency plans in case the new NIC is defective, the NIC is accidentally damaged during installation, or the server does not boot after installation. Alternately, a configuration change made on a remote router may cut you off from the router. By having included contingency plans in your project plan, you are better prepared to solve the problem quickly and efficiently.

In environments in which downtime must be minimized at all costs, contingency planning is even more important. Although the odds of a problem occurring may be low, if a problem does occur, you must be prepared. During a server upgrade, for example, you might have a spare server ready in case the server fails. (Note that you can also use network design to minimize potential downtime. For instance, you might use redundant servers.)

In this lab, you will create a project plan for replacing the NIC in the Windows 2000 Server. Your project plan should include task breakdown, which is the division of the project into smaller parts, and dependencies, which is a list of tasks that depend on the completion of previous tasks. You should also have contingency planning to cover situations such as the following: a defective NIC, drivers that are not available for the NIC, a NIC that is damaged during installation, a server that is damaged during installation, and a server that cannot boot after installation of the NIC. Last, your plan should contain a timeline, the resources, and the project milestone.

After completing this lab, you will be able to:

➤ Make a project for a network upgrade

➤ Perform the network upgrade

16

Materials Required

This lab will require the following:

➤ Pencil and paper, or planning software such as Microsoft Project 2000

➤ A computer running Window 2000 Server with a NIC configured as a domain controller with an IP address of 192.168.1.1

➤ Administrator access to the Windows 2000 Server

➤ An extra NIC (with a driver disk, if necessary)

➤ A client computer running Windows 2000 Server or Windows 2000 Professional with a NIC configured with an IP address of 192.168.1.2

➤ Access to the client computer with an ordinary user account in the domain

➤ A functioning network between the two computers

➤ A Phillips head screwdriver

Estimated completion time: **20 minutes**

ACTIVITY

1. Power on both computers. To verify that the network is working properly, log on to the client computer with the ordinary user account in the domain.

2. Write by hand the project plan that will cover the activities in Steps 3–9, or use project planning software such as Microsoft Project 2000.

3. Power down the Windows 2000 Server computer and remove the power cable.

4. Remove any screws, and open the case of the Windows 2000 Server computer.

5. Unscrew the NIC from its slot in the computer.

6. Place the new NIC in the slot.

7. Attach the NIC to the system unit with the Phillips head screwdriver to secure the NIC in place.

8. Replace the cover and reinsert any screws removed in Step 4.

9. Plug in the computer and turn it on.

10. To verify that the network is working properly, log on to the client computer with the ordinary user account in the domain.

Certification Objectives

Objectives for the Network+ Exam:

This lab does not map directly to an objective on the exam. However, it does teach a skill that is valuable to networking professionals.

Review Questions

1. What is the purpose of identifying milestones in a project plan?
   a. They indicate when project staff changes must occur.
   b. They mark significant events of the project's progress.
   c. They offer a quick assessment of how successfully the project is staying within budget.
   d. They help predict the end result of a project.

2. Which of the following are examples of resources related to a project plan that proposes to upgrade the network cards inside each workstation on a network from 10 Mbps to 100 Mbps? (Choose all that apply.)
   a. NIC device drivers
   b. a team member's time
   c. IP addresses
   d. NICs
   e. hubs

3. Which of the following are examples of stakeholders of a project whose purpose is to upgrade an entire network from 10 Mbps to 100 Mbps? (Choose all that apply.)
   a. network users
   b. network software vendors
   c. high-level managers who approved the project
   d. IT staff who helped implement the change
   e. network cabling vendors

4. Which of the following tools might you use to assess the success of a project whose purpose is to upgrade an entire network from 10 Mbps to 100 Mbps?
   a. Network Monitor
   b. Sniffer
   c. Microsoft SQL Server
   d. System Monitor

16

5. Which of the following obstacles could halt or seriously impair the progress of a project whose purpose is to upgrade the NICs in all workstations on a network from 10 Mbps to 100 Mbps?

    a. the use of two different NIC models

    b. the use of different installation personnel on different shifts

    c. management's requirement that the cost of each NIC remain under $75.00

    d. a group of defective NICs

Lab 16.3 Observing a Network Upgrade

Objectives

Observing a network upgrade is an excellent way to see how they are done in the real world. Depending on the project, you might be able to see only a small part at any one time. For larger projects, the networking professional is more likely to have a formal project plan; for smaller projects, the plan might be very informal.

After completing this lab, you will be able to:

➤ Explain how a network upgrade is performed

Materials Required

This lab will require the following:

➤ Pencil and paper

➤ A person (such as a network professional or your instructor) willing to allow you to observe a network upgrade

> Estimated completion time: **2 hours**

Activity

1. Visit the site performing a network upgrade.

2. Ask the person who is allowing you to observe the upgrade to discuss any project plans they might use during the upgrade.

3. Ask the same person to discuss any contingency planning they might have done as part of the upgrade.

4. Record any changes occurring at the site. For example, the upgrade might involve replacing Category 3 cable with Category 5 cable. Another change might involve altering the IP addressing scheme.

5. Record the time required for the network upgrade.

_____

6. Send a thank you note to the person who allowed you to observe the upgrade.

Certification Objectives

Objectives for the Network+ Exam:

This lab does not map directly to an objective on the exam. However, it does teach a skill that is valuable to networking professionals.

Review Questions

1. Which of the following best describes process management?
   a. recording and analyzing the time and resources required for each task in a project
   b. assessing network statistics before and after a project is completed
   c. monitoring the needs of users prior to the beginning of a project, then later assessing how the project's completion met their needs
   d. planning for and handling the steps required to accomplish a goal in a systematic way

2. Which of the following projects is most likely to be driven by a company's security needs?
   a. doubling the RAM in a key file server
   b. installing a firewall on a connection to the Internet
   c. upgrading the version of client software on each workstation
   d. changing from the use of static IP addressing to DHCP on an entire network

3. What is one good technique for assessing the feasibility of a suggested project deadline before the project begins?
   a. begin calculating task timelines from the deadline, working back to the start of a project
   b. issue a survey to key staff asking their opinion on the suggested deadline
   c. use the Web to research similar projects completed by other companies
   d. calculate the ratio of the number of project milestones to the proposed project duration, in months, to check that it does not exceed 2:1

4. In a very large company (for example, one with over 10,000 employees), which of the following staff is most likely to decide whether a project such as an entire network upgrade will be funded?
   a. network administrator
   b. IT director
   c. chief executive officer
   d. accountant

16

5. Which of the following situations might necessitate changing all the IP addresses on a company's networked workstations?

a. The company has moved from one geographical location to another.

b. The company has hired 50 new employees.

c. The company has decided to use NAT for all connections to public networks.

d. The company has decided to establish a Web server with e-commerce capability.